A New World

the history of immigration into the United States

A New World

the history of immigration into the United States

Duncan Clarke

THUNDER BAY
P·R·E·S·S

Published in the United States by
Thunder Bay Press
An imprint of the Advantage Publishers Group
5880 Oberlin Drive, San Diego, CA 92121-4794
www.advantagebooksonline.com

Produced by PRC Publishing Ltd
Kiln House, 210 New Kings Road
London SW6 4NZ

© 2000 PRC Publishing Ltd

ISBN 1-57145-280-X

Library of Congress Cataloging-in-Publication Data available upon request.

Printed and bound in China

1 2 3 4 5 00 01 02 03

Contents

Introduction

For people in the Old World, North America was a vast unknown land of opportunity and freedom—of thought, practice, movement, and discovery. To peoples from the restricted and tightly controlled European kingdoms, the New World enticed them with hopes and dreams of fortune and advancement—and terrified them with tales of the unknown. The first colonizers faced their future with courage and ignorance, but managed to forge a toehold of control over the immediate environs which gradually spread outwards across the continent as more settlers joined.

Settlers came from all points of the Old World: England, Scotland, Ireland, Wales, France, Germany, Poland, Italy, the Netherlands, and Switzerland plus a few Greeks, Russians, and other Slavs. By the start of the American Revolution there were about two and a half million settlers already living in the Thirteen Colonies. Of these around sixty percent were of English origin and the remainder from a mixture of other nations.

For some ten years or so after the Revolution only some 5,000 settlers a year arrived. But then the numbers began to climb and the immigrants started to arrive. They came because of three principal reasons: in 1815 the Napoleonic Wars ended and many people found themselves dispossessed by the ravages of the war, they had nothing to return home for and only the New World for hope. In the 1840s Ireland along with the rest of Europe, suffered the terrible potato famines which devastated the crops leaving them inedible. However, in Ireland more than anywhere, the people relied on the potato crop and they starved in their thousands. Those who could, scraped the money together for a passage to America. The third main cause was the Industrial Revolution which mechanized so many labor-intensive jobs and deprived workers of their living.

The difference between settlers and immigrants seems minimal but is important. Broadly speaking, settlers arrived in a land (in this case America) to tame the wilds and then to put down roots and cultivate the soil. They established towns and drew up boundaries, they were pioneers, exploring the land, often at great personal risk. Immigrants are more obviously economic migrants who arrive in numbers, often driven out of their homeland by extreme hardship. They were not pioneers in the true sense—they were arriving in an already established society and had to find their own place therein. Immigrants often settled together in ethnic areas where they set up an environment and a way of living that was as much like the old homeland as possible.

By the time the large numbers of immigrants started to flood the shores of America the land was largely explored, and cities and towns were established from the Atlantic to Pacific coasts. The immigrants arrived hoping to carve out a new and better life in the "land of opportunity." They were often escaping poverty and grinding hardship in their home countries. This book is about their story; this is the story of the immigrants who had nothing to lose, because staying at home in Europe was a short road to misery and death, whereas the gamble of the New World offered the chance of limitless wealth and opportunity.

Of course, the Native Americans had lived in North America for some 30,000 years before any visitors or colonizers arrived. Their ancestors, centuries earlier, had crossed the land bridge from Asia to North America before the continents split apart. Their largely itinerant civilizations occupied vast areas, migrating southward to populate North and South America, successfully living off the land and hunting the abundant wildlife. At the time when the first European colonists arrived in America, there were over 200 different tribal groups. There is

little academic dispute that it is these people who were the ancestors of the Maya, Aztec, Incas, and Native American tribes of North America and that they developed in isolation—although plenty of thinly supported theories have been proposed in the last fifty years to argue against this. Whether it was by Japanese, Chinese, Ancient Egyptians, Phoenicians, Carthaginians, Romans, or Jews, the "diffusionists" believe that migrating seafarers contacted—and helped in the development of—the ancient civilizations of the world. There is little to suggest that any of these theories is true; until that is, the more viable theory of development of Native Americans in isolation.

Certainly, it was the Native Americans who were there to greet the first European settlers. Indeed, many of them generously welcomed and helped the new arrivals by showing them pure waters, good hunting grounds and safe lands. Although there was conflict between the settlers and the natives, for many of the native population the arrival of the Europeans also presented an opportunity for lucrative trade. The French, in particular, saw their role in North America as a conduit through which fur and other commodities could be traded by the native population. As a result, the French population of North America was ultimately smaller than the English-speaking.

However, apart from the deliberate death and destruction that the Europeans brought with their advanced military equipment, the Europeans also brought inadvertent death through disease. Many of the most common ailments in Europe, to which the European had developed an in-built tolerance, were unknown in the New World and the native population, therefore, had no natural immunity. The arrival of these diseases caused the death of many thousands, further weakening the ability of the Native American tribes to resist the European incursion.

Reluctant settlers

Not all the colonizers arrived willingly. The largest such contingent were the Black slaves, ruthlessly captured and transported, from (mostly) West Africa and Sub-Saharan Africa, across the Atlantic (the "Middle Passage") to the West Indies and America. The slaves comprised almost twenty percent of the total population (about 690,000 out of some 3.5 million) in 1790. Their forced labor was used primarily to grow and harvest the New World's agricultural wealth—tobacco and cotton. But they were also sent down the mines to extract the new-found mineral wealth that was starting to emerge from under the soil.

The plight of the slaves is well-known; less obvious, but in the early days more important in terms of numbers, were other unwilling arrivals. These were the indentured servants, all of them by and large white, European, and poor. In the days before slaves, the early colonists relied on indentured servants to do much of their menial work. These were people who wanted to escape poverty and oppression in Europe but were too poor to pay the passage across the Atlantic. The contract would bind them for—usually—between three and seven years in return for their passage and board and eventually on the expiry of the contract, a small plot of land. A few were taught a trade but the majority were agricultural laborers. Masters worked them ruthlessly to extract the maximum possible labor before the contracted term expired.

Needless to say, many did not live to receive their final payment as the mortality rates due to dangerous and hard work as well as new diseases took their toll. Furthermore, when slaves started to arrive in North America, the latter were more valuable even though they cost more to buy, but then they became property and could be traded or kept indefinitely. Indentured servants had greater legal rights and, of course, the guarantee of freedom if they survived their term, but they could be beaten, humiliated and traded by their owners with little hope of relief.

Once free, the shortage of women allowed most female servants to marry, but men usually remained impoverished dependants of their former master. At the end of their term many were reduced to squatting on frontier land; relatively few achieved genuine prosperity. In the seventeenth century most indentured servants had been poor Englishmen, but in the eighteenth century the Irish increasingly took their place. It has been estimated that well over half of the new European labor arriving in America before the outbreak of the Revolution came in as indentured servants.

Opposite, Above: Polish and Czechoslovakian emigrees boarding ship at Southampton, England, while on their way to America, c.1921.

Opposite, Below: Under way at last. Emigrants on deck enjoying the fresh air, c.1890.

Another source of forced immigration to the New World was the total of around 50,000 convicts who chose transportation to America over imprisonment.

Immigration law

In the earliest days anyone who could get to America could stay provided they were sanctioned by the local authorities where they landed. The regulation and inspection of immigrants was considered to be the responsibility of the individual ports and states. But as the numbers of arrivals increased regulation became necessary, however the first federal law concerning immigration was not promulgated until 1819 and even then it did not control the people themselves. It merely laid down that full records and statistics (name, sex, occupation, and country of origin) should be kept as to the numbers of immigrants on board ship, and the number that died on the journey. It also set standards for their steerage conditions. Further amendments were passed in 1847 and 1848 but these only concerned the condition of the sailing vessels.

When immigrants started to arrive in numbers as refugees from European conflict, and also with gold rush fever in 1849, locals, especially in New York the biggest port of entry, got increasing worried about the illnesses they brought with them. Devastating diseases such as cholera, smallpox, and typhoid fever could wipe out entire populations. Consequently, new immigrants were closely scrutinized and quarantined or moved on as necessary. Soon this became the job of the local health inspector who would visit the vessel in harbor to inspect the passengers and examine the ship's records for details of deaths at sea before allowing the ship to dock. The steamship companies were made to be responsible for screening their passengers before leaving Europe, so in theory nobody with a long-term or dangerous disorder had passage. Practice, of course, was an entirely different matter.

By the beginning of the 1880s the Supreme Court was deeply concerned about the question of immigration and recommended that Congress get involved by taking on full authority and responsibility for immigration. In 1882 a federal immigration law was enacted to levy a 50c tax on all aliens landing at U.S. ports. Furthermore all states became responsible for inspecting immigrants arriving at their ports. Also, for the first time immigration was restricted by nationality in the 1882 Chinese Exclusion Act. Undesirable aliens were to be denied entrance, including in particular "any person unable to take care of himself or herself without becoming a public charge." (Prostitutes and convicts were already barred from entering the United States by law in 1875.)

Then, in 1885, the Contract Labor Law was promulgated to stop American employers advertising for contract laborers abroad and to stop immigrants entering the country at the behest or encouragement of American employers.

In spring 1891 a new tougher immigration law was passed which looked to exclude anyone suffering from contagious disease or who carried a criminal record for polygamy or "moral turpitude." Anyone entering the country illegally or who became a public charge within a year due to a pre-existing medical condition, would be deported. The Secretary of the Treasury became personally responsible for immigration matters.

The law for the steamship companies was toughened too, now anyone they brought who was refused entry was their responsibility, which meant they had to pay for their food and lodging while in detention and then the cost of the return passage to Europe. After 1893 each passenger was required to answer twenty-nine questions concerning personal details before being allowed to board the ship. They also had to possess at least $30. The steamship companies, anxious not to incur unnecessary costs, employed doctors to give immigrants a cursory examination. Passengers were also often routinely disinfected (along with their baggage) and vaccinated. Nevertheless, in the worst periods, the mortality rate on the voyage was ten percent—which on the largest ships containing 2,000 passengers was 200 souls. Medical inspectors would board the ship once in harbor but before docking, and a quarantine examination would be conducted for the first and second class passengers—U.S. citizens were exempt. Steerage passengers would be sent to an inspection station such as Ellis Island.

Prepaid tickets for passage to the United States were easy to come by both in America and Europe—agents roamed the countries freely selling tickets. The ticket guaranteed no

Major historical factors affecting early immigration to the U.S.

1846	Irish Potato Famine
1848	German revolution suppressed
1849	California Gold Rush
1855	Financial crisis and famine in Sweden
1861–65	U.S. Civil War discourages immigrants
1880s	Russian Jews fleeing persecution
1890s	Mexicans go to California for work
1914	Outbreak of World War I in Europe

Opposite: With the New York skyline in the background, two Czechoslovakian women and a baby arrive on board the S.S. President Harding *in February 1939, to start a new life in the United States.*

Above: Even in the mid-Atlantic, the crowded decks were preferable to conditions in the overcrowded and fetid holds; early twentieth century photograph.

Left: With Manhattan and freedom so close across the harbor, two Jewish immigrants manage to look composed despite the examination ahead of them at Ellis Island, c.1920.

Opposite, Above: Seated patiently on deck a Czech family arrives at Ellis Island on board the S.S. Lafayette *on August 23, 1920.*

Opposite, Below: Transatlantic ships carried as many passengers as possible to make the most of this lucrative trade. These immigrants were photographed packed on deck, c.1900.

The ocean liner Prinzess Irene *lying at anchor off Ellis Island after bringing her cargo of immigrants safely to America, c.1890.*

specific ship or berth, just the price of passage itself. In 1900, to provide a measure of control over this freelance operation, it became necessary for an immigrant to get a passport from local officials plus a visa for the United States from an American consular office or from the local consul at the port of departure.

In 1903 the Secretary for Labor and Commerce took over responsibility for immigration, (it remained his domain until 1940). At the same time Congress put an exclusion on anyone who was working to, or wanted to, overthrow the U.S. government, this included all known foreign anarchists who were considered undesirable aliens.

In 1907 the head tax on immigration was raised to help pay for the medical attention immigrants needed, and the exclusion list was extended to encompass unaccompanied children, anyone with tuberculosis and anyone who through mental or physical disability could not earn their own living in America.

After the hardship of World War I, many Americans were anxious that immigration would not be allowed to resume on anything like the previous scale. Many organizations were formed to rally the cause and were supported by the labor unions who were worried about cheap foreign labor taking their jobs. The effect was that in 1917 new legislation was passed insisting on an English literacy test for all immigrants over sixteen (except those fleeing religious persecution). Also listed were thirty-three classes of foreigners who would not be granted permission to live in the United States, including, primarily Asians. This restricted immigration for a time but after 1921 numbers climbed again. That year the law was made stricter still by establishing temporary quotas limiting each nationality to three percent of its existing foreign-born numbers.

Three years later the National Origins Law set provisional annual quotas at two percent of each nationality as recorded in the 1890 census and a limit of 150,000 annually from non-Western hemisphere countries. Then the most resounding block on immigration was promulgated—from now on every prospective new citizen had to be examined at the American consular office in his/her country of origin. Finally, in 1929, the quota system was fully and permanently promulgated; the numbers of immigrants from each country were rationed by that nationality's proportion of the U.S. population as published in the 1920 census.

More acts and laws were brought in over the years refining and defining those allowed to enter the United States, but the laws already mentioned are the ones which really limited the influx of immigrants.

New York

With its large, safe, deep harbor, New York was the principal East Coast port for transatlantic shipping and consequently the point of arrival for many new immigrants. Between 1786 and 1892 fully two-thirds of the immigrants to America came in through New York; consequently it was here that the first federal laws concerning the arrivals were implemented. In the earliest days those with diseases were sent to the Marine Hospital on Staten Island. But New Yorkers grew increasingly worried about the diseased cargoes arriving and discharging their cargoes largely unchecked. Furthermore the immigrants attracted numbers of unsavory fraudsters and thieves who preyed on the naïve arrivals, often depriving them of all their worldly goods (such as they were). The situation grew desperate, and German and Irish immigrant societies were set up to try and protect their newly arriving countrymen. These societies convinced New York State to create a Board of Commissioners of Emigration to protect the arrivals from the swindlers thronging the wharves—much to the latter's fury. The Board was established on May 4, 1847, and set up the Emigrant Hospital and Refuge in the East River where sick and non-contagious patients could be treated. Also placed under the Board's control was the Marine Hospital.

Nevertheless the numbers arriving—roughly 1,000 immigrants a day—continued to rise beyond reasonable control of the local inspectors and benevolent societies. For example, in 1850, near on 2,000 vessels containing 212,796 immigrants arrived in New York alone: of these 117,038 were Irish; 45,535 were German; and 50,223 from elsewhere. New measures had to be taken. The Board of Commissioners of Emigration needed a holding and examination point and leased for the purpose Castle Clinton, a fifty-year old fort. Built between 1807

Castle Garden, formerly called Fort Clinton, at the southern tip of Manhattan Island as seen in about 1890. The fifty-year old fort served as New York's immigration center between 1855 and 1889, by which time the center was so notorious for corruption that it was closed. For the following year immigrants were processed at the Barge Office, Battery Park while administrators considered other locations for dealing with the increasing flow of aspiring citizens.

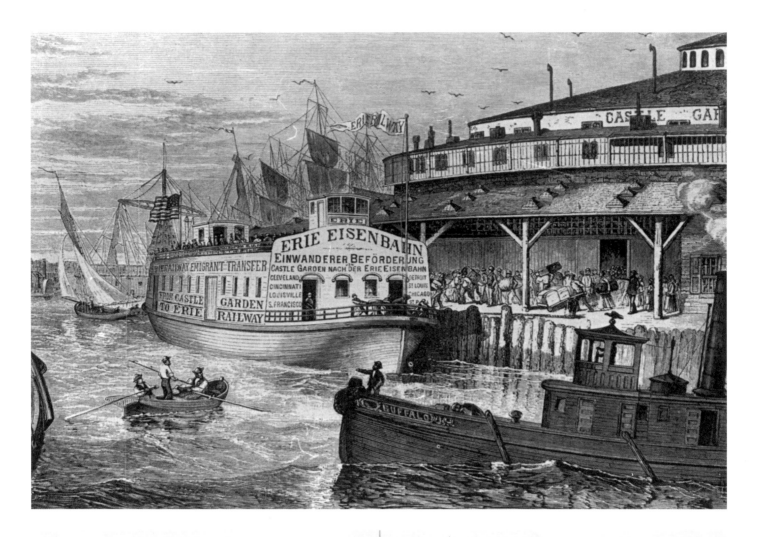

and 1811 to defend New York against possible British invasion, the circular fort was part of a coastal fortification system. Originally called the West Battery, it contained twenty-eight guns and was built by the federal government. In 1815 the fort's name was changed to honor George Clinton, New York's first governor.

The threat of British invasion had receded by 1822 and the federal government gave the fort to New York City. Renamed Castle Garden it became a leisure park for New Yorkers. The venture was unsuccessful, though, and instead the city opened it as the first immigrant receiving station on August 1, 1855. It was open for five years during which time almost seventy percent of all immigrants arriving in America landed there.

Over time the sheer numbers of immigrants and the stresses of dealing with them and the attendant corruption of the administration and officialdom around them forced Congress to rethink the problem from scratch. As a result Castle Gardens were closed in 1890. Then, for a year, while other options were considered, all immigrants were processed under the auspices of the new Federal Bureau of Immigration at the Barge Office, Battery Park.

Ellis Island

Set way out in upper New York Bay, within sight but beyond reach of Manhattan island and New York, lies Ellis Island, the immediate destination point of millions of would-be Americans. There, between 1892 and 1954 over twelve million immigrants arrived in the United States for the first time. After extensive building works, the construction of docks and dredging of deep water facilities the doors of the Ellis Island Immigration Station officially opened for business on Friday, January 1, 1892, on the site of an old naval ammunition store. Simultaneously, immigration stations were established at other major ports including Boston and Philadelphia, as well as San Francisco on the West Coast. At Ellis Island, the work had cost an enormous $500,000—a reflection of the seriousness with which the federal government viewed the immigrant problem. At any one time up to 850 people worked there and even these were inadequate at peak periods.

Only steerage passengers were examined at Ellis Island, first and second class passengers were rapidly and politely checked before being transferred to New York, unless they were obviously ill in which case they went to Ellis Island for further inspection. Once ashore, the steerage passengers were assembled into groups of thirty, each wore a name tag with their ship's manifest number. Then they were ushered to the Main Building's huge reception room where they would be assigned an interpreter (each spoke an average of six languages, but some a lot more). The steep stairs to the Registry Room were the first test of physical ability. Then a doctor looked at each individual—face, hair, neck, hands. If not satisfied he would chalk a large letter on the immigrant meaning, check further. Unsurprisingly, there were times when entire groups would be disinfected before further examination. The next test was the most dreaded exam and concerned the eyes—specifically doctors were looking for trachoma, a disease that could cause blindness and death—and, more to the immediate point, meant certain deportation.

Particularly heart-rending was the plight of sick children—aged 12 and over would be sent back across the Atlantic alone to their departure port, and released there to fend for themselves; children under 12 had a parent to accompany them. Whole families were split this way.

Even after passing the medical exam the ordeal was not over. The next inquisitor was an inspector, ship's manifest in front of him and interpreter beside him. His job was to check the aspiring immigrants answers against the twenty-nine items of information already submitted back in Europe. Known as the "primary line" inspection, each interrogation took about two minutes at the end of which, if satisfactory, each approved immigrant received a landing card. By this stage only two percent failed to pass.

The successful immigrant needed money. With landing card in hand as proof of acceptance he/she went to the Money Exchange where six cashiers exchanged whatever currency or bullion was produced for the day's official rate (as posted on a blackboard) in U.S. dollars.

The next step was top buy a railroad ticket to their destination if it wasn't New York. After arranging for their baggage to be sent on, travelers waited in marked areas for each railroad station until they were called for the requisite ferry and the start of their new life.

Opposite, Above: The romantic and exciting arrival in the New World. A woodcut view of Castle Garden made in 1874, showing an immigrant transfer barge docked outside.

Opposite, Below: In fact the truth was much more austere as this undated photograph of Castle Island shows.

Chalk marks at Ellis Island Immigration Center

X	high front right shoulder mental defect
X	low front right shoulder suspicion of deformity or disease
X	in a circle definite disorder
B	possible back problems
C	conjunctivitis
Ct	trachoma/eye disease
E	eyes
F	face
Ft	feet
D	goiter
H	heart
K	hernia
L	lameness
N	neck
P	physical and lungs
Pg	pregnancy
S	senility
Sc	scalp

Immigrants would be examined further, the mentally ill and physically feeble would be deported without compunction

Below: The magnificent immigration receiving and holding complex of Ellis Island was built after the devastating fire of June 1897, which destroyed the previous wooden buildings. Between 1892 and 1954 over twenty million immigrants entered the United States through its cavernous halls.

Immigrant numbers varied according to political circumstances in Europe. In 1898 Ellis Island processed 178,748 immigrants, four years later the numbers had risen to 445,987 people.

The wooden building of the immigration processing center was completely destroyed by fire in June 1897. Amazingly, despite the inferno, nobody lost their life. For the two and a half years it took to rebuild the facilities, immigrant processing returned to Battery Park. Congress voted $600,000 for rebuilding bigger and better fire-proof facilities, but this had to be upped to $1.5 million by the time the complex was completed to include much bigger administration and hospital facilities. Even these larger facilities proved inadequate in peak periods.

Ellis Island reopened for business on December 17, 1900. However corruption was rife within the building with immigrants threatened, cheated, and exploited before they even reached the mainland. Within the year the venal goings on had reached the ears of President Theodore Roosevelt who ordered an immediate clean-up starting with many at the top. New contracts were put out for food, baggage, concession railroad tickets and money exchange.

During World War I immigration from Europe stopped and Ellis Island served as an internment center for German sailors and suspicious aliens; and again in World War II. Immigrant processing stopped entirely on Ellis Island in 1954.

Left: Ellis Island ferry house as seen from the sea on July 29, 1938.

Left, Below: Immigrants' landing point, Ellis Island circa 1910.

Below: A contemporary photograph of historic Ellis Island—the chief immigration station of the United States of America from 1892 until 1943.

Right: Lady Liberty's view of Ellis Island as she saw it in 1966. Since the days of mass immigration the Statue of Liberty has become a National Monument.

Below: An overview of Ellis Island receiving station. It is now part of the Statue of Liberty National Monument and features an immigration museum.

Above: The loads of incoming wagons being discharged by reservists on September 7, 1914.

Right: Successful immigrants on Ellis Island waiting in line to leave on the ferry for New York and all of America beyond, c.1900.

Right: New arrivals outside the main building on Ellis Island in 1907.

Below: The dreaded medical inspection on which successful entry to the United States depended, photograph taken around 1900.

Opposite, Above left: Immigrants awaiting medical examination at the Immigration Building on Ellis Island in 1904.

Opposite, Above right: Inspectors particularly examined the aspiring immigrant's eyes for signs of disease.

Opposite, Below: Those who failed the medical but were not sick enough to be refused entry were put into quarantine. Here the men were segregated behind a chain link fence and rope barrier, c.1910.

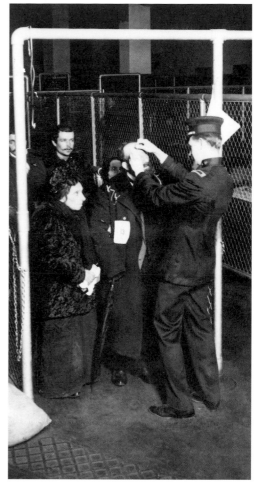

Above: Another examination, this time new arrivals are showing their papers to a board of examiners.

Left: In August 1923 rows of hopeful immigrants wait to be "processed" for entrance to the United States.

Left: The entire entry process involved long periods of waiting for inspection and examination as this photo from 1907 taken in Ellis Island receiving station shows.

Below left: Hopeful immigrants waited patiently under the stars and stripes in the main detention room pending investigation of their visas and other papers.

Below: By 1964 the Great Hall at Ellis Island was quiet and the worn benches were left to bear silent testimony to the millions who successfully passed through to a new life in a new land.

Right: The Great Hall on Ellis Island now houses the Museum of Immigration.

Below: The Registry Hall on Ellis Island full of hopeful people in 1905.

Opposite, Above: Immigrants lined up at Ellis Island processing booths.

Opposite, Below: On September 24, 1920, Ellis Island was overcrowded to almost three times its capacity and had to be temporarily closed until the congestion was relieved. Incoming immigrants had to be held aboard their vessels and hundreds of immigrant families were without sleeping quarters. These lucky people are awaiting release.

Above: Children playing in a wagon on a roof top playground at Ellis Island Immigration Center, c.1905.

Left: Four immigrant children hold American toys at Ellis Island on their first Christmas in the United States, 1918.

Below left: A group of women immigrants on Ellis Island. During their detention they are doing embroidery under the direction of the Matron, c.1920.

Opposite: A young, unnamed, immigrant on Ellis Island in 1905.

Above: A welfare agent fitting an immigrant with clothes supplied by various social service organizations—no charge was made for the service, 1931.

Right: A group of male immigrants wait in line to speak with an immigration officer in the early 1900s.

Opposite, Above: After acceptance as a new citizen, immigrants changed their foreign money for American dollars.

Opposite, Below: Officials asked immigrants a list of questions and checked their answers against previously given information. A record was made of every one.

Above: Immigrants standing in line in front of a money exchange window on Ellis Island in 1911.

Right: Many improvements were made to the Ellis Island facilities in 1925. This is the new dormitory for women and children containing sixty beds and all the latest sanitary arrangements.

Below, Right: View of the immigrant sleeping quarters on Ellis Island in 1923.

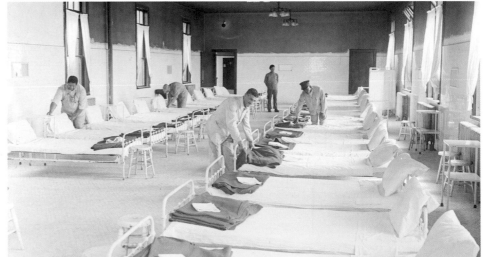

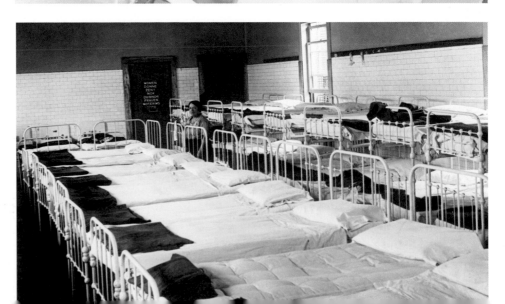

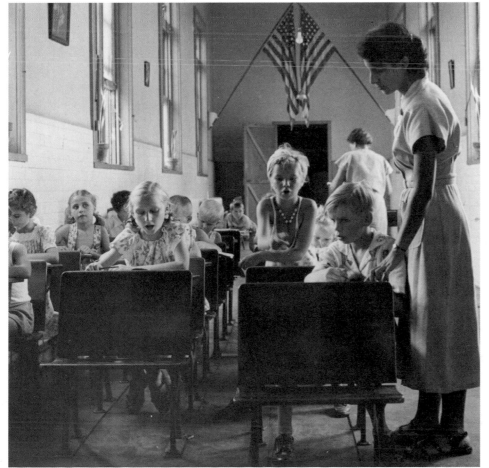

Above: An interior view of the dining room on Ellis Island taken in 1984.

Left: Under the American flag a teacher instructs young immigrants in the classroom at Ellis Island as they await news from the immigration authorities, c.1955.

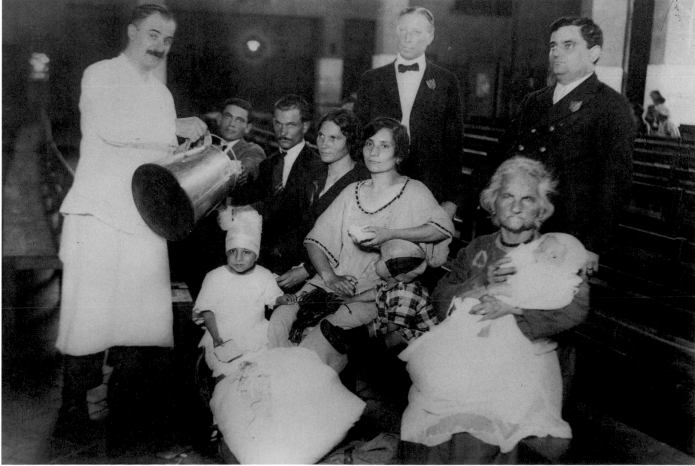

Above: Immigrants awaiting approval of their entry into the United States crowd the lunchroom for their midday meal.

Left: Immigrants being served dinner at the Ellis Island station, November 18, 1920.

Opposite, Above: Women and children being served a welcome drink, c.1920.

Opposite, Below: A man serving refreshments from a large jug to immigrants on Ellis Island in August 1923.

Above: Immigrants in a dining hall on Ellis Island in August 1923.

Right: Successful applicants wait in the railroad room, each is tagged and waiting for ferry boats to the different railroad depots depending on where they were heading.

Opposite, Above: New citizens looking toward Manhattan while waiting to be transferred and become residents of the United States, October 30, 1912.

Opposite, Below: A man hands out bibles to newly arrived immigrants at Ellis Island in 1911.

CHAPTER 1 # The First Settlers

Opposite, Above: A German map tracing the voyages of Christopher Columbus (1446–1506) to the West Indies and the Caribbean Sea.

Opposite, Below: English colonist John Smith (1579–1631) lands in Virginia.

Today, identifying who "discovered" America has become more complicated than in the past; in the same way as theories have been proposed to suggest that Native American culture was affected by seafaring migrants, so too has it been suggested that there were precursors to Columbus. Look at the name "America" itself. The New World was given the name "America" by the German cartographer Martin Waldeseemüller in 1507 after the Florentine explorer, Amerigo Vespucci, who was the first explorer to claim that the New World was actually a continent. Vespucci was a noted charlatan, and his claims were based upon a sensational account of his voyages in which he claimed to have beaten Columbus to the discovery of the New World. Eventually, his claims were disproved, but by that time the name "America" had become accepted. Today, the "discovery" of the Americas is claimed (usually by authors hoping to become bestsellers) by many people—from the Japanese and Chinese to the Basques (fishermen off Newfoundland), Irish (St. Brendan), Scots (the mysterious "Albans"), and even the Welsh (the followers of Prince Madoc).

The very earliest travelers to arrive in the Americas are now generally agreed to have been the Vikings, sailing the cold North Atlantic waters via Iceland and Greenland. Indeed, statues and celebrations have attended the official launch of "Leif Ericsson Day"—July 15— but it seems that the Norsemen only visited for a short time. Whether their settlement was permanent and finished off by war or illness, or temporary—perhaps they came merely to hunt wildlife and fish the teeming waters—they were not present in the seventeenth century when the first influx of successful settlers took place. Probably the major difference between the Viking age and that of the Spaniards, the Portuguese, the English, the French, and the other European states involved in the colonization of the New World, is that the Europeans now had the means to secure a domination over the hostile environment—both physical and human— that they encountered.

Not unexpectedly the English were by far the largest group of immigrants in Colonial America, constituting about sixty percent of the population of European descent and somewhat less than half of the total population in 1790, taking into account African Americans but not the unknown number of Native Americans. The English arrival and dominance of the new lands came about through increased national wealth and a desire for more, natural curiosity, and during a period of largely internal peace and security established by Queen Elizabeth I. Virginia was the first colony to be settled permanently and the first pioneers had a long and hard struggle. Many colonists died and others found life so hard that 300 of the original settlers returned to England in the first nine years of settlement.

The greatest need for England was to persuade her citizens to make the dangerous transatlantic crossing and take up the challenge of a new life. The inducement was land. For the poor but worthy this was a huge attraction—Elizabethans were quick to realize that a new colony would not thrive if all the citizens were criminals and prostitutes intent on a life of ease and dishonesty. In Virginia English settlers were able to farm on a scale long unavailable to any but the very wealthy back home. Also there were no ancient laws and precedents restricting land usage, anyone could take the land and farm as they wanted—and no feudal landlord to pay tithes and homage to either! The first successful settlers therefore, were artisans and tenant farmers, whose life in England was restricted by lack of land and funds, but who had skills with which they could earn a living if given the chance. Virginia presented just that opportunity.

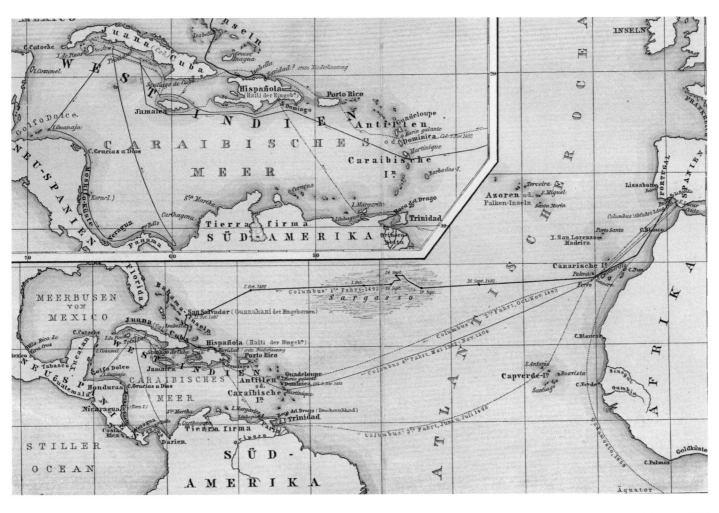

*Dutch colonial officer Peter Minuit
(1580–1638) purchases Manhattan Island
from Man-a-hat-a Native Americans, for trinkets
valued at $24; from a painting by Alfred
Fredericks*

In 1605 two English companies were charted with the specific intention of colonizing America. One was based in London, the other in Plymouth. After exploration, the latter briefly attempted a settlement at Sagadahoc (now Maine), but the London Company founded the first successful settlement on the James River, Virginia, on May 24, 1607. The settlement contained 105 souls who had arrived in three ships—the *Godspeed*, *Discovery*, and *Susan Constant*; (another 39 had died on the Atlantic crossing). Life was extremely tough for these people, but three years later the settlement was established enough to be named Jamestown—it was later abandoned. But at this time and for some years afterward, even the settlers had no idea of the sheer scale and size of the continent they now called home. The Appalachian Mountains were the very limit of geographical knowledge and even their extent was unknown, let alone anything beyond.

A number of colonists went to the New World with the intention of spreading the word of God as well as to escape religious persecution and intolerance. A small minority, albeit an important one, of these English migrants were Puritans and Pilgrims emigrating in family groups in the seventeenth century. Most were yeomen, husbandmen, and artisans impoverished by population increases, economic change, or personal circumstances.

The most famous of these were the Pilgrim Fathers, refugees from religious discrimination in England, who landed at Plymouth Rock on December 16, 1620. Their voyage on the *Mayflower* across the Atlantic was reckoned a good one as only five of the 149 on board died on the crossing. However, during the following winter half the crew and half the passengers died as the effects of scurvy and other diseases. By the following year, only four of the eighteen married women survived.

There were a number of factors that were fundamental in the ability of sixteenth and seventeenth century Europeans to sustain their presence in the Americas as opposed to their tenth and eleventh century forebears. The first of these was, without doubt, the technological advances in weaponry that had occurred over the previous 500 years. While the Vikings had been armed with weapons—such as swords and spears—which were not wholly dissimilar in destructive power to the weapons that were available to the Native Americans, by the start of the fifteenth century the Europeans were equipped with guns and armor which made their military effectiveness much greater.

A second factor in the establishment of European settlement at the start of the sixteenth century was that, rather than the small numbers which the Vikings had brought, huge numbers of adventurers and settlers (many of whom were drawn by promises of instant wealth), took the hazardous journey across the Atlantic Ocean. While not all found the gold promised by the promoters of expeditions, once suitable crops—notably tobacco and sugar—had been identified, so the fertile land became in itself a magnet to those wishing to cultivate the land and build a new future for themselves. The attractiveness of the New World was all the greater during the turbulent sixteenth and seventeenth centuries as a result of the religious strife that redefined the map of Europe in the years after the Reformation.

The French and English in particular enthusiastically explored North America in the hopes of finding mineral wealth, especially gold, in the quantities that the Spanish and Portuguese were enjoying in South America. But none was found and it was this very lack of obvious wealth, which meant that, while the European nations were happy to trade with the native population of North America, there was not the same impetus to conquest. French involvement with North America started shortly after the discovery of Newfoundland. Temporary settlements were established to cure and dry the vast shoals of fish (primarily cod) caught close to the mainland, and while the fur trade with the native Americans developed, again, this did not require the creation of permanent settlements.

The French stronghold was initially Quebec and then Montreal (1642). In this area the French also developed strong trading links based on the export of fur. From their base at Quebec, French explorers took European intervention into the North American heartland. In 1673, Jacques Marquette (a Jesuit) and Louis Joliet headed southward to the Mississippi, claiming the entire length of the river for France. Nine years later, in 1682, Rene Robert Cavelier, Sieur de la Salle, continued the southward exploration of the Mississippi, finally reaching the river's delta. He claimed the river delta for France, christening the region "Louisiana" after the French king, Louis XIV. In 1718, another Frenchman, Jean-Baptiste Le Moyne, Sieur de Bienville (1680—1768), founded the city of Nouvelle Orleans (a place which is today better known as New Orleans).

While the French were establishing themselves on the St. Lawrence and down the Mississippi, other developments were occurring on the eastern seaboard. In 1609, Henry Hudson, an Englishman employed by the Dutch East India Company, while exploring for the elusive Northwest Passage, sailed up a river—the future Hudson River—and claimed the territory for the Dutch. Nieuw (New) Holland was established around Long Island Sound in 1614 and, twelve years later in 1626, one of the most important land deals in history saw Peter Minuit purchase the island of Manhattan from the local Native Americans. The area, which was named Nieuw Amsterdam, is believed to have cost no more than the equivalent of $24.

Further up the Hudson River, the Dutch also established Fort Orange; this was later to be renamed Albany by the British and is still the state capital of New York State. The Dutch presence in the New World was, however, destined to be short-lived as the European rivalry between the Netherlands and Britain resulted in the latter seizing the Dutch-occupied region in August 1664 and rechristening it New York. The Dutch governor at the time was the one-legged and vile tempered Peter Stuyvesant. The primary Dutch reason for settlement was trade and, consequently, the actual number of Dutch settlers was few. Unlike other nationals, the Dutch arrivals were normally employees of the sponsoring company—in this case the Dutch West Indies Company—and received no grants of land.

Apart from the Dutch, representatives of a number of other European nations, including Swedes and Germans, also lived in New Holland, as did some English Puritans who had settled on Long Island to get away from oppression at home. After the Dutch surrendered their right to govern in 1664, their nationals were allowed to remain in the country.

Of all the major players in the colonization of the Americas, it was the English (and later the Scots) that were the last to make their presence felt but were, ultimately, to become the dominant European power in North America and in the West Indies. Although English support had seen Cabot discover Newfoundland relatively early, domestic troubles—religious

Crowds hoping to emigrate to America waiting outside the Government Medical Inspector's Office in London, July 1850.

turmoil resulting from the Reformation, two weak monarchs after Henry VIII and, following the succession of Elizabeth I, the almost constant threat of European intervention in England (culminating in the Spanish Armada in 1588), meant that England's primary concern at this time was its own territorial security.

This is not to say that England ignored the New World. This certainly was not the case but, rather than acting to acquire land, English sailors, most notably figures like Sir Walter Raleigh, acted as pirates, seizing the treasure that the Spaniards had looted from South and Central America. In 1583 Sir Humphrey Gilbert took possession of Newfoundland in the name of Queen Elizabeth I, but this ownership was short-lived and no effort was made to establish a permanent settlement. The first English attempt to establish a permanent colony in the New World was the ill-fated Roanoke Island settlement in North Carolina founded by Sir Walter Raleigh in 1585.

The next phase in the English colonization of North America came with the establishment of Jamestown in 1607 when 105 settlers arrived under the command of Captain John Smith. This settlement was to form the basis of the province of Virginia. The origin of this settlement was the granting of a Royal Charter by King James I on April 10, 1606, to the London Company. Led by Sir Thomas Smythe, this company soon changed its name to the Virginia Company in order to exploit the anticipated riches of the area. In December 1606 three ships carrying Virginia Company colonists—the *Susan Constant*, the *Discovery*, and the *Godspeed*—sailed for the New World.

Following the ultimately successful settlement of Virginia, other English colonies were soon established, or at least authorized. Of these early settlements it was the arrival of the Pilgrim Fathers—the 102 Puritans on board the *Mayflower*, who landed in November 1620 at Cape Cod (in as yet unnamed Massachusetts)—which was perhaps the most significant. These English settlers had already fled to Holland to escape religious oppression, then further emigrated to the New World so they could pursue their Puritan faith in peace. They drew up and signed the "*Mayflower* Compact." This agreement promised that the settlers would be obedient to the laws of their leaders. This established the principle of "government by the people," one of the basic precepts of democracy. In November 1621, the Pilgrim Fathers celebrated their first harvest in the New World, a celebration which continues each November to this day as Thanksgiving Day.

Further colonies followed. In 1623 New Hampshire was founded, although its early history was interlinked closely with neighboring Massachusetts. In 1629 King Charles I granted to Robert Heath the colony of Carolina; this had originally been Spanish and was later to be divided into North and South Carolina. Boston was founded in 1630 and this was followed in 1634 by the creation of Maryland. Connecticut was established in 1635 and Rhode Island in 1636. English power was further enhanced by the take-over in 1664 of Nieuw Amsterdam, Nieuw Holland and Delaware from the Dutch. The last-named state, originally investigated by John Cabot in 1498, was first settled permanently by Swedes in 1635 as Ny Sverige (New Sweden); Swedish rule was, however, short-lived, and in 1655 control passed to the Dutch. Delaware was incorporated into Pennsylvania from 1682 until 1775.

Both Protestants and Catholics sought a refuge from persecution in the Old World. Many of the earliest English settlements, for example, were the result of Puritans—a more extreme version of Protestantism than that officially practiced in Britain—seeking the space to be able to practice their religion in freedom. Pennsylvania itself was founded by the Quaker, William Penn, in 1681, while Philadelphia, Pennsylvania's state capital, followed two years later. The last of the English Thirteen Colonies—Georgia—was established by James Oglethorpe in 1732.

The rise of British power in northern Canada and along the New England coast posed an ever-growing threat to the French dominance along the St. Lawrence and the Mississippi. It was inevitable, therefore, that the rivalry between these increasingly important world powers—already at war in Europe—would develop into open hostilities in the New World.

On the western seaboard, following the earlier explorers who had sailed up the coast of California, it was only in the mid- and late-eighteenth century that explorers sailed further north. The crucial figure in the exploration of the sea between California and the Arctic Circle was a Dane, Vitus Bering, who was working for the Russians and after whom the straits between Alaska and Russia were named. It was through him that the Russians came to have a presence in North America. Subsequently, the coast of the area known later as Oregon Country was sailed by Captain James Cook, one of the most famous of all the late eighteenth century British explorers who was to be a crucial figure in the development of British influence in the Pacific from 1778.

It was inevitable as both England (and later the United Kingdom) and France developed overseas empires that war would ensue between the two countries wherever their interests coincided. Often these conflicts were an adjunct to the major wars that afflicted Europe from 1660 onward, but even when a nominal peace existed in Europe, away in the colonies strife could continue unabated. In North America this imperial rivalry had two immediate consequences. First, both Britain and France constructed a network of forts to defend their territory; second, alliances were forged with potentially friendly Native American tribes in order to gain tactical advantage.

The first major European war between Britain and France to have consequences in the New World took place during the War of Spanish Succession (1701–14). In Europe, there was concern about the growing power of the French state under Louis XIV and, in 1702, Britain joined the Grand Alliance against France and the latter's ally, Spain. The war in Europe culminated in French defeat at the Battle of Blenheim. Much of the action was not in the future United States, but in what was to become Canada.

The War of Spanish Succession was ended by the Treaties of Utrecht (1713) and for the French it was a watershed. Their colonial possessions in North America, strung along the St. Lawrence and the Mississippi, were now sandwiched between two areas dominated by the English—the Hudson Bay region and New England; furthermore, the British colonies were both more populous and better organized in terms of manufacturing industry.

In 1756 the Seven Years' War broke out, known as the French and Indian Wars in North America, this conflict was to witness the almost total elimination of French power in North America. The Treaty of Paris, signed on February 10, 1763, effectively ended French influence on the American mainland and was a reflection of their military weakness, so cruelly exposed on the battlefield. France ceded all of Canada to the British, along with all land to the east of the Mississippi. Britain also gained Florida from Spain.

English Quaker reformer and colonist William Penn (1644–1718) making a peace treaty with Native Americans in October 1682.

CHAPTER 2 Slavery

Opposite: Prince Henry of Portugal (1394-1463), known as Henry the Navigator, popularly credited with instigating the Portuguese exploration of the West African coast in the fifteenth century. Slaves were taken on these voyages and sold for use in Portugal.

At the time of Independence the population of the United States was some 3.5 million (not counting the unknown numbers of Native Americans). The largest part of this figure was, naturally, of English descent. The second largest group, comprising almost twenty percent of the total population, were the African American descendants of those who had survived the "Middle Passage," of whom around 690,000 were still enslaved, the remainder so-called "free persons of color." While this book is planned to examine willing immigrants, it is impossible to discuss the subject without referring to slavery. This chapter, therefore, examines briefly the history of slavery and its involvement in the history of the United States.

The start of the slave trade

Within decades of Portuguese ships first reaching the West African coastline in the fifteenth century, the largest enforced population movement the world has seen was already underway. Over the next four centuries some ten million or more Africans were shipped under the most horrendous conditions imaginable, to live, work, and die in a new and alien world. However, contrary to popular perception, scholars now estimate that only some six to seven percent of these Africans were landed on the North American mainland.

The Portuguese, situated at the far western boundaries of the Mediterranean world, yet benefiting both from their long experience of sailing well beyond the relatively calm seas of the Mediterranean to trade with ports in Britain and northern Europe and from their intimate knowledge of Islamic North Africa, were exceptionally well placed to exploit the new possibilities for Atlantic exploration made possible by advances in maritime technology in the fourteenth and fifteenth centuries. Inspired as much by the prospect of short term commercial gains as the long term goal of outflanking the Islamic rulers of the Middle East by discovering a sea route to the Indies and the gold mines of "Ethiopia," Portuguese—and to a lesser extent Catalan and Castillian Spanish—ships began to raid the Moroccan coast and the newly rediscovered Canary Islands in the fourteenth century. These voyages bought back trade goods including animal hides, wood products and dyestuffs, but also an increasing number of slaves obtained by raiding.

Permanent colonization of the Canary Islands began in 1402–05, setting a pattern for the exploitation of other Atlantic islands with the establishment of agricultural production using the forced labor of Africans. After the Portuguese captain, Gil Eannes, successfully returned from a voyage beyond Cape Bojador in 1434, breaching a previously much feared frontier of the known world, successive voyages pushed further down the African coast, making contact for the first time with populous regions and established local kingdoms. The gold producing regions of the Gold Coast were reached around 1470, with regular trade beginning further east with the kingdom of Benin in 1485–86, and Diego Cão, on a voyage sponsored by the crown, making contact with the kingdom of Kongo in the early 1480s. By 1488 Bartolomeu Dias reached the southern tip of the African continent, opening up Portuguese trade into the Indian ocean. The islands (all uninhabited except for the Canaries) discovered in the course of this exploration, notably Madeira, the Cape Verdes, and São Tomé, were first exploited by the gathering of wild products, but it soon became apparent that with the use of slave labor from

A view of Lisbon in 1640. In 1510, King Ferdinand of Spain authorized the purchase of 250 Africans in the slave markets of Lisbon to be carried to his territories in New Spain. The Atlantic slave trade was underway.

the Canaries and the African mainland they would support rich harvests of sugar, wine, and other highly valued goods.

Thus even before Columbus's voyage of 1492 revealed the presence of a previously unknown continent, the Portuguese and Spanish were using African slaves in plantation agriculture on the Atlantic islands. Other slaves, estimated at around a thousand per year, were being brought back for sale in Lisbon. At first the Portuguese simply seized their captives in raiding parties sent ashore, but they soon found that African forces using canoes were able to offer surprisingly successful resistance. In 1447 for example, the Danish captain and most of the crew of a Portuguese vessel were killed by local people in a naval battle off the island of Gorée. After these early setbacks the practice of negotiating with local African rulers and winning their consent to engage in trade of both slaves and goods became the norm throughout the history of the Atlantic trade. The Portuguese found well-established commercial markets and trade networks which they could tap into and extend. For example they bought slaves in Kongo and indigo dyed textiles in both Benin and Ijebu (a Yoruba-speaking kingdom in southwestern Nigeria) and resold both in exchange for gold on the Gold Coast. It seemed a natural extension of these developments to turn to African labor to exploit the agricultural potential and mineral wealth of the colonies the Portuguese were establishing in Brazil, and the Spanish throughout their vast new possessions in the Caribbean and the American mainland. In 1510 King Ferdinand of Spain authorized the purchase of 250 Africans in Lisbon to be carried to his territories in New Spain. The Atlantic slave trade was underway.

Africans were not the only source of "unfree" labor available to the colonists of the Americas. Both Native Americans and Europeans were also used. Labor from these sources however was to prove neither as suitable nor as effective in the majority of cases. The Native American population of the Caribbean and South America, and rather later, of North America, was devastated by a combination of disease, the exceptional brutality of the colonists, and the destruction of existing systems of agriculture and commerce. In most areas population numbers collapsed to a fraction of their former levels. Although in the sixteenth century there was a thriving slave trade in prisoners captured from the unconquered parts of the Caribbean and during the conquest of Mexico, and numerous more localized systems of enslavement persisted elsewhere, Spanish laws and the pressure of missionaries prevented the enslavement of the majority of the subjugated Native American populations. Moreover, most Native Americans slaves lacked the skills needed and were unable to adjust to the patterns of labor required of them. Although they continued to be employed as servants and were integrated as a subject labor force in the colonial economies of Spanish America and Brazil they were not a substitute for African slaves. Often Native American laborers worked on the same plantations as African slaves but performed only seasonal labor and unskilled tasks.

The immigration of Europeans, either as free workers or as indentured servants, was a potential second source, particularly once the British, Dutch, and French had established colonies in the Caribbean and North American mainland. However, the available supply of such workers was limited—no European countries at this period had the surplus of urban poor that was to fuel the mass emigration to the Americas in the nineteenth and early twentieth centuries that will be dealt with in later chapters. Indentured servants, who signed contracts obliging them to work for a period of years (usually between three and seven) in return for their passage and board on arrival, as well as a small plot of land on expiry of the contract, were comparable in cost for masters in the West Indies with slaves bought from Africa. In 1695 an indentured servant cost Jamaican planters in the region of $15–25 plus transportation fare, while a slave cost around $30. Many thousands of Europeans did come to the Caribbean as indentured servants, but mortality rates through exposure to new diseases and often harsh frontier labor conditions were high. Moreover, the planters found it inconvenient to release the survivors and grant them land, thereby creating growing numbers of troublesome smallholders. It was far better from their perspective of economic self interest to import Africans who were not only relatively more resistant to tropical diseases but could be denied all rights and kept in slavery indefinitely.

A Puritan Couple. Although states such as Pennsylvania and Rhode Island, which were settled by religious nonconformists did not develop economies directly based on slavery, they had less scruples about supplying the slave colonies in the West Indies and their ports supported significant numbers of slavers.

Slave traders and the slaving nations

The history of the involvement of a succession of European powers and their colonies in the business of shipping Africans as slaves to the Americas is a complex one. It is inextricably bound up with far wider issues of the shifts in relative economic strength and maritime power of the participating nations, the vagaries of numerous European wars, changes in the attitude of governments towards issues such as regulated versus free trade, and the possibilities offered by the differing situations in their various colonies and bases in both Africa and the Americas.

Although Portugal and Spain pioneered the development of colonies in the Americas, the Spanish were prevented by the Treaty of Tordesillas, signed after Papal mediation in 1494, from establishing colonies in Africa. This left the Portuguese with a monopoly of the transatlantic trade until the closing years of the following century, while the Spanish colonies were reliant on purchasing slaves shipped by other powers. The Spanish Crown's attempt to regulate and profit from this position by the sale of a series of import license contracts, known as *asiento*, contributed to European rivalry over the trade while failing to furnish sufficient slaves to meet the virtually insatiable demands of her vast colonies. Although the Dutch vigorously attacked the Portuguese monopoly throughout the seventeenth century, the continued expansion in demand for slaves, and the overall growth of the trade meant that Portuguese slavers carried ever increasing numbers over the following centuries. Recent figures by Rawley, based on Philip Curtin's pioneering census indicate total shipments by the Portuguese to be in the order of 4.2 million Africans, rising from under a quarter of a million in the sixteenth century, to a peak of over 1.9 million in the eighteenth century, and a further 1.45 million in the nineteenth century before the trade was finally halted in the 1870s.

The far-reaching Dutch assault on the maritime empire of the Portuguese and Spanish came in the course of the Eighty Years' War (1568–1648). By the 1630s and 1640s Dutch naval superiority had allowed them to take both the Pernambuco sugar-plantation region of Brazil and important African slave supplying areas, including Gorée, the fort of El Mina in the Gold Coast and coastal regions of Angola, from the Portuguese. Although the Portuguese subsequently regained control of Brazil and the Angolan ports, the Dutch were able to take a substantial share of the slave trade. Among the Dutch colonies established in this period, including New Amsterdam, only Surinam on the South American mainland became a large slave-using economy, but the Dutch role as a major maritime power was secured. The relatively barren Dutch-controlled Caribbean island of Curaçao became a major entrepôt for the illicit supply of slaves to the French Caribbean and Spanish America. The Dutch scholar Johannes Postma has estimated the total number of Africans carried by the Dutch to be just under a half million.

French slave traders, based in the ports of Nantes, Bordeaux, La Rochelle, and Le Havre, carried slaves from Senegambia, the Windward Coast, the Bight of Benin, and Angola, to both French Caribbean colonies and the mainland of South America. French slave trading was insignificant until the end of the seventeenth century, reaching a peak in the final decades of the eighteenth century, before the loss of her main slave using colony in Saint-Domingue in the 1790s, and French defeat in the Napoleonic war two decades later, brought an abrupt end. Over the century as a whole it is estimated that French slavers carried something over a million people, making it the third largest participant in the Atlantic trade. By far the largest number of French-imported slaves, along with numerous others bought by other slavers, went to labor in the sugar plantations of Saint-Domingue (present day Haiti). Astonishingly this single colony is now thought to have been the second largest importer of slaves after Brazil, taking nearly ten percent of the total. The French were also significant participants in a much smaller scale eighteenth century and early nineteenth century trade in slaves from Madagascar and South East Africa to plantation economies established on various small Indian Ocean islands.

Although British slave trading took place as early as the notorious voyages of John Hawkins in the 1560s, the organized participation of the British on any scale began with a series of companies granted successive royal charters to engage in slave trading and other African trade in the latter part of the seventeenth century. The Royal Africa Company, chartered in 1672, played a major role in maintaining the string of forts on the African coast and exported some 89,000 slaves between 1673 and 1689. After that date the company's monopoly was increasingly challenged by new independent traders. Slavers from the ports of Bristol and Liverpool now overtook those based in London, although London remained both an important slaving port and the center of the European sugar trade. By the 1730s the British were the dominant slaving nation, a position they maintained until abolition in 1807. Between 1690 and 1807 they transported in the vicinity of 2.8 million African slaves.

Although the supply of provisions to the slave societies of the Caribbean had long been the economic mainstay of the colonies of New England, and the southern colonies were themselves of course based on slave labor, the direct participation of the states of North America in the transatlantic trade itself was relatively minor and of only about fifty years' duration. Beginning as late as 1760, American slave traders carried some 425,000 Africans, a large proportion of whom were landed in Brazil and Cuba. A smaller illicit trade to these two countries continued into the 1860s. The major U.S. slave trading ports were Newport, Providence, and Bristol, as well as Rhode Island, Boston and Salem in Massachusetts, and, to a lesser degree, New York.

The Middle Passage

No discussion of slavery is complete without some words about the conditions of transportation—although the sheer horror of the conditions endured by millions of Africans in the course of the Middle Passage can easily overwhelm any attempt to describe it. It certainly cannot be mitigated by pointing out that the slavers' crews, and white indentured servants, suffered similar appallingly high mortality rates on transatlantic voyages. Assessments of the relative mortality rates of different routes or different periods, relevant as they no doubt were to slavers' profits, are too abstract to approach the intensity of terror and almost unimaginable cruelties deliberately and routinely imposed in the interests of those profits.

The English abolitionists who in 1788 first published and distributed the notorious print depicting the arrangement of slaves packed together on the Liverpool ship, the *Brookes*, "like books on a shelf" as a contemporary viewer put it, captured the essential basis of the Middle Passage. Nowhere else was the slave society's convenient myth that the slaves were goods not human beings so thoroughly expressed. A witness who sailed on the *Brookes* in 1783 recorded that they packed in over 600 slaves on the 320-ton ship, with over seventy dying on the crossing. Although the majority of slave ships were rather smaller, the deadly confinement was the same. As the ship lay at anchor off the African coast, the carpenter and crew installed the wooden slave decks into the holds that had previously been filled with cargo. Before each purchase the captives were stripped and subjected to a rough and intimate examination by the ship's surgeon in an effort to weed out those already sick. Those selected were often branded with a dealers mark. Once embarked the slaves were slotted on these decks, with only four feet or so of headroom. Men were usually chained in pairs, held at wrist and ankle, while women and children were sometimes allowed to move around the ship by day. All the slaves were usually bought on deck twice daily for an exercise period and forced to perform a shuffling dance under the crew's whips. Food consisted of rice, beans, or yams, palm oil, and a small ration of water. Those who refused to eat or otherwise disobeyed any commands were brutally punished. Slave ships stocked crude metal braces used to force open the mouth so that food could be forced down the throat. Although some captains forbade the crew from interfering with the women, there was a constant danger of rape. Recalcitrant slaves were whipped, clubbed, or simply cast overboard. A constant watch was kept to prevent suicide or rebellion, with savage reprisals following unsuccessful attempts. After a revolt on the American ship *Kentucky* in 1844, forty-six men and one woman were hanged, mutilated while still alive, then shot and thrown into the sea.

It is likely that the traumatic impact of the experience itself killed many, a cause contemporary observers recognized as "melancholy" from which many never recovered. Dysentery, known as "flux" was a major killer, as were yaws, scurvy, smallpox, measles, and "fever." Opthalmia was also a regular problem—on the French ship Le Rodeur in 1819, thirty-nine slaves who went blind were simply thrown overboard. The barely trained doctors that slave ships carried in an effort to minimize the economic cost of these outbreaks seldom made any significant difference.

As might be expected, the longer the slaves were kept in such appalling conditions the higher the rate of attrition. The proportion of people who died on individual voyages varied between a low of around two or three percent to upwards of twenty-five out of every hundred. Shipwrecks could exact an even higher toll—in 1737 only sixteen slaves out of 716 survived the wreck of the Dutch ship Leusden. Also, large numbers weakened by the journey died while awaiting sale in the ports of the Americas. In Jamaica it was estimated that between 1655 and 1737, of the 676,276 slaves recorded on arrival, 31,181 died while still in the harbor. Other unfortunates did not survive much longer—one captain reported to his ship owners that their credit in the Indies could be harmed considerably as so many of their "parcels" had expired within twenty-four hours of sale.

Once they had arrived in the New World, mortality rates were still appalling. It has been estimated that, in the Caribbean as a whole, one in three newly imported Africans died within three years of arrival, while in Barbados between 1764 and 1771 around 35,000 slaves were imported but the total population grew by only 5,000. Planters worked on the assumption that they would have to replace at least five percent of their labor force annually. The ratio of men to women in these slave societies varied, with Barbados, for example, having a much higher percentage of women, and hence a larger locally-born Creole slave population than on the other islands. In all of them, however, the conditions were such that, until abolition, in contrast to the situation on the North American mainland, there was no prospect of the African population reproducing, and a large influx of new slaves was needed each year to maintain the existing numbers.

North America

Slavery was crucial to the development of many of the colonies established in North America. It was the forced labor of Africans and African-Americans, assisted in some cases by that of impoverished Europeans imported as indentured servants, that opened up the vast new territories to the production of crops and laid the basis for the future prosperity of the United States. Today, the descendants of those original African survivors of the Middle Passage form a substantial percentage of the population, still struggling in many cases with the bitter legacy of racism and injustice left by the era of slavery. Yet the American colonies were relatively late in their involvement in the slave trade and accounted for a surprisingly low proportion of the total. It is only in the last few decades that scholars working with the details of historical records have established that the number of slaves imported into the mainland of North America was probably a little over half a million. This amounts to about six percent of the Atlantic slave trade, and is substantially lower than the figure for some of the larger Caribbean sugar plantation colonies such as Cuba. For only a brief period after the Revolution and before the abolition did the American colonies account for a substantial proportion of those Africans crossing the Atlantic.

Many American colonists, seeking to found new communities on ideals of liberty and equality that contrasted with the poverty and oppression they had left in Europe, were conscious of the disparity between these aspirations and the reality of a reliance on slave labor. Whilst this prevented neither the development of slave-based plantation economies in the American South, nor the direct and indirect involvement in slave trading by merchants in northern colonies, it did serve to stimulate both a continued undercurrent of legislative opposition in the post-Independence era and the elaboration of a self-justifying ideology of paternalism in the ante-bellum (i.e. pre-Civil War) South. Despite the many brutalities and the all-pervasive injustices, the worst excesses of plantation slavery in the Caribbean—with its appalling death toll of African lives—were far more rarely found. Taken as a whole, the slave societies of the North American mainland were the only ones in which a locally-born Creole population was able to sustain itself, despite the struggle to work and the constantly threatened heartbreak of forcibly separated families. That the black population rose from less than 7,000 in 1680 to 1,377,080 in the first post-abolition census of 1810 owes as much to natural increase as to slave importation.

Before the Revolution: slavery in the American colonies

There were small numbers of slaves in the mainland colonies, working as both domestic servants and agricultural laborers, almost from the first years of European settlement. Some of the earliest seem to have been bought by the Dutch. Records of a colonist, John Rolfe, cited by the historian James Rawley, noted the import of slaves in Virginia in 1619. This was, however, an isolated incident and it was with the spread of tobacco growing after about 1670 that more regular slave imports began. Before this the colonies had been largely reliant on white indentured servants. Mostly young men hoping to escape poverty in England, Germany, and Ireland, these servants were bound to work for their master for a fixed term, usually three to five years. A few were taught a trade but the majority were agricultural laborers. Masters worked them ruthlessly to extract the maximum possible labor before the contracted term expired. Contracts could be extended further as punishment for indebtedness or attempts to run away. Many did try to escape and suffered whippings, branding, or bodily mutilation if captured. About half of all indentured servants in the Chesapeake colonies died before their contracts expired. Once free, the shortage of women allowed most female servants to marry but men usually remained impoverished dependants of their former master.

After 1680, the settlers switched towards an increasing reliance on slave labor and the number of new indentured servants fell in both proportional and absolute terms. The percentage of Africans in the population of Virginia rose from seven to forty-four percent, and that of South Carolina from seventeen to sixty-one percent in the years between 1680 and 1750. In part this was due to changing circumstances in the domestic labor market in England, that reduced the supply and raised the cost of indentured workers. At much the same time British merchants, in the form of the chartered Royal Africa Company, opened up access to the Atlantic slave trade on a wider scale. In simple economic terms, the relative price of slaves improved markedly, although it remained more expensive to buy a slave than to take on an indentured servant. Slaves, however, could be kept in perpetual servitude and so represented a

"The First Cotton Gin."

better long term investment. Moreover, it was generally felt that they were better suited to labor conditions and so more likely to survive. It was also felt to be more difficult for slaves to escape successfully as it was harder for them to blend in with the free poor—the presumption, despite the presence of growing numbers of free blacks, was that all Africans were slaves.

There was, at first, a degree of uncertainty about the legal position of these newly imported slaves. Many slave-holders were particularly reluctant to allow their slaves to become Christians in case it should subsequently be established that this was a cause for emancipation. However, beginning with Virginia's first major slave code in 1680, laws were enacted over the following decades by both southern and northern colonies that restricted the rights of both slaves and free blacks. Slaves and the children of slave women were bound for life; they required written permission to carry arms or leave their master's land; and the possibilities of manumission were severely constrained. Free blacks were prevented from voting, from marrying whites, and from testifying in court against whites. Scholars have argued that these evolving laws reflect both increasing racial prejudice and the growing dominance of the interests of slave-holders on whose continued prosperity the colonies were dependent. There is considerable evidence that in the early years and in frontier zones of spreading colonization, blacks and poor whites interacted on a much more tolerant basis than would later become the norm. Isolated cases of slaves marrying poor white women have been documented from seventeenth century Virginia.

The circumstances of their labor were the dominant factors in determining the differing life experiences and the possibilities of community development facing slaves in differing regions. Only a minority worked in conditions similar to those of sugar plantation slaves in the Caribbean. It was only in South Carolina and Georgia, where the large scale irrigation needed for rice growing (similar to the demands of sugar cultivation) required a large and intensively worked labor force, that holdings of 100 or more slaves became commonplace by the late eighteenth century.

Absentee planters on these estates, and those that subsequently developed to produce cotton on the Sea Islands, usually used the "task" system, under which each slave was set a job for the day and was free to stop once he or she had completed it. As in the Caribbean, this permitted the slaves to develop a substantial area of economic independence, and for this reason alone it was not popular with planters elsewhere in the South. Tobacco, the dominant crop of Virginia and Maryland, did not require the same concentration of labor. More than half the slave-holders in this area owned five or fewer slaves, living and working in far closer contact with the master than was normal on the minority of large plantations. Significant proportions of the white population in most districts owned no slaves at all. The plantation aristocracy of large scale slave owners, important and influential though they were in Southern society, were by no means the norm. In the North there were a very few large estates and the overwhelming majority of slaves worked as servants, craftsmen, or farm hands, owned in groups of only two or three. Slaves performed a wide variety of skilled tasks. In Virginia in 1648 one master was reported to have available for hire as skilled workers over forty slaves pursuing various trades. Although this was far from typical, as the number of white laborers increased so did hostility to the competition posed by the hiring out of slaves in this way. Nevertheless, the contribution made to local economies by the labor skills of both slaves working on the plantations and those living in towns was considerable.

Revolution and Independence: a false dawn for Abolition

The era of the American Revolution has been described as bringing the first major challenge to American slavery. Thousands of slaves were able to take advantage of opportunities the disruptions of war offered to make a break for freedom. Of perhaps greater long term importance, the whole institution of slavery, which had previously seemed beyond reproach, became the focus of sustained criticism. In turn this provoked slavery's apologists to advance new claims in its defense, and although this is hard to quantify, perhaps stimulated a gradual alleviation of some of the worst hardships of slave conditions. These defensive moves succeeded in re-entrenching slavery in the South, and assisted in its expansion as new states were

Opposite: A slave family, South Carolina.

colonized to the west. The decades immediately following the Revolutionary War, saw the largest sustained importation of new slaves in American history.

In his recent history of American slavery, Peter Kolchin has outlined a number of developments that combined to cast doubt on the previously almost unchallenged acceptance of slavery as a social institution. He points in particular to the rapidly changing climate of intellectual life in Europe and America from the mid-eighteenth century. Usually called the Enlightenment and closely associated with advances in both scientific and economic rationalism, intellectuals in this period began to question received ideas on such important issues as cruelty, and the appropriate treatment of fellow human beings.

The notion of human rights began to be expressed for the first time during this period. Attitudes to the unrestricted infliction of punishments on the human body began to change. Many of these then novel ideas found expression in the Declaration of Independence and the newly drafted constitution for the independent United States.

While many seemed to have no problem with exempting blacks in general and slaves in particular from these newly valued rights, others called into question the whole fabric of ideas about the supposedly natural inferiority of Africans that had grown up in the justification of the slave trade. Perhaps, they suggested, the so-called "slavishness" they perceived in the contacts with blacks was a consequence of slavery and not some natural moral condition. Isolated cases of clearly intellectually talented slaves, such as the poet Phillis Wheatley, and the mathematician Benjamin Bannecker, excited great interest. Thomas Jefferson wrote of the latter in 1791:

"I shall be delighted to see these instances of moral eminence so multiplied as to prove that the want of talents observed in them is merely the effect of their degraded condition, and not proceeding from any difference in the structure of the parts on which intellect depends."

Eighteenth century thinkers came to regard the newly elaborated economic principles of free trade, the primacy of the market, and freedom of contract, outlined in Adam Smith's influential book *The Wealth of Nations* (1776), as not just natural laws but moral imperatives. The contradictions between slavery and these new tenets were arguable, but seemed increasingly apparent, providing a ready explanation both for specific crises such as struck the tobacco growing areas, and more general malaise such as the perceived inefficiency of slave labor. Religious sentiments, as we see when we consider the abolition movement in the following chapter, also played a key part in calling into question the "peculiar institution" in the South. Both the Quakers' intellectual opposition to slavery and the growing unease displayed by some members of the Methodist and Baptist churches as religious revivals spread through the South in the closing decades of the century were increasingly important factors. The founding fathers of the independence movement moved in the climate of these new ideas, and were, to differing degrees, profoundly influenced by them. Although slavery was to continue to flourish for several more generations, it could never again be taken for granted.

If the intellectual climate of the age challenged the slave system, the circumstances of the war itself offered many slaves a more immediate and concrete prospect of liberty. Although calls were made by rebels to arm the slaves and allow them to fight in exchange for their freedom, opposition from planter interests succeeded in suppressing any effective proposals that would lead to organized participation by slaves on any scale. Slave enlistment was permitted in Maryland, and in New York slaves who served for three years were promised their freedom. Other slaves were obliged to enlist in place of their masters. More significant, though, was the effect of an appeal made in November 1775 by the Governor of Virginia, promising freedom to slaves who took up arms with the British. Although only a few thousand were ever able to reach British forces and take up this offer, and many of these perished from smallpox and other diseases, throughout much of the South slaves took advantage of the turmoil to flee in huge numbers. It has been estimated that in South Carolina, for example, slave-holders lost some thirty percent of all their slaves, and no doubt a considerably higher proportion of adult males.

One of the most marked effects of the Revolutionary era was to translate the economic divide that had long existed between the slave-based societies of the South and the states of the North, where slavery was economically marginal, into a growing sense of a moral and social divide based on attitudes towards slavery. While action taken in the states of the upper South, such as Virginia, Delaware, and Maryland, to ease some of their slave laws, such as the restriction on manumission, had some effect (in Delaware for example three quarters of blacks were free by 1810,) the legal basis of slavery was upheld. In contrast, Northern states, where slavery was far less economically important, began to pass graduated emancipation acts, allowing all slaves born after the passage of the acts to become free once they reached adulthood. As half-hearted as these measures were, in combination with an increasing tendency towards voluntary manumission by Northern slave-holders, they ensured that virtually all Northern blacks were free by the early decades of the nineteenth century. These acts were augmented at the national level by passage of laws barring the extension of slavery in newly colonized areas, such as the act of 1787 covering the present states of Ohio, Michigan, Indiana, Illinois, and Wisconsin. Both Congress and a number of states moved to prohibit the import of new slaves, although Congress was prevented by a compromise agreement at the Constitutional Convention of 1787 from introducing such a ban until 1807. It was this delay that allowed the planter-dominated states of the lower South to make the following two decades a new peak for American involvement in transatlantic slave trading.

Cotton, paternalism, and plantation slavery

For the majority of blacks in the South the hopes for freedom aroused during the Revolution were to prove illusory. Despite the growing hostility in the North, slavery lived on, apparently strengthened and extending across a massive new region of the continent. The key to this expansion, and to the surge in demand for slaves, was cotton. The development of the cotton gin in 1793 prompted a rapid expansion of cotton growing across the Southern states and financed the opening up of huge new areas to agriculture. From a mere 3,000 bales in 1790, cotton production rose to 178,000 by 1810, and exploded to over four million bales by 1860. By this time it was overwhelmingly the largest export of the United States, and it both fed the textile mills of England and laid the basis for the subsequent industrialization of America. Over the same period there was a comparable dramatic surge in the number of slaves, from 697,897 in 1790 to some four million by 1860. Around a million of these slaves were forcibly relocated to supply the labor needed to open up the new cotton-growing states to the west. An internal slave trade developed, breaking up families and slave communities. Once again, large plantations with 100 or more slaves were exceptional, the majority working quite close to their masters on properties with fifty or fewer slaves. Frederick Law Olmsted, who published an account of his travels through the South in the 1850s, noted details of both large and small plantations. As well as the elegant white-pillared great houses on large estates of 1,500 or more acres, he saw far more modest establishments. One such was:

> ". . . a small square log cabin, with a broad open shed or piazza in front, and a chimney made of sticks and mud, leaning against one end. A smaller detached cabin, 20 feet in the rear was used for a kitchen . . . . About the house was a large yard, in which were two or three China trees, and two fine Cherokee roses; half a dozen hounds; several black babies; turkeys, and chickens; and a pet sow . . . . Three hundred yards from the house was a gin house and stable, and in the interval between were two rows of comfortable Negro cabins."

However, it was the big planters in their great houses with their retinues of domestic servants and field hands, who framed the ruling ideology of slavery in the South. Lesser slave-holders and poor whites took a lead from them. Particularly after the emergence of an overwhelmingly American-born slave population, less alien to the planters in the culture and more or less adapted to the circumstances of slave life, planters came to view the slaves in a different way. Taking a lead from those who were resident with their family on their plantations for much of the year, interacting on a daily basis with both domestic slaves and field hands, it became normal for the slave-holders to extend the idea of family to their slaves and think of themselves as benevolent patriarchs, presiding, sternly but justly, over often recalcitrant "children."

In response to the growing attacks of Northern abolitionists, they asserted that their slaves were not only happy and contented, but far better off than if they had been free. They pointed not just to the alleged advantages of their position compared with their fate as slaves or war victims in Africa (ignoring the extent of the contribution the slave trade had made to the promotion of these in Africa itself,) but to the relatively far worse material conditions of the laboring poor in areas of Europe transformed by the Industrial Revolution. While the self-serving nature of these arguments, and the facility with which they glossed over the continued brutalities of slave life were readily apparent, the nature of the relationships that developed between slave-holders and slaves was a complex one, often filled with mixed emotions on both sides. There is ample evidence that real affection did develop, that many masters and mistresses, however self-deluded about the cares and woes of looking after "their people" did in many cases take real trouble and undergo considerable expense, for example in securing medical treatment for favored slaves. As abolitionists pointed out, of course, favored treatment of a few failed to mitigate even the continued injustice of their position, let alone the hardship and exploitation suffered by the many. But that was not how the planters saw it. They generally took a keen and detailed interest in all aspects of their slaves' lives. Numerous diaries and correspondence make clear their very real feelings of shock and hurt when favored slaves ran away or committed some other offence. The extent to which they had deceived themselves was only revealed in the Civil War, which Eugene Genovese in his classic book *Roll, Jordan Roll*, called "the moment of truth." Among many instances he cites a letter from a Mrs. Mary Jones, a plantation owner's wife, written in 1866 "My life long (I mean since I had a home) I have been laboring and caring for them, and since the war have labored with all my might to supply their wants, and expended everything I had on their support, directly and indirectly; and this is their return." It was particularly painful to many that it was often their most trusted and favored confidants that incited the other slaves to desert to the Union lines.

As for the slaves, their attitudes to the masters were often ambiguous. The same masters who beat them and split up their families could protect them from the ravages of the slave patrols manned by brutal poor whites. In keeping with the paternalist ethos, many masters made a point of personally handing out the rations of food and distributions of clothing, while hiding behind their overseer to administer punishments. Many slaves and former slaves demonstrated considerable, and we might consider unjustified, loyalty to their master and his family in the Civil War and its aftermath. Perhaps the best anecdotal account of these ambiguities and the fears they provoked in the slave-holders is provided by an incident cited by Genovese. An anxious mistress asked one of her favored slaves if they would cut her throat when the Union troops arrived. She can hardly have been reassured by his answer that they would not. Instead, they would go to the neighboring plantation and kill the master there, while the neighbor's slaves would call to deal with her!

Moving behind the self-serving ideology of the slave-holders, life for plantation slaves in the American South was hard. People struggled to build and sustain a family, a community, and a religious and cultural life, while fulfilling the work demanded of them in a way that would avoid the ever-threatened punishments. Field labor was the lot of the majority of slaves on the plantations. The amount of work this required varied according to the seasons and the pace of the crop. Generally planters favored the "gang" system in which a group of slaves, both male and female, supervised by a driver appointed from their own ranks, worked from sunrise to sunset. In the hottest times a two-hour break might be allowed following the midday meal. As slave owners constantly complained, it was rarely possible to compel these gangs to work as fast or as efficiently as desired. A white overseer organized the gangs and set the pattern of labor, but would rarely bother to supervise directly except in crucial periods such as the harvest season. At such times the normal hours of work would be extended and pressure exerted through both additional punishments and the prospects of a festival meal on completion. Normally field workers had Sundays off, and in some cases Saturday afternoons, and planters who tried to deny their slaves these accepted rights risked stirring up considerable counterproductive resentment. When Sunday work was needed at exceptionally busy periods, some masters paid the slaves small sums. Few plantations were large enough to provide full-time work for slaves with such specialized skills as carpentry and metalwork but most had one or more slaves who could carry out these tasks when required. In some cases they were hired out to neighboring planters, and in their free time could earn money for themselves. Some plantations, however, sustained a whole array of such specialist slaves, making them virtually independent of the sur-

rounding community for their labor needs. George Washington's home house in 1786, for example, had four carpenters, four spinners, three drivers and stablemen, two smiths, two seamstresses, a waggoner, a carter, and a gardener.

A colonnaded plantation house in the old South. In fact only a minority of slaves worked on big plantations, many more were settled in smaller groups on less wealthy farms.

The successful building of a family and community life in slavery was the key to the remarkable expansion in the slave population of the South in the ante-bellum years. They were, as we have seen, despite the hardship of plantation life, the only slave community in the Americas able to reproduce itself in this way. The slave quarters, usually a cluster of small two-room houses set some distance away from the planter's house, provided the main site where these families could develop. Usually made from logs daubed with mud, with shuttered windows, these rudimentary and uncomfortable houses mostly accommodated a family unit of four to six adults and children. Most took considerable pride in maintaining these houses, using their spare time to make furniture, add on stock pens, and improvise a range of household items to add to those bought with their scanty savings or acquired from the planter's cast-offs. Near the quarters the slaves had small gardens where they could work in the evenings and on Sundays, in which they could raise corn and vegetables to supplement the rations distributed by the planter, and, in some cases, even raise modest amounts of cash crops for sale. Planters often commented bitterly in their correspondence on the amount of energy and initiative the men and women put into working their gardens compared with their lackluster performance in the daytime. An alternative slave economy developed, although it never took on the scale found in Jamaica, in which slaves marketed their crops and those who had special skills in areas such as sewing, baking, or carpentry were sometimes able to accumulate considerable sums.

Although masters had an obvious financial interest in encouraging their slaves to have children, the majority allowed the young people to select their own marriage partners. They did however prefer that their slaves married within the plantation wherever possible, believing that off-plantation unions encouraged divided loyalty and provided too ready an excuse for slaves to be moving around the countryside. Nevertheless, enough masters attempted to intervene and impose marriages with partners of their choosing for it to be a regular event and a

Black workers plant sweet potatoes on James Hopkinson's plantation, Edisto Island, North Carolina.

recurring source of bitterness. Of more general concern was the fact that slave marriages, even if blessed by a preacher, had no legal validity. They were often celebrated by both the planter's family and the slaves with considerable festivity and feasting, and any subsequent adultery was taken as a serious matter by all parties, but the union created could be dissolved at will by the master if it suited him to sell one of the partners. Pregnant women and nursing mothers were expected to work for all but a few weeks, with young children often bringing babies to the fields to be suckled. From birth until about the age of twelve or so children played around the house together with those of the master, supervised only by the older children. Often they had to scramble for food at lunch time from a communal trough in the yard. Perhaps the most important lesson they had to learn emerges repeatedly from slave narratives—their parents coached them again and again in the ways of appeasing the master and avoiding the scourge of his whip. Their childhood came to an abrupt end when the master decided they were old enough to be sent to the fields. At this point, too, if as happened all too often he was short of funds, they could be sold away. Masters did often try to keep families together when convenient, but their financial interests all too often overrode any humanitarian concern.

In the areas of religion, folk beliefs, and cultural life, blacks were, in general, able to preserve sufficient autonomy to provide a distinctively African input into what was to become African-American culture, while also exercising a considerable and still growing influence over American culture more generally. Slave masters, once they were reconciled to the idea of slaves becoming Christians at all, sought to control and restrict access to those preachers who would uphold the status quo. Slaves listened to many sermons on the theme of obedience to the masters in all things. In the ante-bellum South the Baptists, Methodists, and Presbyterians, acting on the urging of wealthy planters mostly moved away from even their earlier limited opposition to aspects of slavery. Their support for segregated congregations, and to a lesser extent for black preachers, did, however, provide a space in which the spiritual concerns and more vocal worship of the black community, both slave and free, could find expression. In public services the black preachers had to be careful to confine their comments to spiritual matters, but in the night time prayer meetings held in a secluded spot on the plantations they were free to sermonize on the bible's teaching regarding justice, equality, and the prospects of a brighter world to come on earth as well as in heaven. The Baptist church was particularly popular among the black population of the South, but it was a Baptist worship that took on new forms as a black church, catering to the qualities of religiosity Genovese aptly summarized as "this pride, this self-respect, this astonishing confidence in their own spiritual quality."

If the closer interaction with the larger white community prevented the development of Afro-Caribbean religions of the type that flourished in slave societies elsewhere in the Americas, it has long been clear from the work of scholars from Zora Neale Hurston onwards that the folk beliefs of the black South, influenced as they were by many similar European-orig-inated beliefs in potions, soothsayers, and spells held by the poorly educated whites, nevertheless contained a solid core of African-derived ideas and practices. Voodoo, conjurers, and conjure women, the use of grave dirt as a key ingredient in spells, threads to bind packets of "medicine," bottles to trap spirits, all had their sources in African cultures such as Kongo and Yoruba. Whites as well as blacks consulted African-born healers and conjurers in search of cures, fortune telling, and love potions. Music also explored deep African continuities, from ring-shouts and field-hollers, to the blues and jazz. A slave drum collected in Virginia in the late seventeenth century and now in the British Museum, London, is entirely African in form.

Throughout the antebellum era several Southern states passed laws that increasingly restricted the rights of slave-holders to manumit, or free, their slaves. This action was primar-ily taken in response to concerns expressed by both the planters and poor whites about the growing number of free blacks. In the years before 1810 the free black population in the South had grown quite rapidly. In Virginia for example, according to the historian Peter Kolchin, the proportion of free people among the black population rose from under one percent in 1782, to 4.2 percent in 1790, and 7.2 percent—amounting to a total of some 30,570—by 1810. Some of these were able to earn sufficient money to purchase freedom for themselves and their close family, while many others were freed by the masters out of idealism in the years immediately after the Revolution. Still others were selectively freed, as a favorite, a mistress, or a child of a slave-holder.

The majority of these free blacks were in the North, and in the upper states of the South, where some ten percent of blacks were free in 1810, while in the deep South states less than two percent had been freed. Even in the North free blacks were subject to discrimination and mostly confined to menial occupations, often prevented from voting, and restricted in their movements across state lines. Free blacks in the South lived largely in the towns and cities, par-ticularly in Washington D.C. and Baltimore, where many worked in factories, as domestic servants, or as artisans. In the rural areas they were small scale farmers, casual laborers or craftsmen. In the deep South, however, in Louisiana and South Carolina, there was a small and unrepresentative number of free blacks, mostly of mulatto or mixed race origins, who occu-pied many skilled positions, and in a minority of cases, owned substantial wealth. Many of these were the descendants of families of French and Spanish colonists who looked on them-selves as among the social elite of towns such as Charleston and New Orleans. Like other wealthy people at the time, these free blacks were themselves often slave owners. Genovese notes that the wealthiest of them was August Dubuclet of Iberville Parish, who had ninety-four slaves on a plantation of over 1,200 acres. In the years before the Civil War, and particularly after the passage of the Fugitive Slave Act in 1850 strengthened the laws which allowed escaped slaves to be returned to their owners in the South, life for all free blacks became still more difficult as white hostility and the dangers of re-enslavement increased.

Abolition

Although some of the first public support for the abolition of slavery came from American Quakers, it was in Britain that the decisive developments, which would ultimately lead to abo-lition throughout the Atlantic, took place. In the 1750s Britain was the dominant economic and maritime power of the western world. The transatlantic slave trade was expanding annually in a vain effort to meet the insatiable demands for labor in the New World. Britain had the major share of this trade, with ships from Bristol and Liverpool carrying tens of thousands of Africans each year to the Americas. Britain's own sugar plantation colonies of the Caribbean flourished. Slavery seemed securely established as one of the cornerstones of a period of unprecedented economic prosperity. Only the most radical and apparently eccentric voiced public criticisms. Yet within sixty years Britain would pass laws ending the slave trade in all her colonies. Both diplomatic and military action throughout the nineteenth century would become focused on the further goal of persuading or compelling other nations to follow the same path. The world's biggest slave trading nation was to become the prime mover behind the ultimately successful suppression of the trade.

The reasons for this dramatic shift in policy were varied and complex. Although Britain's commercial rivals in France and America were, from the start, suspicious that the underlying motivation was to weaken their own economies and interfere with their shipping, in Britain itself it was widely accepted that pure altruism lay behind the change towards abolition. It was seen, in numerous historical accounts of the abolition movement that were written in the nineteenth century and first half of the twentieth century, as the triumph of good over evil. The abolitionists, inspired by humanitarian interest in the welfare of Africans and backed up by the forces of a new economic liberalism, had outargued and outvoted the reactionary forces of the sugar lobby; the absentee planters, and the slave traders of Liverpool and Bristol. Recognizing that this was the morally right policy, successive British governments had then acted to enforce it worldwide as the slave trading era gave way to a new and more far reaching period of Imperialism. It was only with the decline of the British Empire in the aftermath of World War II that new voices were heard arguing that this picture was unduly complacent and self-serving. In his pioneering book *Capitalism and Slavery* (1944), Eric Williams suggested that the importance of the humanitarian motive had been greatly exaggerated. Instead, he argued, Pitt, the British Prime Minister, supported the abolition bills primarily out of a concern to shore up Britain's own competitive position in the sugar industry and undermine that of her French and Spanish rivals. British sugar-producing islands in the West Indies were, unlike Cuba and those still retained by the French after the loss of Saint-Domingue, well stocked with slaves already. Britain had alternative, and potentially more competitive, sources of sugar in the East Indies. By 1807, against the background of the Napoleonic wars, there was an overproduction of sugar in British colonies. Britain, he claimed, acted to abolish the slave trade because it suited the economic interests of the day.

Although Williams' account was a useful reminder of the economic background of abolition, specific aspects of his analysis have been heavily criticized, in particular his suggestion that a glut of sugar existed. More fundamentally, he failed to demonstrate any clear link between the supposed economic pressures and the actual timing and procedures of parliamentary and legal action against slavery. The view of Williams and his followers that abolition was a response to the declining economic significance of the West Indies and of slave-carrying in British trade has been refuted by more recent research demonstrating that this decline occurred after—not before—1807. Attention has therefore shifted back towards more nuanced accounts of the abolitionist movement and the intellectual climate it helped create.

Sporadic attacks on the morality of slave trading were made even as Britain was entering the trade on a significant scale. In 1665 Richard Baxter argued that those who "catch up poor Negroes, or people of another land, that never forfeited life or liberty, and to make them slaves, and sell them . . . , one of the worst kinds of thefts in the world, and such persons are to be taken as the common enemies of mankind."

Such voices were, however, rare and of no significant influence. It was not until the following century that the broad-based opening up of intellectual life, known today as the Enlightenment, began to provide an arena for a more sustained and effective critique of slavery. Even then however, although it was criticized by such eminent public figures as John Locke and Alexander Pope, and awareness of the brutalities of slave life was increasingly widespread in intellectual and political circles, few considered seriously the prospect of abolition. The Evangelical revival that spread throughout England in the mid-eighteenth century, with its emphasis on the study of the Bible and the spread of working class literacy that it promoted under the leadership of John Wesley and the Methodist Church, was of crucial importance. Wesley was a vociferous and uncompromising opponent of slavery, castigating it as a fundamental source of injustice and cruelty. While the Quakers were important in the leadership of the abolition movement, it was the efforts of Methodists and other nonconformist churches

that provided the mass support for abolition in Britain throughout the following decades. A further dimension was added to the religious and humanitarian critique of slavery with the growing feeling that it was an outmoded and economically inefficient method of labor organization. This radical view found its most influential support with the publication, in 1776, of Adam Smith's classic text of market economics, *The Wealth of Nations*.

The first moves towards the organization of an abolition movement in Britain began with efforts to alter the legal position of blacks on British soil. Although there was no labor demand for African slaves in Britain, many of the wealthy absentee landlords of West Indian sugar plantations had brought favored slaves to work as domestic servants in their town houses and country estates. By the 1770s there were some 15,000 such slaves in Britain, together with a smaller number of mostly impoverished free blacks concentrated in London and other port cities. In 1765 Granville Sharp, a junior civil servant, came across a fugitive slave, called Jonathan Strong, stumbling beaten and almost blind in a London street. Together with his brother, who was a doctor, Sharp took the man in and nursed him back to health. However, two years later, the owner, a lawyer from Barbados by the name of Lisle, discovered that his slave had survived and arranged to have him kidnapped and sold to a West Indian planter. Before he could be exported Sharp filed a petition for assault against Lisle, which the slave owner countered by issuing a writ accusing Sharp of stealing his property. Although Lisle backed down in response to public outrage before any legal ruling took place, this public concern was itself evidence that the tide of popular opinion in Britain was running against the planters. A second case brought by Sharp on behalf of another fugitive ended inconclusively, with the Lord Chief Justice, Lord Mansfield, reluctant to do anything which might offend either the planters or the London public. A more decisive outcome had to await the action taken by Sharp on behalf of a third fugitive, James Somersett, in 1772. This case was to become a landmark judgement in British legal history, although it did not, as some abolitionists claimed at the time, and some accounts have subsequently argued, in itself result in the legal abolition of slavery in Britain. Despite considerable prevarication and reluctance, the

Richard Allen founded the African Methodist Episcopal Denomination. The reluctance of many white churches to accommodate the needs of black Christians, and their often ambivalent attitudes towards slavery, led to the foundation of independent black churches.

Lord Chief Justice finally ruled on June 22, that since there was no positive endorsement of slavery in British law, it could not be upheld through the courts. The ownership rights claimed by the master under the law of the colony of Virginia could not override British common law presumptions in favor of the liberty of individuals. However, while this was a major setback for slave-holders and seriously challenged their ability to flaunt their slaves in their mother country, it did not directly liberate the slaves already in Britain, it merely prevented them being returned forcibly to the Indies.

In the years after 1772 concern with the abolition of the slave trade went from being the preoccupation of a vocal minority to a major focus of public interest. The organization of this upsurge in abolitionism was greatly assisted by widespread outrage at the outcome of the notorious *Zong* incident of 1783. The courts upheld a claim for reimbursement brought after the captain of the slave ship *Zong*, allegedly suffering from an epidemic and a shortage of water, had 232 sick slaves thrown into the sea, hoping to recoup his losses through a claim from the insurers. The Lord Chief Justice's ruling that in law the owners were as entitled to compensation as if horses had been jettisoned brought home to a wide public the nature of the Middle Passage. In response to this case six prominent Quakers formed a committee to promote "the relief and liberation of the Negro slaves in the West Indies and for the discouragement of the Slave Trade on the coast of Africa." Granville Sharp, along with Thomas Clarkson and Josiah Wedgwood, the leading pioneer of the industrial production of pottery, founded the "Society for the Abolition of the Slave Trade." In 1787, Wedgwood designed and widely distributed some 200,000 copies of a pottery seal for the society, whose motif was a kneeling enchained African, with the words "Am I not a man and a brother?" Clarkson gathered a huge dossier detailing the procedures and abuses of the trade, which was to provide valuable ammunition as the dispute with the planters and their apologists became more bitter.

William Wilberforce, a well connected young member of Parliament, was persuaded by Clarkson in 1787 to become the leader of a parliamentary assault on slavery. It was his influence with leading political figures that led the Prime Minister to appoint a Committee of the Privy Council to investigate the slave trade the following year. Clarkson was able to lay much of his evidence before this committee, persuading them that, in spite of the rosy picture of slavery presented by the planters' supporters, they should recommend the subject for a full debate. The efforts of the abolitionist movement to mobilize popular sentiment through public meetings and the distribution of anti-slavery pamphlets and prints bore fruit in a deluge of petitions to Parliament from all regions. Women played a prominent role in the organization of popular opposition to slavery. Nevertheless, in Parliament the debate had to be postponed because of Wilberforce's poor health, and when the motion in favor of abolition was moved it failed by a majority of 163 votes to 88, benefiting from the deep purse of the sugar lobby.

The following year, however, when the issue was returned, the weight of public concern was reflected in the passage of a resolution by the House of Commons calling for the total abolition of the trade. The second chamber of Parliament, the House of Lords, was a major obstacle to change, acting to delay the bill's further progress and to defeat a subsequent bill that proposed to abolish "the supply by British merchants of slaves to foreign settlements." Continued delay seemed likely as the pro-slavery camp was boosted by reaction to the excesses of egalitarianism in revolutionary France. The outbreak of war with France at first promised still further delay, but in its aftermath, with British forces in control of French and Dutch colonies in the Caribbean, and the example of the massacre of whites in Saint-Domingue showing the apparent risks of inaction, members of both Houses of Parliament were more receptive. A coalition government lead by the pro-abolitionists Grenville and Fox was formed in 1806. The same year a partial Abolition Bill was finally passed, prohibiting the sale of slaves to foreign lands or their importation into the newly gained colonies in the Caribbean. The following year saw the passage of a more sweeping measure under which from January 1, 1808, "all manner of dealing and trading in slaves" was "utterly abolished, prohibited and declared to be unlawful" throughout the British Empire. The penalties of a large fine and forfeiture of the vessel were quickly increased. In 1811 slave trading became a crime punishable by transportation or death.

The success of the abolitionists, remarkable though it was, was as yet only a limited one. The slaves in the British colonies of the Caribbean had not been set free and the other nations of Europe and the Americas were still actively involved in the transatlantic trade. With regard to the existing slaves, at first Wilberforce's successor as leader of the movement, Thomas Fowell Buxton, hoped that cutting off the prospect of new slaves would lead the planters themselves to improve markedly the conditions of their workers out of self-interest. It soon became clear that this was not going to happen. An Anti-Slavery Society was established in 1823, and in response to continued popular pressure, the British government passed laws to reform slave conditions throughout the British West Indies. Among these was the abolition of the whip and of flogging female slaves, the freeing of all female children born after 1823, the granting of a day off for religious instruction, and a limit on the working day to nine hours. Instead of complying with these measures, the planters did all in their power to delay their enactment, provoking a series of major rebellions among slaves throughout the British colonies. The bloody suppression of these revolts, the harsh reprisals taken against captured rebels and their sympathizers in the colonies, particularly the hanging of forty-seven slaves in Demerara in 1823, and the execution of 100 more in Jamaica in 1832, outraged public opinion in Britain. Helped by the influx of new members of parliament following the extension of the franchise in the Reform Bill, decisive action was finally taken. The Bill for the Abolition of Slavery became law on the August 29, 1833. The continued influence of the planters was, however, marked by the granting of £20 million in compensation for the loss of their "property" and the requirement that the freedmen be obliged to serve a further seven years as apprentices.

Eager to take effective steps to limit the trade still carried on by the other maritime powers, during the early years of the nineteenth century Britain was able to use the rights of search and seizure—in force during the continuing Napoleonic wars—to harass any slavers intercepted off the African coast. The dubious legal basis for some of these actions, however, added to the suspicion and skepticism with which the authorities of France, Portugal, Spain, and America regarded the British conversion to the humanitarian cause. When peace returned, the question of restricting or abolishing the slave trade became inextricably bound up with issues of national pride, commercial rivalry, and maritime rights, greatly assisting the attempts by pro-slavery forces to delay any effective controls. In 1816, British attempts to draft an international treaty setting up a permanent bureau to effect abolition failed in the face of French and Russian opposition, and it became increasingly clear that the only way forward was to negotiate individual treaties with each of the main nations involved.

Under pressure from the British, in 1817 the Spanish signed a treaty under which they received substantial compensation in return for an agreement to outlaw trading by Spanish nationals north of the equator with immediate effect, extending to below the line from 1820. The Portuguese agreed only to ban trading north of the equator. In order to enforce these treaties and to exercise the limited rights of search, they authorized a small squadron of ships to patrol the West African coast. Courts were set up under the joint jurisdiction of the treaty nations to decide the fate of captured vessels. However, even when they succeeded in capturing a slaver, no conviction could be obtained unless the ship was found to have slaves actually on board. Later modifications allowed ships demonstrably equipped for slaving to also be seized, but even this could be circumvented by measures to reduce the incriminating evidence.

France finally signed the first of a series of treaties in 1831 but continued opposition to British intervention with the free passage of French ships largely overrode the growing pro-abolitionist sentiment in the country. Eventually, it was alarm at the challenge to French commercial and imperial interests in Africa posed by the tactic adopted by the British in the 1840s of signing anti-slavery treaties with local African rulers that prompted the French to send their own naval vessels to interdict slavers. Even then there is little evidence that this force made any serious efforts against the trade.

The British naval patrols captured 1,287 ships between 1825 and 1865, releasing in the region of 130,000 Africans, most of whom were set ashore in the colony at Freetown, Sierra Leone, originally established under the sponsorship of Granville Sharp, as a refuge for the free blacks of Britain. This was only a modest proportion of the total enslaved, and it was clear that the patrols alone would never suppress the trade. More progress was made in concluding treaties with slave importing countries and this succeeded in closing off the markets. By the 1850s Cuba was the only substantial remaining outlet, and much of the remaining trade was carried on by American-flagged ships. The outbreak of the Civil War allowed the British finally to agree a right of search with the American authorities and take action against this last vestige of the transatlantic trade.

Although abolitionist attacks on the morality of slavery had been made almost from the earliest days of colonization in America, it was in the years after independence that the issue of the future of slavery moved to take up center stage as the defining issue of national politics. The hopes for an end to slavery raised during the Revolutionary War had proved false and the dramatic expansion of cotton production had instead generated a huge increase in the number of people held as slaves throughout the American South. The split between the slave-holding Southern states and the increasingly hostile North widened over the course of the early decades of the nineteenth century as disputes arose over the admission of new states to the Union and over slave-holders attempts to recapture fugitives. The emergence of an organized Abolition movement in the North, uniting both blacks and whites in an often bitter struggle, was to be a key factor in keeping the issue at the forefront of public attention and mobilizing support to push for new measures in Congress.

Pro-slavery apologists in the South became increasingly extreme as their national and international isolation increased. The attempts at political compromise intended to hold the Union together in the face of these irreconcilable conflicts finally collapsed at the end of the 1860s with the attempted secession of the South. Although the resulting Civil War was fought primarily to restore the Union, it rapidly became apparent that victory for the Union forces would involve the ending of slavery and a victory for the Abolitionists. Black soldiers, recruited in their tens of thousands, played a key role in that victory.

The abolition movement

Quakers in Pennsylvania were the first settlers in America to publicly oppose slavery. As early as 1688 a number of them printed "The Germantown Protest," which stated that: "Now, tho' they are black, we cannot conceive there is more liberty to have them slaves, as it is to have other white ones . . . And those who steal or rob men, and those who buy or purchase them, are they not all alike?" Such sentiments continued to be expressed in Quaker circles over the following century and had a degree of impact on the passage of laws restricting slave imports in Pennsylvania and Massachusetts, it was only in the years after Independence that an organized abolition movement developed more widely. It built on the opposition to slavery that had been expressed by many of the leading figures of the Revolution and was assisted by the growing harassment of anti-slavery activists throughout the South. The movement brought moral and intellectual opposition to slavery together with the opposition of those who had suffered and continued to suffer its impact. Blacks were not, as pro-slavery apologists had argued, reconciled to and even happy in their lot as slaves. Rather, it was black hostility to slavery that laid the foundations for abolition. The historian Herbert Aptheker has called African-Americans "the first and most lasting abolitionists" arguing that "their conspiracies and insurrections, individual struggles, systematic flights, maroon communities, efforts to buy freedom, cultural solidarity, creation of anti-slavery organizations and publications—all preceded the black-white united efforts."

The abolition movement was the first modern mass campaign to be organized in America, and it involved the mobilization of both workers and intellectuals, men and women, blacks and whites, on a national scale. The American Anti-Slavery Society, founded in 1833, brought together abolitionists from New England, where William Lloyd Garrison was the most prominent activist, with those from Philadelphia, and from the newly opened up states of the Midwest. It was the pinnacle of a network of more than a thousand societies: the regional such as the "New England Anti-Slavery Society;" state organizations in New York, Rhode Island, Massachusetts, Ohio, and Pennsylvania; city groups in Boston, Providence and elsewhere; women's societies, of which the Boston and Philadelphia Female Anti-Slavery societies were prominent; youth groups; college societies; and denominational religious bodies.

A key aspect of the work of many of these groups was to publicize the cause through the printing and distribution of pamphlets, books, and newspapers and to raise funds to continue these efforts. *The Liberator*, edited by William Lloyd Garrison and published in Boston

A scene from the 1927 film version of Uncle
Tom's Cabin.

from 1831 to 1865, was perhaps the most influential and effective of the regular newspapers, but others included *The Philanthropist* in Cincinnati, and *The Anti-Slavery Standard* in New York. Although the circulation of all these journals was quite limited, they were widely read and their articles frequently cited or reproduced in more mainstream publications.

Pamphlets and books, which had to be clandestinely distributed in the South at considerable personal risk, were read in their thousands throughout the country. The opinions of prominent abolitionists such as Wendell Phillips, Frederick Douglass and Angelina Grimke Weld were circulated through pamphlets to hundreds of thousands of readers. Harriet Beecher Stowe's *Uncle Tom's Cabin*, read by millions worldwide, is only the best known of many anti-slavery books published at this period. Frederick Douglass was born a slave in Maryland in 1817, but after a number of unsuccessful escape attempts succeeded in fleeing to Massachusetts in 1838. After an address to an antislavery convention in Nantucket in 1841 revealed the eloquence of his public speaking he became one of the most prominent black members of the movement.

Forced to flee to Europe on two occasions to escape possible arrest, his speeches and writings, including his autobiography, first published in 1845 as *Narrative of the Life of Frederick Douglass, an American Slave*, were hugely influential. For many others, public lectures were also an important means of spreading the word, with long speaking-tours attracting hundreds, or even thousands, of listeners daily. Agents were hired to carry the message to more remote areas, often risking abuse and attacks. Women were prominent as activists in the movement and many abolitionists, from William Lloyd Garrison to Sojourner Truth, were also ardent supporters of women's rights. Truth (1797–1883), freed when slaves in New York State were emancipated in 1828, drew big crowds with her talks on both abolition and women's rights, while Garrison caused considerable controversy with his defense of the right of American women delegates to attend the "World Anti-Slavery Convention" in London in 1840.

Alongside this continuing propaganda campaign, the abolitionists took a number of more direct actions against slavery. These ranged from raising money in response to appeals from freedmen or women to help purchase their family members, through assisting fugitives,

Henry "Box" Brown arrives in Philadelphia.

to John Brown's outright assault at Harper's Ferry. Many of the more radical abolitionists opposed the practice of paying slave-holders to sell people, but few were able to resist the often heartrending appeals made by freed mothers on behalf of children left behind in captivity.

The Fugitive Slave Law of 1793, allowed slave-holders to regain possession of any fugitives they could apprehend in the North. Although it became increasingly ineffective in the face of state personal liberty laws and often hostile public opinion, the presence of slave catchers was a constant threat to both fugitive slaves and free blacks. In 1850, as part of the deal with Southern states known as the Missouri Compromise a new law was passed strengthening these powers and obliging U.S. marshals to assist in the capture of fugitives. Members of the abolition movement played a vital role in sheltering runaway slaves and intervening where possible to prevent their return to slavery. Sometimes, as in 1854 when a Boston crowd tried unsuccessfully to rescue escapee Anthony Burns, obliging the government to send troops to escort the slave catchers on board a ship returning him to Virginia, this involved direct intervention, but equally often it required the financing of legal challenges.

An elaborate informal system of guides and refuges was developed to help fugitive slaves reach the British colony in Canada where they would be safe from any legal efforts to return them. This network, known as the Underground Railroad, helped conceal fugitives on isolated farms or provide them with the names of urban sympathizers where they could seek refuge for a few days before they could be guided to a suitable border crossing point such as Detroit or Buffalo. Even when slave-holders or their agents were not in direct pursuit, rewards were generally offered for their capture and fugitives had to be concealed or disguised to prevent their falling into the hands of professional or opportunist slave catchers. In some cases the organizers of the "Railroad" took the dangerous step of traveling far into the South themselves to assist escapees, risking imprisonment for slave-stealing or, especially if they were black, a real threat of lynching.

Harriet Tubman (c.1820–1913) was the best known of many who risked everything in this way. After reaching the North herself around 1849 she made a total of nineteen journeys from her home in Auburn, New York, to lead others, including her own parents, to freedom. In total Tubman, called the "Moses of her people," helped an estimated 300 people reach Canada.

Although earlier estimates that suggested tens of thousands benefited from the dedicated help of these selfless "conductors" were probably exaggerated, their contribution nevertheless extended far beyond the direct benefits to the individual men and women assisted. Each successful escape brought welcome publicity and a boost to the morale of the abolitionists while arousing further anger and bitterness among their opponents in the South. The more spectacular and newsworthy the escape the greater the benefit from the ensuing publicity. The case of Henry "Box" Brown was perhaps the most extraordinary of many dramatic escapades.

By the 1850s it was apparent to all that while the abolition movement had been successful in keeping the issue at the forefront of public attention the prospects for real progress in the South were further away than ever. Harassment of free blacks and anti-slavery activists by both vigilante groups and legal restrictions in the region was increasing. The passage in 1850 of a strengthened Fugitive Slave Act had demonstrated that anti-slavery forces in Congress were prepared to make concessions in the face of Southern pressure. In this context abolitionists began to despair of peaceful means and moved towards more radical measures.

This was the context in which John Brown led what seemed to many to be a desperate and suicidal assault on the system. Although Brown has been portrayed by conservative historians as a fanatic and even a madman, his actions were informed by the recognition of the violence inherent in slavery and the ultimate necessity of using equally violent means to challenge it. He was not an isolated fanatic but a respected member of the movement and a close friend of Frederick Douglass, Harriet Tubman, and many other leading figures. While Douglass and others may have questioned the wisdom of his tactics at Harper's Ferry they recognized the rationale of his resort to force in the attempt to rally opposition to slavery in a period of unprecedented national turmoil. W. E. B. Du Bois, writing in 1909, noted that "John Brown worked not simply for the Black Man—he worked with them, and he was a companion of their daily life, knew their faults and virtues, and felt, as few white Americans have felt, the bitter tragedy of their lot."

Brown, who was born in 1800, achieved nationwide notoriety when he led his five sons into Kansas to fight against bands of proslavery thugs who had murdered several abolitionists. In a fight at Pottawatomie Creek, on May 24, 1856, Brown and his sons avenged these murders by killing five of the terrorists, before successfully beating off a counter-attack a few months later by a larger party of proslavery vigilantes from Missouri. Although Brown had long been considering a plan, discussed with colleagues such as Douglass, to form a band of armed resisters who could attack and harass pro-slavery forces from the shelter of the Allegheny Mountains, along the lines of guerrilla movements in the twentieth century, his attack, when it finally came on Saturday October 16, 1859, led to a fatal trap. With twenty-two followers armed with pikes and rifles, Brown seized control of the armory at Harper's Ferry. A train which Brown allowed to pass through the town quickly spread the alarm and the rebels were surrounded by local militia reinforced by a company of Marines under Colonel Robert E. Lee. Ten of Brown's men, including two of his sons, were killed in the fighting that followed and by Monday the wounded Brown had been captured and charged with crimes including treason and murder. He was hanged forty days later. Despite the dismal failure of his attack the impact on the abolition movement and the climate of opinion in both the North and the South was electric. Brown's death was marked by intense debate over the issue of slavery across Europe and America and he become the most famous martyr of the abolition campaign. As Du Bois commented, his time in prison and the debates provoked were "the mightiest abolition document that America has ever known."

Congress, compromises, and the abolition struggle

The precarious mutual accommodation reached between pro- and antislavery interests in the immediate aftermath of the Revolution was threatened over the following decades by disputes over two major interrelated issues. The first was the status of free blacks in the North, and the impact upon them of both the attempts by slave owners to use the law to recover fugitives who had succeeded in escaping to non-slave states and of restrictions on the rights of free blacks to

*Opposite: John Brown (1800–59), the
American abolitionist, going to his execution at
Charlestown, Virginia. The song in memory of
his exploits during the Harper's Ferry Raid,
"John Brown's Body," was a popular marching
song with Union soldiers.*

enter certain states. The second was the admission of new territories to the Union. These issues first came to a head in 1819 when Congress began to debate the admission of Missouri, taking on a particular intensity because the proposed new state threatened to upset the existing equilibrium of twenty states, ten of which were free and ten slave-holding. Missouri's state constitution not only provided for slavery but also barred any immigration into Missouri of free blacks from other states. As abolitionists pointed out, this violated the article of the Constitution granting equal privileges and immunities to all citizens. Authorities as eminent as John Quincy Adams, then Secretary of State, felt that Northern states such as Massachusetts would be justified in passing retaliatory measures that similarly discriminated against citizens of Southern states, leading to a de facto dissolution of the Union. In the event, the so-called Missouri Compromise was reached, under which the state would be admitted along with its existing proslavery laws but slavery would be prohibited in further areas of the Louisiana Purchase territories north of latitude 36' 30." The admission of another slave state would be balanced by the simultaneous admission of Maine, which had previously been a part of Massachusetts.

The same issues resurfaced with even greater intensity thirty years later with the acquisition of vast new territories from Mexico following the Mexican-American War. Between August and September 1850, Congress passed a series of five measures, negotiated by Senator Henry Clay of Kentucky, which became known as the Compromise of 1850. The slave trade was abolished in the District of Columbia and the admission of California as a free state was approved. New Mexico and Utah were to be opened to settlement by both slave-holders and non-slavers, while Texas, already admitted as a slave state, was to be compensated for giving up claims to adjoining territory. Most controversially, the new and strengthened Fugitive Slave Act was passed, adding considerably to the bitterness of abolitionist disputes and arousing unprecedented popular support for fugitives in the North. The failure of these measures to diffuse the increasing hostility between North and South was emphasized by the forcing through by proslavery interests in 1854 of the Kansas-Nebraska Act, allowing settlers to formulate their own position on slavery thus breaching the 1820 Accords for the prohibition of slavery north of 36' 30." Disputes over this measure precipitated the final collapse of the Whig party and a re-alignment with antislavery Democrats from which the new Republican party emerged in July 1854. In 1857, a ruling finally emerged from the Supreme Court in the long-running Dred Scott case, arguing that the Missouri Compromise was unconstitutional since Congress lacked the power to prohibit slavery in any part of the Union.

Slavery became the issue around which the growing differences between the South and the remainder of the Union coalesced. The wider economic interests of the increasingly industrialized Northeast with its demand for protective tariffs, and the Congressional support for free homesteads in the expanding territories to the West, came to seem increasingly at odds with the old-fashioned plantation economies of the South. Despite the passage of the Fugitive Slave Act, the ability of planters to enforce what they regarded as legitimate ownership rights over their "property" had been undermined by public opposition and the passage of personal liberty acts by state legislatures throughout the North. A split in the Democratic party along North-South lines in the 1860 Presidential election opened the way to election for the Republican nominee, Abraham Lincoln, on a platform of support for Northern economic interests and continued, if limited, opposition to slavery. Moves by Southern states to secede from the Union followed rapidly and the long postponed confrontation began with the Southern attack on Fort Sumter in Charleston, South Carolina, on April 12, 1861.

The Civil War and Emancipation

The continued absence of any large-scale slave rebellions in the Confederate South allowed both conservative historians and nostalgic former slave-holders to perpetuate the false assertion that the majority of slaves were happy in their role and had made no effort to contribute to the Union cause. In fact however, as W. E. B. Du Bois pointed out in writing as early as 1835 of a slave "general strike," the wartime actions of a substantial proportion of the black people of the South were a major factor in the achievement of their own liberation. In this they were

Opposite: Abraham Lincoln (1809–65) making his inaugural address, surrounded by notables of the Civil War days.

assisted not only by the wider strategic logic of the war situation, but also by the continued pressure on Lincoln and Congress from abolitionists, and by the action and example of black soldiers in the Union armies.

Despite the pivotal role played by the issue of slavery in dividing the combatants and symbolizing the wider differences that had emerged between the Union and the Confederate South, the issue at stake from the outset was not the continuation or abolition of slavery but the preservation or break-up of the Union. In the early months of the war Lincoln repeatedly emphasized that the Republican Administration would not take any measures to outlaw slavery in existing slave states. This position was crucial to avoid alienating both important Northern Democrats and the key pro-Union slave states of Maryland, Delaware, Missouri, Kentucky, and the breakaway Unionist segment of Western Virginia. This pragmatic position remained Union policy for some time and it was only as the war dragged into an apparently prolonged stalemate in the latter part of 1862 that Lincoln's actions began to become more attuned to his personal opposition to slavery.

If there was no dramatic upsurge in outright rebellion among the slaves it is clear that many were able to keep reasonably informed about the progress of the war and take numerous minor individual acts of resistance and self-assertion. Taken together, these actions and attitudes both effectively weakened the Confederate war effort and sapped the already weakened confidence of the slave-holders in the future of their social system. The letters and journals of both men at the front and women at the plantation houses are full of evidence of an all-pervading anxiety over the continued loyalty of their most trusted slaves and the sense of betrayal felt when the extent of their own self-deceit over the true nature of paternalistic slave-holding could no longer be ignored.

Once the Union forces approached any district the pretence that master-slave relations were continuing as normal broke down, work in the fields and houses virtually ceased, and the flow of runaways to the Union lines became a flood. The issue of what to do with all these fugitives helped prompt a grudging reappraisal of policy by federal officials. At first some pro-slavery Union officers even allowed slave-holders to cross Union lines to reclaim their property, provoking outrage and internationally damaging publicity from abolitionists. In May 1861, however, Major-General Benjamin F. Butler in Virginia issued an order that fugitives were to be given employment and effectively they became free. The second Confiscation Act of July 1862 made it an offence for any member of the armed forces to give up fugitive slaves. By this time, as the war progressed, the sheer numbers of runaways and refugees caused considerable logistical problems, with many people suffering real hardship in camps behind Union lines. As General Ulysses S. Grant advanced into Missouri, thousands of refugees almost swamped his often hostile troops. Some of these found work in the hospitals and kitchens of the army camps, or building trenches, while others worked as paid laborers in liberated areas.

The question of employing free blacks and escaped slaves in the ranks of the Union army also involved an often reluctant administration in a gradual accommodation with the realities of the war situation and the initiatives of large numbers of individual African-Americans who insisted on their right to serve. Racist prejudices ran deep in many parts of the army, and the remarks of General Thomas G. Stevenson made in the Sea Islands in 1863, that "he would rather have the Union forces defeated than win with Negro troops" were only an outspoken expression of quite widely held views. In the early months of the war attempts by both blacks and whites to organize black volunteer regiments were rejected, in part because it was feared that acceptance would have discouraged applications from white recruits. By the middle of 1862, however, attitudes were changing in the face of the continuing need for recruits as it became clear that the war would not be quickly resolved. Additionally, both the Northern media and many members of the Union Army reported back on the widespread assistance offered to the Union cause by slaves and free blacks, particularly in supplying valuable information about Confederate military positions.

The first large scale recruitment of blacks to the Union army was made—without explicit authorization by the pro-abolitionist General David Hunter—in the months of May and June 1862. In the South Georgia and Sea Islands area under his command, he began to organize and train a regiment of some 800 black soldiers. However, after intense debate in the newspapers and in Congress, the administration refused to grant the necessary authorization

and the General was forced to disband the regiment in August. The precedent had been established, however, and later that same month the Secretary for War, Stanton, wrote to Brigadier General Rufus Saxton permitting him to "arm, uniform and equip, and receive into the service of the United States such numbers of volunteers of African descent as you may deem expedient, not exceeding 5,000." A small unit from A Company of this regiment, the First South Carolina Volunteers, saw action in November 1862, after which their commanding officer reported that they "fought with astonishing coolness and bravery."

Throughout 1863, when black recruitment became much more widespread, a pattern emerged of white officers persistently deploying their African-American troops away from front line duties, using them wherever possible for heavy fatigue duties such as the construction of fortifications. Nevertheless, black soldiers inevitably became increasingly involved in actual fighting and the remaining prejudices about their military ability were at least gradually dispelled in the face of mounting evidence of their bravery in combat. Black soldiers, however, faced continuing discrimination from all sides. There were increasing complaints from both the soldiers and their white officers over the disparity in pay between black and white recruits. In 1863 blacks received $10 per month less $3 clothing allowance, while whites got $13 plus $3.50 clothing allowance. It was not until the black soldiers of the Fifty-fourth and Fifty-fifth Massachusetts Regiments had refused all pay for many months, that pay was equalized. On the battlefield itself those who fell into the hands of the Confederates were frequently killed or re-enslaved. Throughout the war as a whole, despite the prejudice and hostility they encountered, some 180,000 African-Americans served in the Union Army, and a further 25,000 as sailors, doing much both to advance the cause of the United States forces and to at least mitigate some of the still widespread negative stereotypes.

At the same time as the Republican Administration was gradually changing its policy on the use of African-Americans in the Union army, Lincoln's pragmatic position on the wider issue of the future of slavery was also being supplanted by an increasingly pro-Abolitionist stance. Among the factors contributing to this were a response to a widening desire for more radical change among a growing sector of Northern public opinion and in the press, together with a desire to undermine international support for the Confederates. To come out decisively against slavery would make it impossible for Britain and France to continue their policy of official neutrality and their attempts to take advantage of the rebellion to recover lost influence in the region. A series of measures were passed by Congress, beginning with the August 1861 Confiscation Act, effectively freeing any slaves used by their masters for military purposes hostile to the Union, and a resolution freeing federal officers from enforcing fugitive slave laws. In April 1862, a law was passed to emancipate immediately all slaves in the District of Columbia, with compensation of $300 per head to the slave-holders. On June 19, slavery was abolished without compensation in all federal territories. On September 22, the Preliminary Emancipation Proclamation gave the rebel states 100 days in which to submit, or the irrevocable emancipation of their slaves would be announced.

Finally the Civil War was officially transformed into a war that would end slavery with the issue by President Lincoln on January 1, 1863, of the Emancipation Proclamation. This historic document declared that all those held as slaves in any state or part of a state in rebellion against the Union would be forever free. Although this was not the de facto abolition of slavery since by definition it covered only those areas outside Union control and did not apply either to conquered areas or to the slave holding states who had remained in the Union, it was of immense symbolic importance. Whatever the legal niceties, the remaining slaves throughout the South now knew that a Union victory would bring the ending of slavery. On the eve of that Union victory two years later Congress on January 31, 1865, passed by a two-thirds majority the Thirteenth Amendment to the United States Constitution which proclaimed that:

"Neither slavery nor involuntary servitude, except as a punishment for crime whereof the party shall have been duly convicted, shall exist within the United States, or any place subject to their jurisdiction."

Opposite, Above: A celebration of the abolition of slavery in Washington D.C.

Opposite, Below: An African-American regiment being reviewed.

CHAPTER 3

Germans, Dutch, and Scandinavians

Above: Two injured sailors from the scuttled
Columbus arriving at Ellis Island.

Opposite, Above: German refugees on board the
S.S. Nieuw Amsterdam *watch the*
Manhattan skyline as they steam up the bay,
December 16, 1938.

Opposite, Below: The officers and crew of the
scuttled German liner Columbus. *They were*
picked up by the U.S.S. Tuscaloosa *and*
transferred in the lower harbor to Coast Guard
vessels to be taken to Ellis Island while a decision
is made as to their status.

By the early 1970s more than twenty-five million Americans claimed German descent, ahead of all other groups except Britain. Although the Netherlands, Sweden, Denmark, and Norway, were less important numerically, they too were among the earliest countries to send significant quantities of migrants to Colonial America and in the early decades of the Republic. In the second half of the nineteenth century German speakers were the largest group to arrive each year, a position they also held for most years between 1923 and 1963. Paradoxically, while the majority of Germans were among the most successful at integrating into mainstream America in economic and cultural terms, some of the earliest arrivals, forming a group that became known as the Pennsylvania "Dutch" resisted much of that assimilation, maintaining many areas of distinct cultural identity well into the twentieth century.

Many of these migrants arrived before the formation of a German nation state under Prussian leadership in 1871, leading to a degree of confusion and statistical uncertainty through the overlap of conflicting linguistic, political, and ethnic definitions. In the nineteenth century and later significant quantities of German-speakers arrived from Switzerland, Austria, and from German communities in Russia, and even Italy. This statistical confusion had its earlier counterpart on the ground with the popular misidentification of Colonial German immigrants as Dutch that arose from hearing the new arrivals describe themselves as "Deutsch" (that is, German), together with a then standard use of the term to describe anyone from the whole length of the river Rhine. When large scale immigration began in the nineteenth century relations between the established Germans in Pennsylvania and the new arrivals were one of the problematic areas to be negotiated. As non-English speakers different problems of language and identity faced the Germans migrant communities than their Irish contemporaries. In the twentieth century the two world wars confronted German-Americans with new difficulties and hastened the process of integration.

Germans

Although a few Germans arrived individually in the early decades of the seventeenth century, the true beginnings of German settlement in the Americas can be precisely dated to 1683 when a group of thirteen Quaker and Mennonite families led by their minister Francis Pastorius arrived to settle in the newly established colony of Pennsylvania. Other similar groups of religious dissenters arrived throughout the Colonial era: Swiss Mennonites; Dunkards, an Anabaptist sect from Westphalia; Schwenkfelders; and Moravians. Some seven hundred of the latter arrived in 1741, founding the towns of Nazareth and Bethlehem. Unlike many of the other communities established by sectarian groups in the early Colonial era the majority of these settlements thrived and expanded, setting up new offshoots in neighboring states.

However, despite the attention paid at the time and in subsequent accounts to these dissenting sects, the majority of German migrants at this period were members of the mainstream Lutheran or Reformed churches who were displaced for economic or political rather than religious reasons. They did not begin to arrive in large numbers until the years after 1710 when the so-called War of Spanish Succession between France and Britain led to French

Wahre Jacob.]   [*Aug. 15.*

America draining the Strength of Europe.

An unusual comment on mass migration to America from a German newspaper in a cartoon by Whare Jacob. America is shown draining the strength of Europe—Chorus of powers: "The rascal is drinking up all our soup."

troops sacking Rhineland towns allied to their British foes. A large group of the Rhinelanders, already under pressure from increasing overpopulation and the impact of an unusually severe winter, sailed to Britain, from where some 600 were sent to North Carolina and almost 3,000 to New York to make naval stores. Weakened by their ordeal many died on the journey and the planned settlement in New York rapidly collapsed, but the majority of survivors reached Pennsylvania.

Within a few years of the arrival of these Rhinelanders or Palatines (as they were called in America) European migrant agents and letters home had spread word of the welcoming conditions in Pennsylvania, prompting a growing flow of immigrants. Some three ships carrying Germans were recorded in 1717, a number that doubled to six annually before 1740, and around ten thereafter. Most of these sailed from Rotterdam carrying Germans who had indentured themselves to pay their passage. They were known as free-willers or redemptioners acknowledging the fact that most had bound themselves voluntarily (although of course after a long journey down the Rhine starvation in a foreign port was the only other alternative on offer.) Two contracts were signed. The first committed the migrant either to pay his or her fare on arrival or to agree to be sold as an indentured servant to cover the debt. Once in America, the majority who lacked friends or relatives able to repay their fare signed contracts of indenture with one of the farmers and merchants looking for additional laborers who met each ship on arrival. Contracts usually lasted three to six years, although children under fifteen had to serve until they reached twenty-one. The system was open to abuses: families were separated and extra servitude was often required of those whose partners, parents, or relatives had died at sea to pay for their passage also. Nevertheless the system seems to have been broadly acceptable to most, and the majority survived their contracts to prosper as free farmers and laborers. Significant reforms which brought about the end of the indenture system did not occur the early decades of the nineteenth century when, under pressure from increasingly established local German communities repelled by the worsening conditions as the numbers of migrants rose, several key states introduced legislation restricting the terms of contracts sufficiently to make the enterprise no longer viable.

By 1812 communities of Pennsylvania Germans had spread out to settle across some 15,000 square miles of eastern, central, and western Pennsylvania from the original colony at Germantown. Onward migration over the following decades led to the founding of smaller farming communities in Maryland and elsewhere in the South, in New York State, and especially across the Midwest. Some craftsmen and artisans settled in colonial towns—by the end of the century some ten percent of the adult males in Baltimore were German. Despite the variety of crafts and trades from Europe, in America the majority of Pennsylvania Germans became farmers, earning a reputation for being frugal, hardworking, and unusually open to improved farming methods. Nevertheless apart from some sect members who benefited from mutual aid and cooperation the Germans were not significantly more prosperous than other farmers of the day. They were responsible for some notable innovations including the covered or "Conestoga" wagon so important in spreading the American frontier to the West, the Pennsylvania rifle, and major improvements in barn construction. A distinctive Pennsylvania German culture, drawing on and adapting such aspects of their German origin as rural cuisine, folk music, and religious traditions, developed in the eighteenth century, as did a hybrid Pennsylvania German dialect. Religious revivalism, sponsored by Moravian missionaries and prompting a response by the Lutheran and Reformed churches provided an important focus of communal life. Electoral conflict with the English and Irish, as well as concerns raised by the rising tide of new German migrants in the first half of the nineteenth century led to an increased awareness of ethnic identity and the importance of preserving cultural distinctiveness. At the same time however, growing numbers were adopting Anglicized names, using English for business, and even intermarrying. Numerous societies, of which the Pennsylvania German Society (1891) was the most important, struggled with only limited success against these pressures towards integration. The use of High German in churches, schools, newspapers gradually dwindled, with the spread of public schools from the 1830s a major factor, although the final shift to English in a few rural churches was resisted for a further hundred

Umſtändige Geogra-
phiſche
Beſchreibung
Der zu allerletzt erfundenen
Provintz
PENSYLVA-
NIÆ,
In denen End-Gräntzen
AMERICÆ
In der Weſt-Welt gelegen/
Durch
FRANCISCUM DANIELEM
PASTORIUM,
J. V. Lic. und Friedens-Richtern
daſelbſten.
Worbey angehencket ſind eini-
ge notable Begebenheiten / und
Bericht-Schreiben an deſſen Herrn
Vattern
MELCHIOREM ADAMUM PASTO-
RIUM,
Und andere gute Freunde.

Franckfurt und Leipzig/
Zufinden bey Andreas Otto. 1700.

Above: The title page from a German book, c.1700, encouraging emigration to Pennsylvania.

Left: German-born Albert Einstein (1879–1955) leads a crowd of immigrants in a mural in the Roosevelt Public School, New Jersey. Artist Ben Shahn (1898–1969) painted the mural in c.1936.

years. However uniquely among migrant groups of such long standing the Pennsylvania German dialect still provided a focus for a continued sense of ethnic community throughout the twentieth century, with radio, television, theatre, and the press in south-eastern Pennsylvania all finding at least a limited space for dialect to survive.

Germans in the Era of Mass Immigration

In total somewhere between 65,000 and 100,000 Germans arrived in America during the colonial period, with their descendants making up some 8.6 percent of the population at independence, according to calculations based on the census of 1790. In Pennsylvania Germans were around a third of the total population, but they were also significant minorities in Maryland (twelve percent), New Jersey (nine percent) and New York (eight percent). These figures were to be dwarfed by what followed as the mass immigration era of the nineteenth century saw the pace of German arrivals accelerate rapidly, beginning in the aftermath of the Napoleonic wars in 1816–17 which saw some 20,000 Germans seek refuge from failed harvests and the general economic disruption. The number of German immigrants per decade fell to under 6,000 in the 1820s, then soared to almost a million in the 1850s, reaching a peak of 1,444,181 in the 1880s, before dropping off somewhat earlier than other countries. In the year of 1882 alone over a quarter of a million Germans came to America. A few still came for religious reasons, including some of those who objected to the Prussian enforced unification of the Lutheran and Reformed churches, and a growing number of Jews. Fewer still escaped direct political persecution, including a small but influential number of refugees after the failed democratic uprisings of 1848. The majority however had more general economic motives.

Historians have divided this influx into several phases related to the progress of industrialization in Germany in the nineteenth century. As with other nations background conditions which made possible migration on such a vast scale were also important factors, including improvements in communications and literacy that spread news of the opportunities to be found in America and the advances in transportation that made the journey increasingly accessible at a relatively low cost. The first "pre-industrial" phase lasted from the 1820s through to around 1865 and was primarily a movement of whole families that ebbed and flowed with agricultural conditions such as bad weather, crop diseases, and the level of grain prices. Changing patterns of agriculture contributed to this migration in north-eastern Germany as moves towards less labor intensive commercial crop production on larger estates reduced the prospects of secure employment and prompted many day laborers to emigrate with their families. Other migrants in this phase included small farmers from southern Germany and artisans from towns in the central regions. After this however increasing numbers of people found their established modes of life disrupted not by the occasional failures of the agricultural cycle or the onset of war, but by the spread of industrialization in the rapidly expanding German economy. Population growth made it difficult for expanding families to move into traditional occupational niches. This second early industrial phase comprised mainly rural laborers and their families from the north and east, with fewer established farmers and artisans. A few thousand liberal and socialist intellectuals came as political refugees, the so-called "48ers" after the abortive revolutionary unrest of that year, and attracted attention out of all proportion to their numbers. By the 1890s industrial modernization had progressed sufficiently for factory labor within Germany to absorb rural migrants, and combined with the impact of economic depression in America to bring the era of mass migration from Germany to a close rather earlier than in many other European nations. Smaller numbers continued to arrive in this mature industrial phase, but the numbers of families declined as migrants were mostly industrial laborers seeking temporary opportunities to make higher wages. By the 1930s new migrants were outnumbered by those returning to Germany, but there was a further influx of mostly professional Jewish German refugees whose cultural significance as artists, architects, film directors, and scientists far outweighed their comparatively modest numbers.

Opposite, Above: A customs official attaches labels to the coats of a German immigrant family at the Registry Hall on Ellis Island in 1905.

Opposite, Below: German immigrants arriving at Ellis Island from the S.S. Prince Frederick Wilhelm *on July 24, 1915.*

Areas of German Settlement

The initial points of German residence in the United States in the nineteenth century were determined largely by the shipping routes that brought them. After the collapse of the indentured trade economical transportation early in the century required a viable return cargo, so that many migrants sailed on ships that brought cotton from New Orleans to Le Havre. Later a cheaper but indirect route from Liverpool to New York became popular, while in the final decades of the century the Bremen-Baltimore route used to export American tobacco and a Hamburg-New York route established for the migrant trade took over. Unlike the Irish and Italians, only a quite modest proportion of German migrants remained in New York or other disembarkation ports, although New York remained one of the largest urban centers of German speakers. The Erie canal and Great Lakes route to the Midwest, and the railroads such as the Baltimore and Ohio, and the New York Central were one important factor influencing settlement patterns. Another was the publicity given to certain areas by promoters ranging from published emigrant guides, to German churches, earlier settlers, and the railroads themselves who offered cheap land along their routes to stimulate traffic. Although New York soon had the greatest number of German residents, a position it maintained in the twentieth century, it was Wisconsin that attracted the highest proportion relative to total population. This concentration was part of a pattern of German settlement in the newly established farming areas and frontier cities of the Midwest, particularly northern Illinois, Wisconsin, and Michigan, with smaller numbers in Missouri, Iowa, and Minnesota. Notable urban centers of German residence, aside from New York and its offshoots such as Hoboken and Jersey City, included Milwaukee, Cincinnati, Chicago, Detroit, Cleveland, Toledo, Louisville, and St. Louis. Milwaukee, Cincinnati, and St. Louis were said to form the three corners of a so-called "German triangle" which in the late nineteenth century encompassed a majority of all those of German ancestry born in the United States. Elsewhere there were individual migrants and their families working as merchants or skilled craftsmen in many towns in the South but few significant German communities aside from at the disembarkation point in New Orleans and some farming settlements in Texas.

Occupations

One of the familiar images of German-American migrants was as conservative, thrifty but hardworking farmers who built a prosperous home on the land for their families through a careful application of European techniques unfamiliar to their less successful neighbors. Like all such clichés there was a degree of truth in the stereotype. Where German agricultural workers were able to establish a viable ethnic community large enough to support their own churches and schools and to attract new migrants, community norms did tend to reproduce German customs over time. There was an unusual emphasis on investing in and developing the land rather than exploiting it and moving on. However there is little evidence to suggest that Germans were inherently better farmers, or even that on average they were more prosperous that settlers from other nations. When they were among mixed communities most adapted quite quickly to local norms, and even the clusters of German agricultural settlements that formed in such states as Wisconsin, Missouri, and Minnesota adopted as much from established American farming practice as they rejected.

In fact although a third of all German workers in America in 1870 were farmers or agricultural laborers, statistically they were underrepresented in rural employment and disproportionately worked in industry. By that date Germans made up 11.4 percent of all employees in manufacturing, mechanical trades, and mining. In addition to working alongside Americans and other immigrants in the expanding industries and mines of the day, Germans were active in retailing, baking, butchering, cigar making, the dairy industry, and as tailors and cabinet makers. There were numerous German musicians and artists but relatively few lawyers, teachers, and doctors. Brewing and distilling was one area in which German capital and expertise were utilized to build up a sizeable industry based in such cities as Milwaukee and St. Louis.

Opposite, Above: The great day of arrival in America for emigrants aboard the S.S. Prince Frederick Wilhelm, *July 24, 1915.*

Opposite, Below: The S.S. Prince Frederick Wilhelm *was fully loaded with eager immigrants waiting to disembark.*

The hub of the German immigrant community was Hoboken, just across the Hudson River from New York City, c.1955.

German women of the first generation were less likely to enter the labor force than in many immigrant groups, but those that did largely found employment as nurses, janitors, laundresses, catering staff, tailors, or servants, rather than seeking factory jobs. There were individual success stories—John Jacob Astor (1763–1848) who became a real estate baron, John A. Roebling (1806–69) a designer of the Brooklyn Bridge, Henry E. Steinway (1797–1871), the piano manufacturer, among others—but the majority of German-Americans achieved only modest economic prosperity. Lack of capital inhibited the development of substantial German-owned businesses and skilled craftsmen were increasingly displaced by industrialization. Second and third generation German-Americans moved steadily into white collar employment but it was only by the second half of the twentieth century that significant numbers attained high management positions. By the 1970s their median income was above the national median, but remained below that of Italians, Poles, and Irish.

Community life and culture

For many but by no means all Germans of the first generation religion was at the core of community life, although the religious diversity of their homeland meant that it could not provide the unifying force it did for other ethnic groups such as the Italians and Irish. Although demands for German national parishes were quickly granted conflict over the Irish dominance of the church hierarchy remained a major feature of the history of German Catholicism in America. A shortage of candidates meant that German parishes demands for could not be met and calls for the appointment of German bishops were frequently resisted by the church. Some were finally chosen in the Midwest but controversy over the issue was renewed each time a see became vacant, culminating in an appeal to the Pope for more German bishops in 1890. German Catholic churches supported numerous religious confraternities and secular associations, sponsored orphanages, hospitals and other social facilities for the German community and played a major role in integrating migrants into American urban life. By 1869, German national parishes numbered 705, rising to a peak of almost 1,900 by 1916. Yet their very success in adapting to the needs of Catholicism in America undermined their future as their congregations began to move on to the suburbs and into the mainstream of American society. The anti-German backlash in World War I accelerated the decline of a distinct German Catholic identity, and although German-Americans have remained an important part of American Catholicism Irish dominance of the church hierarchy remains largely intact.

The Lutheran and Reformed churches in America saw divisions within the German community as the new arrivals of the nineteenth century found that the institutions established by their Pennsylvania German predecessors were already uncomfortably Americanized and liberal. They responded by setting up their own rival synods dedicated to the preservation of the German language and what they saw as doctrinal orthodoxy. The most important of these was the Missouri Synod founded in 1847 by C. F. W. Walter, who became known to his critics as "the Lutheran Pope of the West." However even these conservative institutions could only hold back rather than defeat the inevitable Americanization of their members and were ultimately forced to adapt and abandon the use of German language services in the early decades of the twentieth century.

Many German immigrants were not churchgoers at all and for them it was social clubs and organizations that provided the main forum of community life. Mutual benefit associations and voluntary fire and militia groups were some of the earliest of these, but over the years a rich variety developed in all major German-American clusters reflecting the diversity of interests and opinions among the migrants. Masonic and Odd Fellows lodges grew rapidly (over 300 of the 4,800 Odd Fellows lodges were German speaking by 1871) and new German fraternal societies such as the Sons of Hermann flourished. Debating societies, free thinkers, and various political reform groups met regularly. German societies established to assist new arrivals began in New York, Baltimore, and Philadelphia, before spreading to most major cities, providing a means to organize annual German day celebrations, carnivals, and other activities. Most of these events were focused in the German-dominated residential neighborhoods that sprang up in East Coast and Midwest cities. With names like "Little Germany," "Over the

Rhine," and "Nord-Seites," these areas were dominated by German shops and churches. Both impoverished new migrants in slum conditions and well established professionals in substantial houses could be found in these German enclaves which provided a continued point of contact with familiar ways even after many migrants had moved elsewhere. As the twentieth century progressed however the character of most of these areas changed as the majority of second and third generation German-Americans joined the exodus to the suburbs to be replaced by newer immigrant communities.

If people wish to keep up the traditions and beliefs of their home country it is vitally important that a living knowledge of their language is passed on to their children. For this reason schools and their language policy were a key factor in the evolution of the German community in America. Moreover many Germans were unimpressed by the standard of American schooling of the day and it was through their efforts that now familiar aspects such as kindergartens and music tuition became part of the mainstream education system. At first even non-religious Germans were obliged to send their children to German church run schools but the influx of more educated migrants by mid-century made it possible to set up a secular private system. Most of these schools were unable to compete effectively however with the spread of instruction in German within the public school system that took place beginning in Pennsylvania and Ohio in 1839. Yet these schools, attended by a significant majority of German-American children in fact advanced rapid assimilation as they offered only limited language training in German. It was only in a few rural areas and some parochial schools that the entire curriculum was taught in the mother tongue. Instruction in German in public schools attracted considerable controversy with regular attempts by state legislatures to mandate teaching in English and anti-German feeling rising. One unfortunate side effect of the anti-Germanism that accompanied World War I was the virtual ending of even German language instruction throughout America for many years.

The German language press began with Benjamin Franklin's short-lived *Philadelphische Zeitung* in 1732, and by 1860 had expanded to over 250 mostly weekly publications, reflecting the diversity of local, religious, and political interests and opinions of the expanding German-speaking population across the nation. Representing around eighty percent of all foreign language journals published in 1880, the total numbers peaked at about 800 titles in the 1890s before beginning a decline that was accelerated by the war. However total readership of daily titles was probably never much more than ten percent of German speakers. German-American theater, though important in its day, also dwindled away as its audience shifted allegiance to more American pastimes, particularly the growing attraction of the movies. The area where the cultural sophistication of many nineteenth-century German migrants did leave a lasting impact in their new country was music. Singing societies flourished, operas were staged regularly, and Germans played a key role in the early history of many of America's leading symphony orchestras in such cities as Philadelphia, Chicago, and Boston. A further vital German contribution to American culture occurred in the twentieth century when the 1930s influx of German Jewish intellectuals brought to America such seminal figures as the film director Fritz Lang, the architect Marcel Breuer, and more briefly the author Thomas Mann.

German-Americans were often unfairly caricatured as driven only by narrow economic motives and lacking political commitment in America. It is true that they never achieved direct political representation commensurate with their numbers—the only German-American politician of note at a national level in the nineteenth century was Carl Schurz (1829–1906) who was senator for Missouri and secretary for the interior under President Rutherford B. Hayes. However the main reason for this was not so much a lack of political enthusiasm as the diversity and sophistication of political opinion among German-Americans which did not fit well with the "machine" mobilization of a block vote behind a single party which was the norm in American politics of the day. Opposition to nativism and the related defense of German interests against such popular concerns as temperance and Sabbitarianism were the main themes before the Civil War. In the war itself Germans fought on both sides but geography at least put the majority in the Union camp, where they contributed a disproportionate 176,000 soldiers and several important officers including Schurz and Ludwig Blenker (1812–63.) In postwar politics nativism was again a key issue and both parties competed at national level for the German vote. German associations struggled to adapt to the increasing assimilation of the younger generation, with only the Catholic based Central-Verein and a newly established National German-American Alliance (1901–18) retaining influence. German-American brewing interests helped finance opposition to prohibition.

The continual erosion of German identity in America was dramatically accelerated by the events of World War I. The switch from a pro-German line to proclamations of loyalty once America entered the war in April 1917 could not divert a national wave of anti-German harassment. Names of families and towns were hastily changed, there was vandalism of German properties, tarring and feathering of a few unfortunate individuals (even a lynching in Illinois) but the more far-reaching impact was in the collapse of most German-American orga- nizations and especially the virtual ending of German language tuition. Equally important was a widespread recognition that continuing to maintain a strong ethnic identity despite the prac- tical assimilation that was already occurring was counterproductive and damaging to their status as full and loyal Americans. Pro-Nazi interests attracted very little support in the 1930s and there was no comparable anti-German backlash in World War II, if only because by then German-American ethnicity had already faded from public consciousness. The number of German language publications and of German-American organizations continued to decline in the postwar years, with the election of Dwight Eisenhower as president in 1952 a milestone in the evolution of a community that was rapidly becoming one of the least distinctive of the major immigrant groups. In total some five million Germans came to America in the nine- teenth century, with a further two million following in the twentieth. Their contribution to the development of the United States has been massive yet even with the revived interest in eth- nicity in the years since the 1970s for most expressions of German-American identity have remained confined to the occasional festival or parade. Only in pockets of rural Pennsylvania and a few other farming communities does a distinct German-American identity survive.

The Volga and Black Sea Germans

A separate group of Germans arrived during the nineteenth century from Russia and now have something of the order of a million descendants in the United States. Germans settled in large numbers on the Black Sea coast and along the Volga river in Russia late in the eighteenth century, primarily as peasants escaping religious restrictions and the impact of the Seven Years' War (1756–63). They established numerous villages grouped by religious denomination that had little contact with their Russian neighbors. After the freeing of Russian serfs in 1862 the privileges such as exemption from military service that had attracted the Germans were with- drawn and attempts made to Russify the schools, prompting a significant minority to move on to the United States. For those that remained the situation deteriorated further as the Bolshevik government abolished private land holding, and in 1941 Stalin ordered the forcible deporta- tion of the entire people to Central Asia and Siberia. In the 1990s, following the break-up of the Soviet Union and the reunification of Germany, most remaining Russian Germans have returned to their ancestral homeland in Germany.

The first Russian Germans to reach America were twenty-one Black sea German families who reached New York in 1849 before settling in Sandusky, Ohio and Burlington, Iowa. In 1872 one of these returned as a wealthy visitor and was expelled for stirring up discontent. News of his success encouraged a substantial outflow from the Black Sea villages to farmland mostly in South Dakota. A community of Mennonites was established in central Kansas. Volga German Catholic migration began a couple of years later, and under the influence of railroad land promoters most also settled in central Kansas. Volga German Protestant farmers clustered in an area between Denver and Sterling in Colorado. Others concentrated in Nebraska, parts of central New York State, and North Dakota, with smaller numbers throughout the United States. This largest number of migrants was in 1912, but the flow was virtually ended by the out- break of war in Europe and the Revolution in Russia that followed in 1917.

A substantial majority of Russian Germans were farmers settled in small communities that at first mirrored the religious exclusiveness and large patriarchal families they had become accustomed to in Russia. Fathers hired out their young sons for wages before setting them upon their own farms, while daughters rarely worked outside the family farm. Marriage within the local and religious group was very much the norm until well into the twentieth century. There was little contact with other German migrants who tended to disparage the Russians and their strange dialects. Black Sea Germans were heavily concentrated in wheat farming, while most Volga Germans who had had less opportunity to bring capital from Russia were obliged to seek work in construction and other urban sectors, though many of them subsequently resumed farming also, particularly in the sugar beet sector.

A thriving Russian German press, of which the *Dakota Freie Presse* was the most important title, continued into the 1950s. As it did in the main German migrant group the anti-German fever of World War I brought an end to the effort to maintain German language schools, although German was still used in at least some church services until the 1960s. While most Russian Germans in urban areas have become thoroughly Americanized elements of the distinctive family patterns and religious exclusiveness still live on in rural enclaves. Abbreviated forms of the medieval German betrothal and marriage customs they brought with them from Russia continue to this day.

Many Dutch immigrants went by train to the Midwest in 1910.

Dutch

The Dutch were among the earliest Europeans in North America, establishing a colony in 1624, but the number of Dutch settlers remained small until the 1830s. In the nineteenth century, Dutch migration was significant in relation to the small size of their home population but did not take on the mass scale that characterized movement from other European countries such as Germany, Ireland, and Italy. By the 1970s the total number of Americans of Dutch birth or descent was estimated at around four million. However unlike the majority of German-Americans this far smaller numbers of Dutch mostly seem to have been relatively

Cottonwood trees overhanging a pioneer encampment at Council Bluffs Ferry, a crossing place over the Missouri River, Iowa. The ferry marks the start of the long trek across the plains to Utah on the old Mormon Trail, 1855.

successful in retaining an awareness of group traditions over several generations. Historians link this both to the clustering of the colonial period settlers and the character of the nineteenth century inflow as chain migration from a small number of regions to a similarly concentrated settlement pattern in America. Most of these Dutch immigrants were conservative hard working country people motivated by the desire for good farming land who have prospered in America and played a significant part in developing the country's agriculture.

Dutch in the colonial period

When the English explorer Henry Hudson sailed his ship the *Half Moon* up what became the Hudson River in 1609 he was in the employ of the Dutch East India Company, which five years later established Fort Nassau near the site of the present day city of Albany. This trading outpost was declared part of a colony of New Netherlands in 1624, and a second settlement founded at New Amsterdam on Manhattan Island in 1626. In 1655 Dutch territories expanded with the conquest of a small Swedish colony on the Delaware. In total some 6,000 Dutch colonists migrated to the colony before it fell to the British in 1664. These included a few wealthy merchants and ruling officials who instituted and benefited from a feudal land holding system which they dominated as "patroons." Together with the frequently fatal sea crossing and the constant threat from Native Americans this made the colony an unattractive prospect for Dutch settlers. In consequence the majority who arrived were indentured servants, the desperate and poor of Amsterdam orphanages and almshouses, religious refugees, Jews from a failed colony in Brazil, unemployed day laborers etc. Some two thousand English joined the colony from New England, along with French Huguenots, and others, giving New Amsterdam an ethnic diversity that foreshadowed in miniature the history of New York.

The British conquest brought even this sporadic immigration to a halt, with few except the occasional merchant and clergymen to serve the numerous Dutch Reformed churches joining them before the 1830s. Some Dutch Quakers and Mennonites did join William Penn and played a part in the founding of Germantown, but the first phase of Dutch colonization had effectively ended. However despite its unpromising origins the Dutch settlement flourished and expanded by natural growth, so that by 1790 there were 100,000 people of Dutch descent in the United States, eighty percent of them still in the vicinity of New York City. Education for both girls and boys was important to the colonial Dutch and local schools continued to use their native language until the 1820s. The Dutch Reformed Church continued to hold services in Dutch into the mid-eighteenth century and set up two colleges, Rutgers (1766) and New Brunswick Seminary (1784) to meet local demand for clergy. Large families promoted a gradual expansion of farms along the tributaries of the Hudson, as well as into New Jersey and Pennsylvania. The concentration of Dutch in the New York area gave them continued visibility and a degree of influence in the early decades of the Republic. Subsequently there have been three United States presidents, the two Roosevelts and before them Martin Van Buren, who were of colonial Dutch ancestry.

Dutch in the mass migration era

As in several other European countries it was religious dissenters seeking freedom of worship who led the early phases of Dutch emigration in the 1840s. Against a background of rapid population growth, dissatisfaction with the Dutch Reformed church added to immediate hardship brought by the failure of potato crops to stimulate several group departures led by pastors or priests (called *dominee*.) One of the most important of these groups, led by Dominee Albertus C. Van Ralte, took some 1,000 settlers to found a colony they called Holland on the shore of Lake Michigan, while other religious groups, another set up the town of Pella in central Iowa. In total some 5,000 religious dissenters fled to America in the years before 1850, setting up close knit rural communities that were able to preserve aspects of their local tradition over several generations. Agricultural problems induced other Dutch rural dwellers at the same period into group migration as whole neighborhoods or extended family groups seeking better land on the frontiers. The introduction of greater religious freedom in the Netherlands after 1848, together with economic problems and the Civil War in America in the following decades slowed down Dutch migration significantly until the Reconstruction era. When large inflows resumed in the 1880s they largely drew people from the same localities as before in a form of chain migration stimulated by letters, news, and ticket money sent home. Letters praising the opportunities to be found in America were circulated widely, printed in the press and denounced in the churches, so that everyone in the affected areas had either direct or indirect knowledge of someone who had already emigrated. Since economic motivation was the primary driving force in the majority of cases the numbers of migrants rose and fell according to the varying economic conditions of the United States and the Netherlands, with the 1880s peak of some 75,000 closely linked to a severe farming depression in the northern part of Holland. A further 75,000 arrived between 1900 and 1914, about 35,000 in the 1920s, and a surprisingly large 80,000 between 1945 and the mid-1960s largely as a result of continued population growth and the impact of World War II. Over the period as a whole only about one eighth of these Dutch migrants returned home, a lower figure than for many other comparable groups.

Statistics collected by the Dutch government provided unusually detailed information on the Dutch migrants up until 1880, indicating that the overwhelming majority were drawn from the rural poor, with only a small percentage of emigrants from the more wealthy and professional classes. Moreover most of these more prosperous migrants preferred to head for the Dutch colonies of Indonesia or South Africa rather than the more uncertain opportunities of the Americas. Some 30,000 of the descendants of these migrants to Indonesia were granted special permission to enter the United States in 1958 to 1960 after the colony gained independence. Unusually in the final phase of Dutch migration after World War II it was the Dutch government itself that organized and subsidized the exodus from the home country, anxious to relieve problems of postwar reconstruction and provide aid to victims of a disastrous flood in 1953, negotiating an unprecedented exception to the U.S. quota limits.

Occupations and settlement patterns

As we might anticipate settlement patterns and occupational distribution were closely linked among Dutch migrants, with the majority moving to areas in the Midwest and north were land was freely available for farming. Later arrivals and the children of the first generation tended to move more readily to urban centers were they adapted to industrial work or filled whatever other economic niches became available. Although most migrant groups arriving in America liked to settle alongside their fellow country folk where they could ease the problems of adjustment and preserve as much as possible that was familiar, the Dutch rural migrants of the nineteenth century seem to have taken this localism to extremes. Holland was marked by extremely small local subcultures with their own costume, dialects, farming techniques, traditions etc., and many settlers attempted to transplant these local variations intact in the New World by dividing up Dutch enclaves on a strict regional basis. The most extreme example was in the colony of Holland, Michigan, where new arrivals grouped villages named after their home provinces around the core town established by migrants from the Gelderland and Overjissel provinces. Similar regional groupings occurred in the two other major early colonies at Pella and its offshoot at Orange City in Iowa. All of these attracted other migrants, both direct from the homeland and from within the United States, expanding into neighboring counties and moving farther afield again to establish new clusters. Migrants from Orange City, for example pioneered Dutch settlement in Washington state early in the twentieth century. In Wisconsin and Michigan the Dutch drew on the dairy farming tradition of their native land, while in Iowa and the Dakotas they adopted American styles of mixed livestock ranching and wheat growing. In the vicinity of cites many Dutch became truck farmers supplying vegetables to urban consumers.

Of course not all Dutch were rural farmers. Second generation families and later immigrants joined smaller numbers from the first arrivals in the major cities from New York across to the Great Lakes, where they formed small but lively Dutch enclaves in cities such as Chicago, Buffalo, Cleveland, and Grand Rapids. In Chicago only the Groningers on the West Side who

worked mainly as teamsters, refuse hauliers and day laborers were really an urban community, the other enclaves at South Holland and Roseland were farmers eventually swallowed up
and displaced by the growing city. Other Dutch town dwellers worked in (and largely owned)
the furniture industry in Grand Rapids, while large numbers were employed in the textile mills
at Patterson. Some opened small businesses such as shops and restaurants to meet the needs of
the residents in the Dutch enclaves. Dutch women found employment as household servants
and in the service industries but mostly avoided factory work. By the third generation the proportion of farmers had fallen sharply and the Dutch were moving successfully into middle
management, government service and the professions in ever increasing numbers. As other
migrant groups from southern Europe and later African-Americans from the South moved into
the northern cities in growing numbers Dutch enclaves moved outward towards the suburbs,
often in a series of communal shifts that largely preserved a clustered pattern of Dutch settlement, although over the years the overt signs of Dutch origin such as language use largely
disappeared as assimilation increased.

Social and cultural life

Social and cultural life for Dutch-Americans of the first few generations centered around the
church and religious influence on community values was and to a degree remains pervasive.
Over eighty percent of Dutch migrants to America were members of the Reformed Church,
with the remainder Catholics, Mennonites and Jews. Without exploring the arcane details of
doctrinal disputes we can note that two secession groups were prominent both in migrations to
America and within the two major denominations, the Reformed Church in America, which
dates from the colonial era, and the Christian Reformed Church founded after an 1857 schism
in Michigan. By the early 1840s the Reformed Church had abandoned Dutch services but had
a thriving congregation attending in excess of 250 churches, mostly in the New York area. By
1916 the close cooperation that evolved with migrants of the new era had expanded the church
throughout the East and north central states to a total of some 700 churches, some of which
provided Dutch services to the newer migrants. In the main area of nineteenth century Dutch
settlement in the Midwest however the newer Christian Reformed Church dominates. Less
Americanized and therefore more familiar and acceptable to the conservative incomers the
Christian Reformed Church maintained services in Dutch for all except a few urban churches
well into the twentieth century. As part of clannish and insular rural communities the church
contributed to the survival of Dutch and its regional dialects in many areas, although it could
only slow the gradual spread of a hybrid Yankee Dutch and eventually of English. By the 1960s
only an occasional Dutch service could still be found. Urban Dutch lost their language and any
aspects of their culture far more rapidly as work and daily life brought them into regular contact with Americans and other nationalities, although too mostly retained a Calvinist outlook
and values.

In contrast to most other long standing immigrant groups the Dutch, with the active
lead of the Christian Reformed Church, have been remarkably successful in maintaining a distinctive educational system. Several hundred Calvinist founded schools are attended by a
substantial majority of the children from their congregations and both impart a continued link
to the values of their religious tradition and play a key role in promoting higher than average
educational attainment among Dutch-Americans. There were numerous Dutch language
newspapers and periodicals, mostly associated with the Protestant churches, although few survived beyond the 1940s. Politically the Dutch were not sufficiently numerous to form important
voting blocks and with the exception of Dutch Catholics have consistently voted Republican,
sending a succession of Dutch-Americans to Congress from Midwestern states. Nascent Dutch
solidarity that emerged in opposition to the English actions in the Boer war against Dutch
South African colonists at the turn of the century was shattered soon after by the nativist backlash of World War I. With all foreigners suspected of lacking patriotism and incidents where
Dutch were confused with Germans by over excited mobs Dutch language tuition and press
were drastically curbed. Assimilation was hastened by the wartime army experience of many
thousands of Dutch-Americans. The final influx of Dutch migrants in the 1940s and 1950s

was to settle largely in ethnically mixed urban areas and did little to reverse the inevitable adaptation of a Dutch-American ethnic identity which while still a source of pride today lives on largely in tourist orientated festivals and academic study programs.

Scandinavians

Although the number of nineteenth century migrants from each of the Scandinavian countries was far lower than the millions from Germany or Ireland the population pool from which they were drawn was also smaller so the flow represented a significant proportion of the total population. In the case of Norway the 176,000 émigrés in the 1880s were almost ten percent of the entire population, an astonishing loss in a single decade that was exceeded only by Ireland and after 1900 Italy. A lesser but still substantial proportion left Sweden and Finland at the same period. In Denmark both the pattern of agricultural land distribution and the pace of industrialization were significantly more favorable and the percentage driven to migrate substantially smaller.

Sweden

Sweden has the distinction of having established one of the smallest and least known colonies on the North American mainland. Fort Christina, the supposed base for a colony of New Sweden, was built on the site of present day Wilmington, Delaware in 1638. In the 17 years before the colony fell to the Dutch its population hardly exceeded 500, many of whom were Finns or Dutch. Nevertheless there is said to have been a legacy of this unsuccessful colonization in the introduction to America of the log dovetailing technique used to build pioneer cabins. At the Continental Congress of 1776 it was a descendant of one of the handful of Swedish colonists, one John Morton, who cast the deciding vote of his delegation in favor of Independence.

Over the following decades a thriving trade route shipping iron ore from Gothenburg to New York allowed a few hundred more sailors, and other occasional travelers to reach America, but there was no significant migration until the mid 1840s. In the ten years after 1845 economic depression prompted some 15,000 Swedes to emigrate, most of them relatively prosperous and well educated family groups with capital raised by selling their land. A minority of perhaps ten percent were Janssonists fleeing religious persecution. Followers of Eric Jansson, a farmer's son from Uppland who was a fierce critic of the Lutheran Church of Sweden, the Janssonists and their prophet established the utopian colony of Bishop Hill in Henry County, Illinois. Despite the disastrous failure of the colony (which was almost wiped out by a cholera epidemic in 1849, with Jansson himself murdered by a fellow settler the following year) the attention it received helped spread the notion of emigration throughout Sweden.

At the end of the 1860s the effects of growing rural overpopulation that had left large numbers of peasants landless were made dramatically worse by a disastrous crop failure which quickly led to famine throughout Sweden. In a single year twenty-two in every thousand Swedes starved to death. The first large flow of emigrants, some 100,000 people in the five years after 1868, left in response. After that migration slowed, but a second wave of about 90,000 migrants followed twenty years later when imports of cheap American and Ukrainian grain caused a severe agricultural depression. As the Swedish community in America grew migration took on added momentum prompted in part by letters and remittances sent home, bringing a further substantial inflow of some 200,000 in the 1890s, another 219,000 before 1910, and after the war caused a break, 92,000 more in the 1920s.

Most of the early Swedish immigrants were aspiring farmers who settled in the Midwest, particularly in Illinois and the section of the northern Mississippi valley in Minnesota that became known as the Swedish Triangle. Later secondary migrations joined by new incomers established Swedish settlements in Kansas, Nebraska, the Dakotas, and further afield around Austin, Texas, and in northern Maine. As the flow of unemployed laborers and smaller numbers of professionals and their families added to the migration, they joined the influx of second generation Swedes to the cities of the Midwest. By 1910 two thirds of Swedish-Americans were city dwellers. Many of them settled in Minneapolis and St. Paul, but the largest concentration of Swedes was in Chicago, whose 145,000 first and second generation Swedes in 1910 comprised nine percent of the population and made it the second largest Swedish city after Stockholm. In the early years conditions in Swede Town were extremely poor and cholera endemic.

Swedish-American churches never achieved the dominant role in their community that typified many immigrant churches, as many Swedes attended local churches of other denominations or were not churchgoers at all. The largest was the Lutheran Augustana Synod (founded with Norwegian participation in 1860 but subsequently exclusively Swedish) which attracted around one in five Swedish-Americans and was active in promoting education and social welfare. However individual pastors were often of great importance in rural communities and indeed some had led their flock in large groups from Sweden. The Augustana Synod merged with other Lutherans to form the Lutheran Church of America in 1962. Secular organizations were seen by the Lutheran church as a direct challenge to its authority and society or club membership frequently led to expulsion. Nevertheless Swedish-American organizations, most of which catered to the cultural and social needs of the increasingly prosperous Swedish middle class, did attract quite large memberships in the early decades of the twentieth century. Both the church and secular interests were represented in the Swedish-American press which thrived between the 1880s and about 1915 but like other foreign language media was severely affected by the nativist backlash that followed. Although few Swedish-Americans have achieved national political prominence Minnesota has had a succession of Swedish senators and governors since John Lind in 1886. The most notable literary achievement to emerge from the Swedish-American experience was Vilhelm Moberg's trilogy *The Emigrants* (1949–59), although this sensitive account of farming migrants was published before Moberg himself had visited the United States. Nelson Algren is probably the best known author of Swedish descent.

Swedish-Americans tended to have been assimilated relatively quickly into the American mainstream despite a markedly low rate of intermarriage with non-Swedes in the first generation. Most of their children attended public schools and inevitably lost familiarity with their language. After World War I integration proceeded rapidly. Although Swedish-American heritage remains of cultural interest to many, as a living phenomenon it lives on only in a few scattered rural pockets. Elsewhere it finds expression in renewed contacts with Sweden and in the annual celebration of St. Lucia's day (December 13), marked with a procession, singing, and dancing.

Norway

Although they apparently left no lasting impact Norwegians can make a good case for having been the earliest European settlers in North America. Scholars still dispute the extent of their voyages but it is now widely accepted that a group of Norsemen led by Leif Ericsson (born in the Viking colony of Iceland) settled briefly on the east coast of America at a place they knew as Vinland in the year AD 1000. In the colonial era a few hundred Norwegian migrants arrived on Dutch ships, settling near Albany in a colony called Rensselaerwyck. In the era of mass migration that began in the 1820s Norway sent a higher proportion of its population to America than any other nation except Ireland. Some 850,000 Norwegians in total emigrated to America in the 150 years after 1820, the vast majority of them between 1840 and 1915. Scholars attribute this huge outflow to a combination of severe land shortages with a tradition of rural resistance to central government and religious institutions. Only a tiny percentage of Norway's land is suitable for agriculture and as the population expanded in the nineteenth century, plots sizes fell and a growing number of peasants became landless. The urban middle class leadership that had emerged from Norway's successful campaign for independence from Danish and Swedish rule earlier in the century seemed to have little to offer the impoverished peasantry that could compare with the vista of land, freedom, and social equality held out by letters and newspapers from America.

Some of the earliest migrants were involved in a variety of abortive colonizing projects organized by religious dissenters or other social visionaries. Cleng Peerson (1783–1865) led a group of fifty-two settlers who left Norway in 1825 on the ship *Restauration* to found a settlement at Kendall in the thick and inhospitable forests of the south shore of Lake Ontario. Their failure did not deter numerous others, including the internationally known violinist Ole Bull (1810–80), who in 1852 financed the purchase of land for a colony in Pennsylvania which was intended to become New Norway. As with other such failed settlements the publicity they received in the home country stimulated a faster outflow of migrants despite the collapse of the initial project. The early decades of Norwegian immigration were dominated by farming families in search of land, most of whom settled where land was then most readily available in northern Iowa, Wisconsin, Minnesota, and the Dakotas, forming small Norwegian dominated enclaves among similar clusters of Germans and Swedes. By the 1880s the children of these settlers were being joined by new more urban migrants in the coastal regions of northwestern states such as Washington, British Columbia, and even Alaska. Before long a large concentration of Norwegians had formed in Seattle and they dominated the fishing, shipbuilding, and timber industries of the Northwest. Norwegian sailors and shipyard workers also formed a small but long-lived community in Brooklyn.

Although the Lutheran church provided an important focus for ethnic identity sectarian differences were frequent and it was not until 1917 that the three main factions merged to form the Norwegian Lutheran Church of America (dropping the national name in 1946 to become the Evangelical Lutheran Church.) By 1922 they had 492,000 members. A small minority of Norwegian immigrants joined other churches, including the Methodists,

Norwegian emigrants en route to America on board the S.S. Hero *in 1870.*

Mormons, and Baptists. The Norwegian churches established several important higher education institutions including St. Olaf's in Minnesota and Augustana College in Sioux Falls, South Dakota, but most of their flock relied on the public school system for basic education. Inevitably this hastened the integration of the second generation into American ways. Use of Norwegian dropped sharply after the start of American involvement in World War I, prompting a rapid decline in the number of Norwegian language papers and periodicals, although a few significant journals did not switch to English until the 1940s. Most Norwegians adopted a progressive political stance, exemplified by the anti big business rhetoric of Knute Nelson (1843-1923), who served as a U.S. Senator from 1895 until his death, after being elected the first Norwegian governor of Minnesota in 1893.

The best known Norwegian-American literary figure was Ole. E. Rølvaag (1876–1913), a farm worker from North Dakota who later taught at St. Olaf's College. His novels such as *Giants in the Earth* explored the immigrant experience and stressed the importance of preserving a knowledge of nation's heritage in America. In pursuit of this goal a Norwegian-American Historical association was established in 1925. Despite the disappearance of the Norwegian language in America, contacts with the homeland flourish and a sense of Norwegian ethnicity has been retained both in areas of a few big cities such as Minneapolis and in Midwestern settlements.

Denmark

Denmark had a relatively advanced economy by the mid-nineteenth century and as a result did not experience emigration on the same mass scale as its Scandinavian neighbors. Over the whole period from 1820 to 1975 the total inflow of Danish migrants to the United States recorded by immigration statistics was only just over 360,000 as compared with over a million and a quarter Swedes.

A few hundred Danes arrived in America early in the colonial era. A Danish expedition attempting to find the Northwest Passage explored much of Hudson's Bay in 1619, while the Bering Strait is named after the Danish captain Vitus Bering (1681–1741) who discovered it in 1728 while sailing for the Russians. Among the earliest Danish settlers was one Jonas Bronck (d. 1643) who bought from the Native Americans the area of New York that became known as the Bronx. Hans Christian Febiger (1749–96) is remembered as a senior lieutenant of George Washington, and Peter Lasson (1800–59) as a pioneer leading settlers across the Rockies to California.

In the nineteenth century, the Danish government kept exceptionally detailed statistics on emigrants, confirming more anecdotal impressions from other nations, such as the age profile of migrants. The emigrants were mostly remarkably young—only twenty-two percent of Danish emigrants between 1868 and 1900 were over thirty years of age. Danish statistics also allow scholars to quantify the gender imbalance in emigration—96,000 adult men left compared with only around 60,000 adult women, with consequences for population growth and social life in both countries. Denmark proved a fertile recruiting ground for the Mormon church, which financed the emigration of some 20,000 converts, in the process making Utah the state with the largest Danish population in 1860. As with neighboring countries mass emigration began as a rural phenomenon in the 1860s, but the earlier urbanization meant that a higher proportion of Denmark's emigrants came from the towns and the shift towards a predominantly urban migration later in the century occurred rather earlier.

Although in many areas there were just too few Danes to allow the formation of ethnically homogenous settlements, small Danish enclaves did develop in East Coast cities. Often Danes found employment in factories and small companies owned by fellow countrymen before saving enough money to move West and buy land. The first Danish farming community began in Hartland, Wisconsin as early as 1845, with others following across the state and in Illinois, Michigan, and especially Iowa over the following decades. Later in the nineteenth century Chicago became an important focus of Danish settlement, particularly attracting the minority of professionals and businessmen, with other enclaves forming in cities such as Omaha, Council Bluffs, Iowa, and Racine, Wisconsin. Danish immigrant men and women worked across the whole range of employment possibilities open to them in nineteenth century America, with the only statistically significant concentration being in dairy farming, where Danes and Danish-Americans pioneered many significant technical improvements.

Only a minority of Danish-Americans were regular churchgoers and many of those joined other Scandinavian or American denominations, leaving only some twenty percent to support the various factions of the Danish Lutheran Church. Numerous Danish organizations, some small and short lived, others still flourishing, were set up to meet welfare, cultural and social functions, including a nation-wide fraternal order known as Det Danske Brodersamfund (founded in Omaha in 1866), and a Danish-American Heritage Association (1977). A Danish language press flourished in the early decades of the twentieth century but dwindled away to a handful of titles with a circulation numbering only a few thousand after World War II, although some Danish-American periodicals in English remained slightly more successful. Sophus Keith Winter, whose trilogy of novels exploring pioneer life in Nebraska were published in the 1930s remains the most significant Danish-American author in English. Perhaps because they were so widely scattered and relatively few in number Danes seem to have assimilated quite quickly with a very high level of facility in English and of intermarriage apparent as early as 1910. "Danish Days," notably Constitution Day on June 5, and Danish celebrations of Christmas Eve are still held within the family and as festivals in towns marking their Danish heritage.

Finland

Finland had been a Swedish colony since at least the fourteenth century AD, and the first Finns in America were sent from the Swedish region of Varmland to the short-lived settlement of New Sweden on the Delaware River at the end of the 1630s. In 1669 an uprising against the English, who had captured the territory from the Dutch five years earlier, was lead by one "Long Finn." It took several decades more before the small cluster of Finns and Swedes were absorbed into the English colony and apart from sporadic deserting sailors few more Finns reached America until the 1860s. In that decade a few hundred Finns who had earlier settled in Norway began to arrive with Norwegian miners and others in Michigan and Minnesota. In the 1870s some 3,000 migrants came directly from Finland, starting an exodus that swelled to 61,000 between 1880 and 1892, and a further quarter of a million or so from 1893 to 1920. Over sixty percent came from the two provinces of Vaasa and Oulu where industrial development was slowest. Around an eighth were Swedish speakers from Finland's Swedish minority. Return rates were quite high, with around thirty percent eventually moving back to Finland.

By 1900 almost half of all Finns in the United States lived in Michigan and Minnesota, with the remainder mostly spread across New York, Massachusetts, Washington, Oregon, Montana, Wisconsin, Illinois, Ohio, Pennsylvania, New Jersey, and California. A significant minority of Finnish settlers were farmers, while the rest took whatever jobs were available, including domestic service and factory work for women, iron ore mining, salmon fishing, and textile work for the men.

A widespread resentment of centralized pastoral authority lead to numerous splits and schisms in Finnish Lutheranism, culminating in three main churches, the Suomi Synod, the Apostolic Lutherans and the National Lutherans, while the American Congregationalists also attracted a number of Finnish adherents. There was strong Finnish support for the temperance movement, leading to the founding of a Finnish National Temperance Brotherhood in 1888. Numerous other groups attempted to organize and support the migrant Finns, including a Finnish Socialist Federation which was active in several major strikes and labor disputes before World War I. In the same period there was a small but thriving Finnish language press but after the war the virtual cessation of Finnish immigration combined with growing assimilation of second generation migrants brought a marked decline in all aspects of cultural and social activity, challenging the survival of Finnish media, organizations, and churches. Merger with others into non ethnic bodies became inevitable. Ethnicity ceased to be a major issue for the majority of Finnish-Americans as the century passed, although an interest in the homeland and aspects of Finnish culture remained.

CHAPTER 4 Irish

The famous exhortation of America to the Old World to "bring me your tired, your poor, your huddled masses, yearning to breath free" perfectly matches the common picture of Irish immigration. Of the roughly thirty five million emigrants to America between 1800 and 1921, over seven million (or twenty percent) came from Ireland, and many of them were indeed tired and poor. The enduring image of Irish immigration is thus a nineteenth century one. It is of famine-era coffin ships unloading their diseased and starving cargo into the crammed, insanitary tenements of Boston and New York. From there the strong and resourceful struggled towards modest, or occasionally spectacular, success in a burgeoning new nation, while the weak and unfortunate scratched out a precarious, hard existence through back-breaking work and domestic service.

For many Irish immigrants, this was indeed the pattern, but such images reflect only part of the Irish-American story. Not all started out as poor slum dwellers, and many had left their homeland in search of more prosperous and less oppressive lives as early as the seventeenth century. Indeed since the early eighteenth century emigration had become a constant and much lamented feature of Irish life, and it has endured until quite recent times.

Irish emigration was, in short, a varied experience, and it must be noted that the Irish went to many destinations besides America. Many settled in Britain, itself an expanding and wealthy country throughout this period and a greater industrial power than America until the 1890s. Indeed Irish emigration to Britain—which had the advantage of an easier return home to Ireland—has been a more attractive option than America in some periods. Significant numbers of Irish made the long sea voyage to South Africa and more made the even longer journey to Australia and New Zealand. Canada became both a temporary stop before further migration to the U.S. as well as the final destination of many Irish immigrants—especially for nineteenth century Protestant emigrants. Between 1876 and 1921, however, over eighty percent of Irish emigrants went to the U.S. attracted by higher wages (often up to three times those in Ireland), seemingly limitless economic expansion, and the expectation of greater freedom, America had undoubtedly become the favored destination for most.

Emigration was caused by shifting combinations of poverty, religious discrimination, and political subordination, which in turn need to be understood in the wider context of Irish history. Underlying this history is Ireland's proximity to the larger island of Britain, whose various peoples have imposed their political, economic, cultural, and social systems on Ireland in a way that has often oppressed Irish people and constrained Irish development. The Anglo-Irish connection cannot explain all of Ireland's economic problems, nor all of the reasons why the Irish emigrated, but it is an essential starting point. From the sixteenth century until the nineteenth, England, and then Britain, gradually developed into the world's most powerful nation. As Britain's star waxed, Ireland was unable to avoid the harsh glare of its ambition, and British strategic, religious and economic interests affected Ireland profoundly. As a result, many Irish men and women chose, and were sometimes forced, to leave Ireland.

The earliest invasion of Ireland came around 600BC when the warlike Celts began to settle and by around 150BC they had become dominant. They valued learning highly and their Druid priests, their poets and their historians held a high status equivalent to nobility. This intellectual class transmitted orally to each new generation culture and customs (much of it in the form of Brehon law) which survived piecemeal into the modern era. This gave the Irish an

attitude toward family, land ownership and political authority which differed markedly from that of the English. These differences are crucial to an understanding of the centuries of conflict, conquest and control which form the backdrop to the story of emigration.

Christianity was established in Ireland in AD5, largely through the efforts of a Celtic Briton called St. Patrick, it merged with these older Celtic traditions, and Ireland's place on the edge of Europe gave this latest cultural import a distinctive difference. Unlike most of western Europe (including most of Britain), Ireland was never conquered by the Romans. Hence it developed a unique Celtic Christianity rather than adopting the Romanized form taken by the rest of western Europe. For hundreds of years after the collapse of the Roman empire (the so-called Dark Ages) the Irish monasteries maintained vital elements of Christian learning which had been wiped out in most of western Europe, and this Christian Celtic culture survived largely unmolested until the Viking incursions which began in AD795.

This tradition gave the Irish Celts a unified language, religion, and culture, but it failed to provide the political cohesion that had developed in England and France. Over 150 clans with their own kings constantly fought each other for land, cattle, and regional dominance. Tribal rivalry continued unabated through the centuries and led eventually to Dermot MacMurrough of Leinster inviting the Anglo-Norman noble, Richard de Clare, Earl of Pembroke, (also known as Strongbow) to help him regain his lands in 1167.

From this point the influence of England and then Britain becomes inextricably linked to Ireland. These colonizers were not "English" or "British" in a modern sense. They were the recent descendants of Norman nobles who had accompanied William the Conqueror in his invasion of England from northern France barely a century before. They spoke an early form of French, not English, and many of them had come from Wales rather than England. Nevertheless, with their superior organization and weaponry they swiftly established themselves in Ireland: and this effectively established the rule of the English crown and a permanent English presence in Ireland. The Normans quickly set up the feudal structures and laws current in England, and by 1297 had established their own Parliament. However, until Tudor times, this English conquest of Ireland was always haphazard and incomplete. The English tended only to occupy the rivers, plains and coasts, while leaving the hills, bogs, and forests to the native Celts. Trade and agriculture flourished in those areas under Norman rule, but life outside their new towns retained its traditional Celtic flavor.

During the fourteenth and fifteenth centuries effective English control dwindled to a small area on Ireland's eastern coast around Dublin, known as "the Pale." Many of these "Old English" became so immersed in Gaelic ways that the English crown began to lose control over them until in the sixteenth century the Tudor monarchs Henry VIII and Elizabeth I embarked on a program of reconquest with the Gaelic chiefs often taking different sides and positions as the situation constantly changed. The bitterness of these conflicts was further heightened by a new animosity in Anglo-Irish relations—religion. The Reformation had turned England into a largely Protestant country, but despite the efforts of Henry and Elizabeth, it had barely touched Ireland outside the Pale. The common Catholicism of the Gaelic and Old English nobles often led to joint resistance as the English attempted

This sixteenth-century struggle for Ireland culminated in the Ulster War of 1595–1603 by the end of which the old world of independent Gaelic kingship had finally disappeared. As a result of their defeat, effective English control of the whole of Ireland was achieved for first time.

In 1607, still broken by their humiliation and fearful of persecution, around ninety of Ulster's traditional Gaelic Catholic elite (including O'Neill) abandoned their lands and left for France. This "emigration"—the famous "Flight of the Earls"—left Ulster, traditionally the most Gaelic province of all Ireland, open to the Protestant colonization (or "plantations") which have been the cause of so much of Ireland's tensions. The subsequent influx of Protestant settlers was not confined to Ulster (British Protestants settled all over Ireland), but Ulster became the most densely peopled with Protestants. Conspicuous among them were Scottish Presbyterians who settled in the east of Ulster. They made the short crossing from Scotland largely by their own initiative and created a solid Presbyterian heartland in Antrim and Down. Many of their descendants would move on to America in the eighteenth century.

During the seventeenth century Irish society was restructured and the conditions for later Irish emigration were set. The bulk of all Irish land changed hands, from Old English and Gaelic Catholics to new English and Scottish Protestants. This shift of power and wealth was the outcome of a century of war and upheaval on a grand scale, as Ireland became caught up in the wider conflicts of British and European power politics.

The two key episodes were Ireland's involvement in the Civil Wars which racked the British Isles between 1639 and 1652, and William III's "Glorious Revolution" of 1688–91. In the former a fragile coalition of Old English and Irish Catholics rebelled, seeking the return of those lands and privileges already lost, while claiming continuing loyalty to Charles I. For eight years shifting alliances and a confusing array of English, Scottish, and Irish armies caused immeasurable suffering until Charles' defeat in England by Cromwell allowed the Parliamentary armies to turn their attention to Ireland. Few episodes in Irish history are as notorious as Cromwell's campaign of 1649. For not only was he trying to reestablish English control, he also sought revenge for the Catholic massacre of Protestants at the beginning of the rebellion in 1641. Although wildly exaggerated by Protestants, the massacre claimed around 12,000 lives in Ulster and confirmed the view of many Protestants that the Catholic Irish were untrustworthy and savage barbarians. Cromwell's victory was followed by the largest single dispossession of Catholics in Irish history. Unable to pay his army with money, thousands of his English and Scottish soldiers were rewarded with grants of land confiscated from their defeated enemies. The scale of this transfer of land was enormous. Before Cromwell's intervention, Catholics had still held about sixty percent of the land. By the time of the restoration of Charles II in 1660, this figure was probably nearer twenty percent.

Protestant dominance was further reinforced toward the end of the century as a result of the Glorious Revolution. In 1685 James II, a Catholic, had become king, and in 1688 his second wife surprisingly produced a male heir. The prospect of a permanent Catholic dynasty so disturbed the English Protestant elite that a group of nobles invited Mary (James' Protestant daughter from his first marriage) to take the throne with her husband William of Orange. William, the Protestant stadtholder of the Dutch republic, was eager to use the resources of England in his long-running war with Louis XIV of France, and by taking the throne he turned Ireland into the next theater of war for this European struggle. William defeated James' armies at the battles of the Boyne (1690) and Aughrim (1691), and when the Catholic forces were finally defeated at the siege of Limerick in 1691, Protestant Ireland set about securing land and political superiority with vigor.

Religion, rather than ethnicity, was now the defining feature of Ireland, and over the next generation, the Irish Parliament passed a set of laws which discriminated against Catholics in almost every sphere of life. In breach of the Treaty of Limerick, Catholics were excluded from voting or sitting in parliament, and from educating their young in Ireland. Mixed marriages were illegal and powerful incentives were given to those who would convert to the legally established Protestant Church of Ireland. All official, legal and military offices were closed to Catholics, and they were not allowed to bear arms nor buy land. In short, they became non-citizens. Protestants who dissented from the established church also faced political and educational disabilities (albeit on a smaller scale than the Catholics). In their case, weaker ties to the land and more individualistic attitudes to family and independence did lead many to emigrate to America.

By 1782, the British Parliament had been forced to renounce its right to make laws for Ireland and to relinquish its control of Irish trade, which had hindered the Irish economy since the 1660s. However, the head of state was still the British monarch, and his ministers were still able to manipulate the Irish Parliament through the distribution of well-paid government jobs and pensions. By 1793 Catholics had been given the vote again, and most of the penal laws had been repealed, but they were still not allowed to sit in Parliament and the Irish government remained exclusively Protestant and largely aristocratic. This led to the growth of radical republicanism and Catholic discontent—expressed by the United Irishmen and the Defenders.

After severe government repression and a failed attempt at invasion by the French at Bantry Bay in 1796, a United Irish rebellion finally exploded in Wexford and northeast Ulster in 1798. United Irish leaders, such as Wolfe Tone, were usually middle class Protestants who professed enlightened toleration of all religions and the equal rights of all Irish citizens, but the

rebellion took on a sectarian character. Around 30,000 were killed during the rebellion, which finally convinced the British government that direct rule from Britain was necessary. The Irish Parliament was bribed and cajoled into voting for its own dissolution, and in 1801 the Act of Union came into effect. The failure of the rebellion led many radicals and rebels to emigrate to America.

The rebellion and Union left a bitter legacy which defined the religious and political allegiances that persist in parts of Ireland to this day. Although many Protestants were initially against the Union, they rapidly saw it as their best protection against future Catholic rebellions. Conversely, many Catholics had supported the Union—partly because they were promised emancipation as part of the deal, and partly because the Protestant Ascendancy in Ireland had proven itself a far greater enemy to Catholic rights than the British government. But George III opposed the attempt of William Pitt, the British prime minister, to bring in a bill for emancipation, and this destroyed any prospect of Catholics being reconciled to the Union.

In the 1820s, Daniel O'Connell, a brilliant Catholic lawyer from an Old Irish gentry family in Co. Kerry, mobilized growing Catholic economic discontent into a formidable political power to get Catholic emancipation. By means of a "Catholic rent" of a penny per month, the lower classes became part of an organized political body for the first time. The objective of this Catholic Association was Catholic emancipation (i.e. the right of Catholics to sit in Parliament and hold the highest offices of state), but it also set a pattern of lower-class political activity that was to prove highly influential in both Ireland and America. Ultimately, fearing serious unrest, the government of the Duke of Wellington and Home Secretary Robert Peel (both of whom had previously resisted emancipation) passed a Catholic relief bill in 1829 which removed virtually all remaining restrictions on Catholics in Britain and Ireland.

Victory was achieved at a price, a bill to restrict the electorate by raising the property qualification in the counties by five times was passed simultaneously. This decimated the very basis of electoral support which O'Connell had used to achieve emancipation. All but a minority of comfortable Irish Catholics became politically insignificant. O'Connell had created a mass-based Catholic nationalism which changed Irish politics forever, and emigrants took this political tradition with them to America—much to the dismay of elite Anglo-Protestant American politicians. But emancipation had done little for most Catholics, and they soon realized it.

The rapid population growth combined with an agricultural slump after the end of the Napoleonic Wars in 1815 caused rising rents and great poverty among an expanding peasant class. Also, the Protestant elite, deprived of their parliament in 1800, maintained a vice-like grip on local administration, the judiciary, the military, and the professions—all of which were often heavily influenced by the anti-Catholic Orange Order. Finally, there was the continuing injustice of being forced to pay tithes to the Protestant Church of Ireland. These grievances lead to increasing violence in the Irish countryside, with attacks on individuals and property by agrarian secret societies such as the Ribbonmen during the "Tithe War" of the 1830s. They also fueled a massive increase in emigration among poor Catholics from the mid-1820s onwards.

Early settlers

Significant numbers of Irish men and women had started leaving their homeland as early as the seventeenth century. Between 50,000 and 100,000 people went to America in the 1600s, to be followed by up to 400,000 in the 1700s.

The first well-known Irish emigrants of the modern era were the "Wild Geese"—the Gaelic and Old English Catholic elite who fled defeat in Ireland's seventeenth-century wars of conquest and religion. But very few went to the new American colonies of their English enemies—almost all preferred service in the armies of France, Spain, Russia, and Austria. Lower down the social scale, Irish men (and to a lesser extent women) did emigrate to America in the seventeenth century. The majority of eighteenth-century emigrants were Protestants, but as many as three-quarters of Irish emigrants in the 1600s were Catholics. Most of them headed for Virginia and Maryland (which had been founded as a haven for English Catholics

Opposite: May 15, 1878, edition of Puck *entitled "The Difference Between Them." It shows Irish immigrants and Chinese immigrants entering the United States with the Irish intending to stay and the Chinese to stay only temporarily.*

in 1632) rather than the northern colonies. Many also found their way to the West Indies as convicts and indentured servants whose working conditions approximated to slavery.

Surprisingly few Irish emigrated in the seventeenth century despite the massive social upheavals. This was because they were discouraged by the pain of leaving close knit communities, by the hardship of the crossing, and by ancient ties to the land and its culture. Furthermore, most were simply too poor to emigrate as free men, and in any case, Gaelic tradition saw emigration as enforced exile and treated it as a last resort rather than a chance of improvement. Those who knew a little of America were also discouraged by the anti-Catholic attitudes of the American colonists, whose puritanical Protestant vision of Godly communities free from the corruption of the Old World did not include the admission of "papists."

The majority of Irish Protestants who emigrated were Dissenters (so called because they dissented from the legally established form of Irish Protestantism—the Anglican Church of Ireland). They would later become known as Scotch-Irish (a nineteenth-century label). At the time they were simply seen as Irish and usually mixed freely with their Catholic compatriots, who made up about a quarter of Irish emigrants to America in the 1700s.

Most Protestant emigrants were Presbyterians of Scottish stock whose ancestors had come to Ireland in the seventeenth century as part of the plantation of Ulster, but Anglicans, Methodists, Baptists, and Quakers (who naturally went to Pennsylvania) also left Ireland.

Reasons for leaving

From around 1717 up to the American Revolution and beyond, there was a steady stream of Ulster Dissenters crossing the Atlantic. On the eve of the Revolution around 10,000 were arriving in America annually. These immigrants set sail for a variety of religious, political, and economic reasons. Although Irish Dissenters enjoyed a privileged position in contrast to the Catholics they had displaced, they were second-class citizens in comparison to the Anglicans. Like the Catholics (although in less severe form) they suffered discrimination for their religion. Their difficulties increased in 1704 when the Sacramental Test Act (which required all government office holders to take communion in the Church of Ireland) prevented Dissenters from taking public office. They could still vote (as could some Catholics until 1728) but they were effectively excluded from local and national political power. They were also forced to pay a tithe to the Church of Ireland, and their marriages were not recognized by the state. This second-class status encouraged many to leave Ireland for the religious freedom and political liberty which they felt could be found in America. Although the fact that the first large wave of Presbyterian emigration started well after the worst period of intolerance had passed clearly shows it had other causes.

In common with all emigrants, the desire to improve material circumstances also loomed large in their decision to leave home. This motive can be seen in terms of both the pull of American prosperity and the push of Irish poverty. Dissenters and Catholics naturally wished to be free of expensive, rising rents paid to Anglo-Irish landlords, and irksome tithes paid to the Church of Ireland. It is fair to say that the large numbers of Dissenters who emigrated between 1717 and 1720 went primarily because of sharp rent increases following the expiration of generous leases which had initially attracted them to Ireland. Subsequent peaks often accompanied similar rent rises, and a rapidly rising population made competition for land intense. In such circumstances cheap land in an America largely free of established churches was inevitably appealing—especially when it could often be bought for the same as a year's rental in Ireland. Such facts created a popular image in Ulster of a bountiful America which contrasted with the reality of an impoverished Ireland.

Despite economic growth after the 1740s, Ireland was still poor in comparison to Britain and America. Travelers often noted the degraded condition of the peasantry, and Irish intellectuals fretted endlessly about the causes of poverty and its possible remedies. A common complaint throughout the century was that the British parliament imposed severe trade restrictions on Ireland—especially on the Patriots in the 1770s.

One group, however, aroused particular scorn—landlords. Absentee landlords, who drained profits from Irish estates to fritter away in London and Bath, were especially hated, but the class as a whole was regularly accused of failing in its duties. Most ignored contemporary advice on "improving" their estates, which were generally saddled with low levels of re-investment and inefficient agricultural practices which left the land exhausted. Arthur Young, the famous agricultural theorist and travel writer, subjected Irish landlords to withering criticism, calling them "lazy, trifling, inattentive, negligent, slobbering, profligate." Many Catholics and Dissenters agreed, and the latter in particular looked enviously to America as a land of small, independent, landowning farmers who were free of semi-feudal landlord control.

Not all landlords were villains. Indeed, ironically, security of tenure and landlord-tenant relations were generally better in Ulster than elsewhere. And Ulster, while poor in comparison to England, was generally more prosperous than the rest of Ireland as many small farmers supplemented their income by spinning and weaving linen in their homes. But it was precisely this thin financial cushion which allowed them to leave. The near destitution of most peasants usually prevented rather than encouraged emigration (at least until the Famine). Furthermore, many landlords, even in Ulster, did rack up their rents to exorbitant rates when leases were up for renewal—often in a deliberate attempt to clear their estates. These rent increases, perhaps above all else, caused eighteenth-century emigration.

Once the decision had been made to go, the eighteenth century emigrants often faced a difficult crossing, with cramped conditions, stormy seas, and the constant danger of shipwreck. Some were even impressed into the British Navy in mid-Atlantic in times of war. But the horrors of the journey should not be exaggerated—at least not before the Famine era. E. R. R. Green has argued that for the young and healthy, death and disaster were rare, and according to Green, many emigrant letters describe the crossing "pretty well in terms of a holiday." For the unlucky few, adverse weather conditions and badly maintained vessels could drag the journey out for months, but six weeks was the norm for a crossing to Philadelphia. It was there that the real hardship began.

Arrival and settlement—life on the frontier

The Ulster Presbyterians soon began to alter the character of colonial America. Rugged and (usually) God-fearing, they were among the most successful pioneers along the Appalachian frontier. They played a crucial part in opening up the "backcountry" and then provided a market for goods produced in the more developed regions. After they landed in Philadelphia, most journeyed west into central Pennsylvania, following mountain passes and valleys into the western regions of New York, Virginia, Pennsylvania, and the Carolinas.

When the first immigrants found land and settled, they encouraged their families and friends to follow them. This set up a chain, which dragged more and more Irish Presbyterians to America. Ship captains and agents encouraged this profitable trade with rosy accounts of America's opportunities, and the route was soon established as the most obvious escape from an unsatisfactory life in Ireland. By the Revolution, over a quarter of a million of these "Scotch-Irish" had entered America, and at around ten percent of the population, they were the largest non-English, white, immigrant group of the eighteenth century.

Once they had their land, the early Irish settlers often formed tightly knit communities, which dominated many frontier regions. In these groups ingrained Anglophobia and distaste of Episcopalian religion caused divisions with other settlers and led to quarrels with neighbors and local government.

Not all Ulster emigrants became frontiersmen, however. For the numerous single, young men who arrived during this period, the goal was often to work as a clerk or an assistant for a merchant, shopkeeper or trader. The more successful shied away from manual labor and those with an education often settled for school teaching, which was always in demand. Such emigrants naturally settled in the towns and cities, but land remained the main attraction for most well into the early nineteenth century.

Frontier life was harsh and not all emigrants prospered. The extreme climatic and environmental conditions made civilized living difficult, and the neat, wellordered villages of Ulster were hard to replicate in the untamed forests of the American wilderness. Even allowing for anti-Dissenter prejudices, the Church of Ireland clergyman, Charles Woodmason, painted a

bleak picture of the Ulster Irish in South Carolina's backcountry in the 1760s. Half-clothed, half-starved, and filthy, they lived "like hogs" in open cabins, according to Woodmason. They were lazy, drunken, and devoid of all manners, principles, or shame. Whole families lived, slept, and changed in the same room. The girls married at age fourteen and many were not formally married at all. Each had ten to fifteen children and they were regularly exchanged like possessions by the men. There were no courts, churches, or schools—in short, nothing which resembled civilized life to a literate, eighteenth-century gentleman.

For those who settled in more established regions, the reality of emigration was also often harsh. At the bottom of the heap were those who emigrated against their will. Around 50,000 convicts, many of them Irish, arrived from the British Isles between 1718 and the Revolution. Many more poor Irish men and women could only afford to emigrate as indentured servants, usually for a term of four to seven years, or as redemptioners, who arrived in servitude but could buy their freedom back at any time. In the seventeenth century, most indentured servants had been poor Englishmen, but in the eighteenth the Irish increasingly took their place. It has been estimated that well over half of the new European labor arriving in America before the outbreak of the Revolution came in indentured servitude.

On the surface indentured servitude seemed a fair bargain. It was already common practice in Britain and Ireland for the poorer sorts to spend part of their youth as dependant servants in another household. Their passage to America would be paid, and at least they would have food and lodgings, some were even given land by the Virginia Company at the end of their term. But American servitude was much harsher than the British or Irish variety. In the British Isles servants were generally only legally bound for a year and could then move on if things did not work out. Their treatment (which could still be brutal by twentieth-century standards) was softened by custom and by the proximity of kith and kin. Furthermore, the abundance of labor in Ireland made masters less desperate to hang on to servants.

In America, the pressing demand for workers and the investment of the master in the servant's passage meant that they were often treated little differently than African slaves. Indeed masters regularly failed to distinguish between these two types of "property" and indentured servants could be sold or passed on in wills just like slaves. Indentured servants had greater legal rights and, of course, the guarantee of freedom if they survived their term, but they could be beaten or humiliated by their owners with little hope of relief. Some tried to escape, but this was difficult in a country made up of small communities where everyone knew each other. And when caught, the courts, as well as their owners, punished them severely. At the end of their term many were reduced to squatting on frontier land. Relatively few achieved genuine prosperity.

As the century progressed, Irish Dissenters (along with German settlers—the other major European immigrant group) gradually changed the political balance in many colonies. Their rural, frontier settlement pattern, along with their independent-minded religion, led to conflict with Anglo-Protestant settlers and colonial governments in the Eastern seaboard. Their need for new roads and improved defenses against Native American raids clashed with the desire of most coastal colonists for low taxes and minimal militia duties. When frontier demands fell on deaf ears, anger at their perceived neglect could boil over. In the winter of 1763-64, after the widespread Indian raids of Pontiac's War, many Irish frontiersmen rioted and some even marched on Philadelphia. In the North Carolina backcountry, Irishmen were prominent in the "Regulator" movement of the late 1760s. This protest against corruption and taxation was eventually suppressed by colonial troops at the battle of Alamance, but for a time the Regulators held sway over much of the region.

Religion contributed to these quarrels. For while America generally offered greater religious freedom than Ireland, it was not the land of complete religious equality that Irish Dissenters had envisioned, and in some states their official position was similar to that in Ireland. States such as Virginia officially recognized Anglicanism and supported it through taxation borne by all. They also refused to recognize marriages performed by Dissenting ministers. Nevertheless, Irish Presbyterians assimilated easier than most later immigrants. Their use of the English language helped enormously, and despite their religious differences, they were at least fellow Protestants. For the established Anglo-Protestant colonists they formed a buffer between themselves and the Native American frontier, and in the South they were also

Opposite: Miss Sadie O'Connell, one of 545 Irish immigrants arriving in Boston on March 2, 1921. They were the first Irish immigrants to arrive in the United States since 1914.

a welcome counterbalance to the increasing numbers of black slaves. Essentially, their uses out-weighed their nuisance and their numbers were rarely so large as to threaten Anglo-Protestant power.

The Irish radical heritage

Scotch-Irish and Irish settlers arrived with a mentality that distrusted power in all its guises and a desire to be ever vigilant against corruption and tyranny. Their nature valued personal independence and placed public spirit and virtue at the center of politics. Such beliefs naturally led to a desire for checks on the power of the executive and a balance between all the branches of government to prevent any one becoming over-powerful. This was easily translated into opposition to British authority in America and a desire for more democratic government.

Not all of the Irish settlers supported the Patriots. Catholics were especially ambivalent about the Revolutionary cause. Given the extreme anti-Catholic sentiments expressed by the colonists when protesting about the Quebec Act (1774)—which had made Catholicism a legally recognized religion in Canada—many Catholics were naturally reluctant to support them. Among the Irish Presbyterians, local quarrels sometimes distorted the larger patterns of allegiance. Some Irish even deserted Washington's armies and fought for the British under Archibald Campbell in Georgia. In Philadelphia, hundreds of Irishmen joined the Volunteers of Ireland—a loyalist regiment founded by Lt. Col. Lord Rawdon. Rawdon was very proud of his regiment (he knew the Irish made good soldiers) and tried in vain to persuade his superiors to make greater efforts to secure Irish loyalty.

However, the majority of Dissenting Irishmen firmly supported the cause of American Independence—especially the successful commercially-oriented settlers of the Eastern seaboard. Their religious inclination toward Republicanism (combined with their vigorous anti-English sentiments) usually put them at the forefront of revolutionary opposition to British rule. Between a third and a half of George Washington's army may have been made up of Irishmen. In recognition of their valor, Washington once remarked that if he were defeated everywhere else, he would make his last stand among the Irish of his native Virginia. Eight signatories of the Declaration of Independence came from Ulster Presbyterian stock (there was only one Catholic, Charles Carroll) and later their political legacy was continued by Presidents Andrew Jackson, James Knox Polk, James Buchanan, Chester Alan Arthur, and Woodrow Wilson.

The Ulster Irish role in the Revolution did not eradicate tensions between recent settlers and more established Americans. As the frontier moved westward, unequal patterns of representation worsened due to the disproportionate electoral importance of the Eastern constituencies. By the late 1780s, the Irish and German communities were calling for equal representation, and the slaveholding plantation owners and the moneyed elite feared that their interests would be overwhelmed by those of the new settlers. Nevertheless, by their efforts in the Revolution and by their hard work, most Ulster Irish emigrants had secured a firm place in American society by the end of the century.

Irish Presbyterian emigration continued after the war with Britain. About 5,000 left annually in the 1780s and 1790s (most of them for America and Canada) and around the turn of the eighteenth century, political upheaval in Europe cast another wave of emigrants on American shores. When the Democratic and Republican French Revolution led to war with Britain in 1793, those radicals in the British Isles who continued to call for reform were increasingly seen as dangerous subversives. To avoid prosecution many fled to America. Most of the Irish exiles from this period left in the wake of the rebellion that erupted in 1798. Hundreds of defeated rebels, both Protestant and Catholic, either fled to America to avoid capture, or were banished there by the government.

The flow to America started almost as soon as war broke out. In England, Thomas Paine, author of *Common Sense* and *The Rights of Man*, was forced to flee to France (he eventually returned to America in 1802). Joseph Priestly, the famous philosopher and scientist, also left for America in 1794—three years after a "Church and King" mob had burned down his house and laboratory. In Ireland, the government reaction was even harsher, and soon many of

Paine's apostles there were also being forced to leave their homeland. Irish radicals, many of them Ulster Dissenters, had formed a society of United Irishmen in 1791, which called for a reform of the Irish Parliament, political rights for Catholics, and meaningful independence from the British government (although not initially separation from the Crown).

As tensions between radicals and the Protestant Ascendancy government escalated in the mid-1790s, some of the most prominent Irish radicals were forced to flee to avoid imminent prosecutions. James Napper Tandy and Archibald Hamilton Rowan were two prominent escapees. Many of these reluctant *émigrés* would return in time to Europe, but others, however, settled and achieved success. Many who had been involved in the production and dissemination of radical political literature found a niche for their skills in the fevered American political scene of the 1790s and continued their trade.

Indeed the struggle between Federalists and Jeffersonian Republicans was transformed and polarized by this radical influx, almost all of whom attached themselves to the Jeffersons. Their numbers were not large: there were probably less than 1,000 whose emigration came as a direct political result of the rebellion. But as newspaper editors, polemical journalists, and lawyers they exerted an influence on American public life disproportionate to the size of the radical exodus. The Alien and Sedition Acts of 1798, which restricted political rights for recent immigrants, were largely a reaction to the political activity of recent Irish and British arrivals. But the measure could not silence the Irish radicals, and their skills as propagandists and activists were crucial in getting Jefferson elected president in 1800. In doing so they changed the face of early American politics.

Jefferson's victory did not create the democratic nirvana hoped for by the radicals, but it did create a more favorable environment for Irish political exiles—whose anti-English republicanism dovetailed neatly with American patriotism. Many of the Irish radicals who became established in cities like New York and Philadelphia went on to form the bedrock of the developing Irish-American communities in those cities. Through emigrant-aid organizations such as The Friendly Sons of St. Patrick, Irishmen created a network of support that would ease the passage of increasing numbers of Irish immigrants. In doing so they formed a bridge between the older (predominantly Protestant) and the newer (predominantly Catholic) Irish-American communities. This transition took decades to develop, however, and the first 15 years of the 1800s saw little change in the basic composition of Irish emigration. Most were still Protestant, and many were comfortable or middleclass farmers, artisans, merchants, or professionals, who were leaving for primarily economic reasons—often to preserve their social rank and independence. The main difference with late eighteenth-century emigration patterns was the smaller numbers leaving Ireland between 1800 and 1815.

The Napoleonic Wars disrupted the flow of emigrants, not least because of the agricultural boom which it occasioned in Ireland. The wars, which lasted from 1793 to 1815 (with a few brief intervals) made it hard for Britain to supply its ever-growing need for food and provisions. Europe was largely closed to British shipping, and transatlantic trade was risky. Ireland increasingly filled the gap, and as a result prices and production soared. Grain in particular was needed to feed Britain's growing, and increasingly urban, population. This brought new areas of Irish land into production and provided work. Indeed times were relatively good for Ireland as a whole between the Act of Union and the end of the wars in 1815. But many of the lower sorts were finding it difficult to keep up with rising rents and this prosperity was fundamentally fragile, resting on Bonaparte's aggression and the artificial constriction of British sources of supply.

The rising Irish population was putting increasing pressure on the land, and the end of the war caused a slump in prices as Britain was able to buy its provisions more cheaply elsewhere. Once again emigration became the best economic option for many, especially as price changes were encouraging landlords to clear their land for cattle farming. Just when the agricultural labor market needed to soak up the increasing population, labor-intensive grain production became less profitable than beef and dairy production—which needed very little labor. Slowly but surely, these trends altered the composition of Irish emigration and increased its volume.

Thus, the character of the Irish-American community gradually began to change around 1820. Up to that point Dissenting emigrants still outnumbered Catholics, and the predominantly urban nature of Irish-America had not yet taken shape. Communities of Catholic

Opposite: An immigrant family in a tenement
slum in New York, c.1890.

and Protestant Irish were scattered. They mixed fairly freely, and they were as likely to be in the country or in the South as in the Northern cities. Then, in the 1820s and 1830s, increasingly large numbers of poor Catholic emigrants arrived in New York, Boston, Philadelphia, Baltimore, and New Orleans, and by the late 1840s the huge influx of famine emigrants was changing the face of East coast urban America.

The coming of the Catholic Irish

Large-scale Catholic Irish emigration to America began well before the Famine. Population growth, rising rents and postwar agricultural recession were breaking down the traditional Gaelic reluctance to emigrate long before the 1840s. This led to significant growth in Catholic immigration in the 1820s, and up to 40,000 a year were arriving in America during the 1830s. Between 1815 and 1845 at least 1.5 million people left Ireland, and at least half of them headed for America. This trend would have continued even if the catastrophe of the Famine had not occurred. Of the two million or so who emigrated between 1845 and 1855, between a third and a half probably would have gone anyway—a huge number which would still have had a significant impact on America. But the Famine gave an additional, enormous impetus to Irish emigration, and the epic scale and traumatic quality of the Irish exodus to America would not have existed without the Famine.

The high demand for Irish agricultural produce up to 1815 masked deep structural problems in the Irish economy. Besides the rapid and unsustainable growth in population, fluctuations in the linen and woolen industries affected many small farmers and cottiers. In the late eighteenth century, these groups had increasingly relied on money from spinning and weaving in their homes to pay their rising rents and retain a grip on the land. But this type of cottage industry was first disrupted by the French Wars and then plunged into terminal decline in the 1820s and 1830s by the increased mechanization of the Industrial Revolution. In the north, the linen industry survived a difficult re-structuring, and new linen factories in Belfast gave some outlet for excess labor, but in the south the industry largely perished, along with the domestic woolen industry, and many Irish families faced an increasingly difficult struggle to pay their rents. In fact most non-agricultural sources of income were diminishing in most of the country. Belfast suffered the collapse of a briefly successful cotton industry before the mechanization of linen spinning, and many of Ireland's fragile industries (with the exception of linen, glass, and brewing) went into decline.

This happened for a number of reasons. Competition from more efficient British manufacturers was certainly one of them. After 1824, in accordance with the intention of the Act of Union of 1800, Ireland and Britain became one large free trade area and all protective tariffs were removed. Irish industry was henceforth subjected to the full force of open competition with the world's most advanced and efficient industries. But there were more fundamental reasons why Ireland was disadvantaged. For a variety of psychological and practical reasons both Irish and British investors were reluctant to put capital into Ireland. Its lack of coal and iron also hindered the formation of new industries. And although its roads were relatively good, it was slow to develop the extensive canal and railroad system which allowed cheap distribution of bulk goods. Thus, while small pockets of industry survived and even flourished, most of Ireland actually suffered deindustrialization during this period, and its swelling population was increasingly thrown back on the land.

Subdivision of this land to accommodate more and more people only exacerbated the problem of Irish poverty. The practice was barely sustainable even with the high agricultural prices before 1815, but as they plummeted, thereafter survival became ever harder as higher proportions of diminishing crops were sold off to pay rents. Small tenant farmers and cottiers increasingly relied on the potato, and for many paying the rent became simply impossible. Secret societies like the Ribbonmen used violence and intimidation to hold down rents and prevent some evictions, but in the long term, without radical land reform, emigration to the industrial centers of Britain and America became almost inevitable.

As James Brownrigg, the land agent to Lord Downshire's estates in King's County observed in 1815 that the peasantry were unable to pay the high rents but went on to identify

the subdivision of land as the root of the problem and accused the landlords (or at least their agents) of colluding in the process by renting tiny plots to whoever promised the best price irrespective of a realistic assessment of their ability to pay. This had "produced . . . an agricultural population more than four times as numerous as the cultivation of the country required." What was to be done with such a peasantry asked Brownrigg? Turning them out as beggars on the world was "a dreadful alternative," but he saw no other remedy, and with ominous foresight, Brownrigg argued that a reduction in the number of cottiers and small farmers was necessary for improvement and civilization in Ireland.

The outlook for the Irish poor, therefore, was bleak, and before the 1838 Irish Poor Law came into effect there was no regular state or local system of relief except for that provided by charities and by sporadic government aid (often in the form of public works after 1831). Even after 1842, the poor houses that began to appear were so harsh in their restrictions and regime that only the absolutely destitute rather than the seasonally poor would enter. To make matters worse, legislation made eviction of tenants easier and cheaper for landlords, and further legislation increased their ability to distrain (i.e. confiscate property, such as cattle or crops) in lieu of unpaid rent.

Such a history of decline and fall was common in western counties such as Mayo, which was among the poorest regions of Ireland. But permanent emigration was still less attractive in the largely Gaelic speaking and underdeveloped west than it was in the increasingly commercialized and English-speaking east. The free market economic system of money transactions and contracts, which was spreading rapidly through rural south Ulster, the midlands, and the southeast, imbued the knowledge, skills, and information which encouraged and allowed emigration. Improved transport and increasing access to cash were the prerequisites of pre-Famine emigration, for both practical reasons and because they broke down traditional Gaelic psychological reluctance to emigrate. When people began to see themselves as individuals in a wider market economy rather than part of a local world defined by land and family, they became more likely to leave that world in search of work, money, and independence. Much of the west had still not developed in this manner by the time of the Famine, and so migration from this area remained much less common than from the rest of Ireland until then.

Fear of the transatlantic voyage itself, which was especially acute in these communities, contributed to the western reluctance to emigrate. More importantly, almost all preferred to stay on the land they had been born on rather than leave for a strange country. Some even refused free passages despite their wretched poverty, and landlords anxious to clear their estates often noted the lack of ambition among their tenants—who seemed satisfied with a small cabin and a tiny potato plot. The agrarian violence of secret societies to prevent evictions, rent rises, and other "improvements" in Irish agriculture, can be seen as a result of this attachment to traditional ways of living, as can the forced compromise of seasonal migration to Britain rather than permanent migration. Even expansion onto previously unused, poor, acidic soils was preferable to a large, fertile farm in the alien environment of America.

From the late-1820s emigration from other areas soared, however, with around 50,000 leaving Ireland annually for non-UK destinations in some years during the 1830s. Before this point most Irish emigrants still headed for the statistically-invisible destination of Britain, but this was changing rapidly. After a temporary downturn caused by an American recession starting in 1837, emigration reached new heights in the early 1840s, with over 90,000 non-UK emigrants in 1842 alone. The vast majority went to America, often via Canada (which was cheaper) although increasingly on direct passages using the growing Liverpool–New York route.

Nationalist exhortations to stay in Ireland and enjoy the imminent benefits that would come from the repeal of the Act of Union (which Daniel O'Connell promised for 1843) may have had some short-term effects. There was a sharp, short-term decline of around sixty percent between the high of 1842 and the emigration figures for 1843. But in the long term it is doubtful that increasing Irish nationalism had much effect in persuading people to stay. If anything, by heightening dissatisfaction with British rule it may have hastened the departures of the independent-minded who had little taste for servility after the repeal movement failed. Nationalist ideology also gave a ready-made explanation of emigration as forced exile.

The effect on Ireland was to relieve some of the pressure on the land, but even at these levels, emigration could only retard rather than stop the growth in population. Furthermore, many worried, with good cause, that the "wrong" people were emigrating. There were many more small tenant farmers and laborers leaving in the 1840s than in the 1820s, but most took a little money and some useful skills with them. It was still not the very poorest who were leaving for America, despite the noticeable shift of the "typical" emigrant down the social scale.

The view that it was primarily the able and energetic that were leaving while the poorest and weakest stayed behind on their tiny, exhausted plots of land was common and justified. Urban artisans, the younger sons of small farmers, and the more energetic and adventurous of the laboring class comprised the bulk of the pre-Famine emigrants. And these came from the more developed regions of the north, east, and south—areas which often had the lowest population density. The families barely surviving on half-acre potato plots in the densely-populated west were still clinging onto Ireland. This would change amid horrific circumstances after 1845, but for many only death would loosen their grip.

The Famine Emigrants

Irish famines were nothing new. There had been severe ones in the seventeenth and early-eighteenth centuries (notably in 1740–41 when tens of thousands died), and the early-nineteenth century had already seen many partial potato failures and localized famines. But the repeated and sometimes total failures of the potato crop between 1845 and 1850 gave rise to suffering and shortage that were of a qualitatively different order. The calamity completely restructured Irish social life, not least because it set in train a decline in population through death and continuing emigration which was not halted until the 1960s. Around one million died as a direct result of disease and starvation during these five years. Many more left the country. According to David Fitzpatrick, around one million people left Ireland between 1846 and 1850, and another million followed them in the next five years. Another expert, Kerby Miller, puts the figure at over 2.1 million for the same period. Of these nearly 1.5 million went directly to the U.S. and about 340,000 to British North America—many of whom then crossed the border to the south. Thus around 1.75 million Irish people may have eventually settled in the U.S. during this decade.

Such an exodus had huge implications for both Ireland and America. Among them was the growth of Irish nationalism in both countries. For Ireland, it meant the removal of over a third of its population within a decade. The Famine decimated the laborer and cottier class in particular, and marked a major social shift away from the subdivision of land towards larger farms passed down to a single son (which in turn encouraged the emigration of daughters and younger sons). For America it caused the first influx of immigrants on a scale large enough to threaten the Anglo-Protestant character of the country. It also signified a massive injection of labor into a rapidly expanding economy.

The causes of the Famine and the reasons why it led to so much death and emigration are complex. Entirely natural factors such as the potato fungus *Phytophthora infestans* combined with social factors such as extremely high population density, and economic factors such as free market capitalism and an exploitative land-holding system. These in turn were exacerbated by the willful ignorance and callous indifference of key figures in the British ruling elite. Given that in 1845 at least one third of the 8.2 million Irish people were already barely surviving almost exclusively on potatoes, any widespread failure of this crop would inevitably have caused immense suffering. But the prevailing worship of free competition and the common British view of the Irish as lazy, superstitious, morally inferior, and irresponsibly fertile, made effective relief of this unprecedented problem almost impossible.

There is simply too much evidence of government assistance and hand-wringing to uphold claims of British genocide, but after Sir Robert Peel's removal as prime minister in 1846, that assistance was rarely adequate, often inhuman, and usually too late. The hard-heartedness of the new Whig government's responses to heartrending appeals for help are shocking in retrospect, especially after 1847 when hand-wringing increasingly gave way to handwashing. But they occurred in an era when the government's duty to its people was not normally thought to extend to feeding them over the long term. Nor did the government perceive their duty to extended to controlling the sale and export of food by farmers, landlords, and merchants.

As a result, famine relief was increasingly thrown onto Irish localities, which were often completely unable to cope, and famine victims were confronted with the sight of Irish grain,

Mrs. Bridget Casey of County Cork, Ireland, with nine of her children after arriving in New York on the S.S. Berlin on December 2, 1929. She was to join her husband and two older children already residing at Bridgeport, Connecticut. Her second eldest child, Bridget, age nineteen, was left home in Ireland having failed to pass the Immigration Department test.

meat, and other foods, being sold in markets or exported to Britain. While this went on, they begged, starved, or exhausted themselves on unnecessary construction schemes to earn enough money to buy maize imported by the government from America! Such tortuous and perverse relief schemes can only be explained in terms of slavish adherence to free market orthodoxy. By demanding irrelevant, backbreaking work for wages set at the absolute minimum required for survival, and by selling the victims a food not normally sold in Ireland, the government sought to minimize disruption of the "normal" mechanisms of labor supply and food distribution. They were eventually converted to the straightforward supply of free food, but superstitious and irrational attachment to dogma had been shown not to be the exclusive preserve of the Catholic peasantry. Restricting food exports from Ireland would not have come close to making up the potato deficit, but it could have softened its impact at key points—notably in the winter of 1846–47.

When landlords, the churches, and private charity combined effectively to supplement government soup kitchens and public works schemes, they sometimes staved off starvation in their areas. But many landlords were indifferent to the plight of their tenants, and in the poorest areas of the west they were usually overwhelmed even if they were not. After the total failure of the 1846 potato crop people started dying in large numbers, and many of those who could decided to get out. From 1847 to 1853 roughly 200,000 people left each year. These were the lucky ones. Their compatriots were dying in their cabins, by the roadside, or in the poor houses and fever hospitals.

The starving ate grass, herbs, and dead animals to survive (there are even accounts of cannibalism). Bodies went unburied and diseases such as cholera swept the country as the destitute gravitated to the towns and cities in search of food, work, or a passage out of Ireland. From Dublin, Cork, Belfast, and a host of other ports, the tired, poor, huddled masses began leaving Ireland in droves. The flow would not ease up until 1855, and by then around two million had left.

An immediate question arises from this picture. How was such an exodus possible for a starving and destitute population with little state assistance? In fact, eighty percent of passages were paid for by American money sent back to friends and family in Ireland. This was often in response to heartbreaking letters which left the recipients in little doubt as to their kin's impending doom. Fares to New York or Philadelphia from Irish ports ranged from around £3.10s to £4.00 ($17–$20). From Liverpool they were slightly cheaper. This was equal to between two and four weeks wages for a laborer in the U.S., who could expect to earn 75 cents to $1.50 a day depending on the work. Hence, the fare was a significant amount, but it was well within the means of the thrifty and hard working to save enough to bring over their families and friends—especially if the immigrant was doing well and had established himself before the Famine. Between 1850 and 1855 about $30 million was sent back to Ireland to supplement incomes and to send family members over.

Emigration affected all social groups and all regions. Once-comfortable farmers sought to escape the chaos in Ireland while they still had some assets. The destitute sought assisted passages or scrapped together enough money for the cheap crossing to Liverpool in the hope of finding the rest of the fare there. Necessity even prompted large numbers of single women to leave unaccompanied by family groups—a practice that was rare among other immigrant groups but which became accepted in Ireland. From this point on roughly equal numbers of men and women emigrated. In the 1820s and 1830s emigration had been popular in certain areas (such as Ulster, the midlands, and the east coast) and relatively rare in the rural west—it now spread, of necessity, across the whole of Ireland. For the first time large numbers began leaving the remote areas of Connacht and Munster—provinces which thereafter produced the heaviest emigration.

Leaving Ireland was traumatic. Very few would ever return and most realized it. For those staying behind, such a final parting was so akin to the death of the emigrant that they would normally give an "American Wake" (a practice which many Famine emigrants were unable to indulge in). The local village or town would see the emigrant off with a night of dancing, drinking, and singing, which would last until dawn. In the morning the emigrant might be blessed by the local priest and accompanied by friends and family on the first part of the journey. As a sign of their reluctance to leave, they often took the longest route out of the village so as not to hasten their departure. Families were torn apart—indeed, among all the immigrant groups, the Irish had the lowest rates of return. Less than ten percent of those leaving would ever see Ireland again.

The Journey

A common emigrant journey began with a deck passage to Liverpool from Dublin, Belfast, or another east coast port. This was cheap and lasted between fifteen and thirty hours, but passengers were open to the wind, rain, and sea. They sometimes had to stand all the way and were often placed right next to animals. Vomiting through sea-sickness was common, and many arrived wet, ill, and tired. Their trials were just beginning. The bustling port of Liverpool was home to all manner of sharpers, tricksters, and fraudsters, offering an array of "services" to the new arrivals. Dishonest agents sold tickets for passages on dilapidated ships that left weeks or even months after the advertised time, forcing precious savings to be spent on disgusting boarding houses and much-needed provisions to be consumed before embarkation. Many were robbed or hustled out of their money. Some drank it away, and a fair proportion made it no further than the dockside slums. Their descendants formed such a large and concentrated Irish population in Liverpool, that the city's Scotland parliamentary division near the waterfront returned an Irish Home Rule MP (Thomas Power O'Connor) between 1885 and 1929. To this day, Liverpool is the most Irish and Catholic of all English cities.

Once on board, emigrants faced a four to five week journey (if they were lucky). For steerage passengers there were no cabins, only one long communal deck. Stowed away in disgusting, cramped, and filthy conditions, their tiny bunks opened onto a gangway that could resemble a sewer. Diseases such as typhus, dysentery, and cholera were common and easily transferable between emigrants who were often ridden with lice and ignorant of basic hygiene. In stormy seas the hatches were battened down and passengers had to endure the fetid, putrid smells of vomit and excrement in near darkness. Inadequate cooking facilities had to be fought for and many passengers did not bring enough food. Ships were required by law to provide basic provisions and drinking water, but they were often contaminated or in short supply. As the complaints of some passengers show, many relieved the tedium and misery through drink and song. Fights frequently erupted in the confined and competitive environment—often between Protestants and Catholics. This was not a journey for those of delicate sensibilities.

Surprisingly, death rates for the period as a whole were relatively low at around one or two percent, and they were often much lower in the pre-Famine era on the better ships—which lost remarkably few passengers. But death rates could easily rise to ten or even twenty percent during major outbreaks of disease and during the Famine. The very young and the very old were naturally the most vulnerable, but on the "coffin ships" of the Famine era most passengers were at risk. Already weakened by hunger, the chance of contracting a disease increased dramatically—and it was disease rather than straightforward starvation which was the real danger.

Not all vessels of the famine era could be fairly called "coffin ships." Towards the end of the 1840s, custom-built packet ships with three decks for over 400 passengers were being launched in America especially for the emigrant trade, but these were the exception. The enormous demand for shipping of any kind during the Famine led to many unsuitable vessels being used. As Edward Laxton has pointed out in *The Famine Ships*, 5,000 vessels of all shapes and sizes made crossings with Irish emigrants between 1845 and 1851. Ships designed for the timber and grain trade had rough, narrow bunks hastily fitted on arrival to enable them to take a human cargo on the return leg. These bunks were often only six feet by twenty inches. Tiny coasters like the *Hannah* (only fifty-nine feet long!) made repeated voyages from Ireland to New York crammed with over fifty passengers. Some ships, like the *Elizabeth* and *Sarah*, had been in service since the 1760s, and many would certainly have transported slaves in similar conditions half a century earlier.

To make matters worse, winter crossings became imperative, whereas in the past emigrants had been able to wait until spring or summer. The newer, larger ships could usually cope with these conditions, but numerous smaller, older ships, unsuited to an Atlantic winter crossing, were pressed into service to make quick money by evacuating the starving masses. From Dublin, Cork, Belfast, Waterford, Wexford, Sligo, Galway, and Limerick, as well as other smaller ports, ships designed for local cargo traffic began sailing directly to America.

The most horrific passages tended to be on British ships. These usually offered the most wretched conditions, partly because they were allowed to carry three passengers for every two that American ships could. And although shorter, many of the worst passages were those to Canada—especially in 1847. As this passage was cheap (sometimes as low as £2 or $10) it attracted the poorest, most desperate passengers. The Quebec authorities required these coffin ships to dock at Grosse Isle in the middle of the St. Lawrence River to protect its citizens from the full impact of their diseased and starving cargo. Cholera and other diseases spread through Quebec in any case, but conditions on Grosse Isle itself were nightmarish, and if we include those who died shortly after arrival, death rates occasionally reached thirty percent. For those who retained some strength, their joy was great when they finally caught sight of land after weeks (or even months) at sea. The dense green forests of the American coast would have seemed wild and strange but were welcome nonetheless. Ships headed for New York and Philadelphia often sailed along the coast for days before reaching port, and this section of the journey must have been intensely frustrating, as food, water, and stamina were running out. But the sight of land gave renewed hope that a new, and better, life in America was about to begin.

Gaining a foothold in America

The ordeal of the passage did not necessarily end on arrival. For an unfortunate minority a quarantine hospital was their first port of call. At New York, for example, a quarantine ship would approach each immigrant vessel as it approached Staten Island to remove the diseased and dying. Many made it no further, succumbing to typhus, cholera, or yellow fever. Those who survived faced the understandable hostility of Staten Island residents who feared the spread of disease. In 1858, after repeated attacks, the hospital was stormed by locals, who kicked out the patients and burned it down.

Healthier compatriots faced different kinds of hostility across the harbor, where a variety of conmen and fraudsters tried their best to part naive rural Irishmen from their money. The lucky ones with family and friends to meet them at the dockside were led away to relative safety. Those without local connections ran the gauntlet of moneychangers, thieves, and swindlers, whose promises of work or lodgings often proved illusory. "Runners" from nearby boarding houses earned commissions for each new immigrant they procured. Needless to say, their descriptions of the accommodation on offer rarely matched reality. Exhausted arrivals were persuaded and pressured into parting with meager cash reserves for disgusting rooms in nearby "barracks" and tenements—often by fellow Irishmen. Their baggage would be taken from them and locked away to compel payment, but often it was simply stolen. Some were sold fraudulent tickets for onward journeys, and a few single women were seduced or harassed into prostitution.

Organizations such as New York's Irish Emigrant Society (1814) and the Hibernian Society of Philadelphia for the Relief of Emigrants (1790) tried to protect the Irish from such trials by directing them to the better boarding houses and by giving advice on transport and employment. But they were overwhelmed by the scale of the problem. Their lobbying eventually led to protective legislation and the New York Board of Commission of Emigration in 1847. The Catholic Church was heavily involved in the activities of these societies, and religious orders often provided shelter for thousands of vulnerable arrivals—especially single women. Benevolent societies and Irish American newspapers like the *Shamrock* helped find jobs for emigrants and assisted with the transfer of money back home or to a place of ultimate settlement. But all these organizations struggled to cope due to the sheer number of immigrants.

The situation improved slightly in 1855 when Castle Garden on the tip of Manhattan Island was converted into an immigrant processing center. This placed an official buffer between the immigrants and the runners, much to the disgust and anger of the latter. From this date until the opening of its replacement on Ellis Island in 1892, Castle Garden was the first taste of America for hundreds of thousands of Irish settlers. In this huge, teaming, circular building they began their transition from Irish men and women to Irish-Americans.

After disembarking, tens of thousands simply stayed in New York's Lower East Side. The most notorious immigrant ghetto in this area was Five Points, where breweries, stables, liquor shops, slums, and street vendors, jostled for space amid crowded streets and alleyways. Wealthy New Yorkers would visit this "colorful" area as contemporary westerners visit third world countries. When they returned to their spacious uptown homes, they left behind whole families who lived in a single room. This would serve as kitchen, bedroom, living room, and bathroom. Many kept animals, as they had done in the Irish countryside, but in an urban setting, this only added to the filth and squalor.

If Irish immigrants escaped the dockside slums, they often got no further than hastily erected shanty towns on the edge of the cities. There may have been a little more space here for keeping pigs, but housing was just as dangerous, both structurally and hygienically. These improvised villages were also subject to immediate destruction when the city expanded outwards. Striking photographs of luxury apartment buildings towering over ramshackle wooden hovels on the Upper East and West sides of Manhattan before developers cleared them away provide stark evidence of the contrast between rich and poor in nineteenth century U.S. cities.

Shortly after arrival, many immigrants naturally wrote home to their families. Common themes in their letters were the initial loneliness of emigration and the hard work required to succeed in America. Emigrant pioneers never tired of warning siblings and friends of the harsh facts of American life, and anyone expecting easy riches, they warned, would be sorely disappointed. Weak or lazy sons were best kept in Ireland. Good wages could be had in America but for the unskilled the work was literally backbreaking. As an old joke put it, not only were the streets not paved with gold, they were not paved at all, and "Paddy" was expected to pave them! But for those with desirable skills or the aptitude to learn new ones, advancement and security could be had quite quickly. However, for the Catholic immigrants of the 1830s, 1840s, and 1850s the first experience of America was harsh. In this period many more new arrivals came from the unskilled laboring classes. For these people success was not easy and assimilation increasingly difficult. By 1850, the Irish made up forty-three percent of the foreign-born U.S. population. However, this huge influx had already begun to harden negative attitudes to them among Anglo-Protestant Americans.

The geography of Irish settlement

The new Irish immigrants increasingly became an urban people even though they had usually come from rural areas or small towns intimately connected with agriculture. The wide, open spaces of the Midwest did not, on the whole, appeal to a convivial people whose rural landscape had been on a much more intimate scale. Furthermore the small farmers and cottiers who had survived largely on potato plots of a few acres were not equipped with the skills needed for farming grain, corn, or cattle, on large commercial farms of fifty to a hundred acres. Hence, they tended to huddle near the ports where they had arrived. In doing so they were following established and developing trade routes. New York overtook Philadelphia as the main point of arrival in the 1820s, not so much because of conscious decisions to plough new furrows of immigration, but because more of the shipping from Ireland and Liverpool was heading there. Such shifts then became self-perpetuating as chain emigration funded by money and tickets in "American letters" took more and more Irish immigrants to established Irish settlements.

In general, these settlements grew up on the northeastern seaboard from Maryland to southern Maine before moving slowly westward into the industrial, transport, and mining centers of the Midwest. New York, Massachusetts, Pennsylvania, New Jersey, and then Ohio, Michigan, Illinois, and Indiana, became the heartlands of Irish-America (they were quickly followed by California after the Gold Rush of 1849). Within these areas the big cities, especially New York, Philadelphia, Brooklyn, Boston, Chicago, St. Louis, Cincinnati, Baltimore, and San Francisco acquired large Irish populations (as did the port city of New Orleans). But all the cities in this broad northeastern area (and many far beyond) had their Irish communities. For Irish laborers often traveled in search of work or stayed on in a far-off town after laboring on a newly-constructed railroad or canal.

Eminent Irish-Americans had hoped to channel this massive influx along more rural lines, but their schemes to settle the newcomer in new lands to the west largely failed. In 1818 leading Irish Americans sent a memorial to Congress urging it to set aside lands in Illinois for settlement by Irishmen. Rural settlement, it was argued, would act as a barrier to Native American Indian incursions and prevent the uncontrollable growth of disease-ridden, corrupting slums in the cities. The proposal was defeated by eighty-three to seventy-one, and in any case, few Irish families showed much inclination to leave their compatriots for the large, lonely farms of the west.

Aside from the better known urban centers, thousands of Catholic Irish emigrants settled in Louisiana and Texas—initially because they were governed by Catholic states. French control of Louisiana made it attractive to Catholics, and thousands continued to pour into New Orleans after Louisiana was sold to the U.S. in 1803. From there many made their way up the Mississippi and some went to Texas—which was under Spanish control until 1821 and Mexican thereafter. In 1828 two Irish settlements were founded there. James McGloin and John McMullen were granted a large tract of land to bring 200 recent Irish immigrant families from New York to establish the colony of San Patrico. Their attempt to plant urbanized Irish on the open farmlands of Texas was only a partial success, but James Power and James Hewitson's settlement at Refugio was more enduring.

Many Irish Texans went on to play a central role in the separation of Texas from Mexico in the 1830s, such as Sam Houston and Thomas Jefferson Rusk—a member of the convention which declared Texas independent in 1835. Irish-Americans also filled the ranks of the U.S. Army in its struggle with Mexico over Texas in 1846-47. However, religious bonds, American anti-Catholicism, and the promise of land persuaded 300 to 400 Irish immigrants

to fight for the Mexicans in St. Patrick's Battalion. As many of them had deserted from the U.S. Army, they were hanged on capture. A plaque in their memory still exists in Mexico City.

Thus, Irish experiences in America were diverse—especially before the Famine. Irish-America could be rural or Protestant as well as urban and Catholic. It was also more geographically diffused than is sometimes recognized, for the poor Irishmen who could only find jobs as laborers were often drawn away from major urban centers in search of construction projects. Thus, even the smaller American cities had their Irish communities. But in comparison to other ethnic groups and to the population as a whole, Irish-America was increasingly urban, and its concentration in the largest U.S. cities was beginning to alter their nature completely.

The O'Laughon and McCormick homes, Milton, North Dakota, are a little piece of Ireland on the prairies. Both houses have picket fences but one is made of sod and the other is a frame house with a brick chimney, c.1890.

Structure of early Irish-American communities

Early Irish-American communities centered on family and church. They transported the communal spirit of their native clachans and townlands to an alien American setting, and in doing so they created a new form of community which modified traditional bonds of co-operation for an urban setting. Irish national sentiment also played an important part in this community spirit, but early bonds often were initially based on a shared Irish locality, which could form a more important focus for identity than a generalized Irishness. Indeed, distaste for fellow emigrants from another part of Ireland was often pronounced, with those from Connacht particularly looked down upon by other Irish-Americans. But the challenges facing the Irish in their new American homes, including anti-Irish prejudice, gradually gave them a common purpose and identity.

Within the city, neighborhoods were constructed around groups of blocks, which soon became parishes once a church had been built. Irish priests were sent over to minister to these communities and to enforce social morality. With so many young, single emigrants away from traditional economic and parental restraints marriage came at a younger age than in Ireland, and the number of children they produced was high. But the appalling conditions of squalor and dirt led to very high infant mortality rates. Diseases such as typhus, cholera, typhoid, dysentery, and tuberculosis were rampant. Some cities were healthier than others (Boston, with its disgusting cellars was notably worse than Philadelphia in this respect) but all had their wretched corners, and life expectancy was extremely low in these urban slums. Cramped and dirty conditions inevitably led to prolonged sickness and widowhood as well as death, which in the harsh world of prewelfare state capitalism created the need for mutual aid societies. These societies fostered community spirit and co-operation, as did local volunteer fire companies, which were vital in the early wooden tenement slums (or "barracks") thrown up in New York. Membership of volunteer fire companies, as well as militia companies and Irish nationalist organizations enhanced Irish-American identity and maintained links with the old country. They also allowed Irish men and women an escape from the drudgery of their daily lives. The men dressed up in uniforms to attended dinners and picnics, and their officers got the chance to practice their oratory. Other voluntary organizations, such as the Ancient Order of Hibernians, promoted lavish celebrations on St. Patrick's Day, as well as their own dances and picnics. Out of all this activity an Irish American skill for organization and mobilization developed which would serve them well in their struggle up the social ladder.

Irish labor

Irish Americans played a vital role in building modern America. As well as filling the factories of the northeast, the railroads, roads, bridges, canals, sewers, dams, buildings, and all the other elements of a modern industrialized nation were built largely by Irish labor. The spectacular economic growth of nineteenth century America, which had initially encouraged Irish immigration, was then pushed along even faster by Irish labor. Between 1815 and the late 1830s, road building and canals were the focus of much Irish energy. Chief among the early projects was the Erie Canal, which was employing 3,000 Irishmen by 1818. When completed this linked the Hudson river with Lake Erie, opening up the Midwest to further development and confirming New York as the leading port and city in America. Albany, Rochester, and Buffalo, all developed as a result of the Erie Canal and they acquired large Irish populations as a result. By the 1830s, Irish labor was carving across Pennsylvania for the Chesapeake and Ohio canal and contractors were advertising in Ireland for labor. The supply was seemingly inexhaustible.

The next major development was the explosion in railroad mileage from 3,000 in 1840 to 30,000 miles in 1860, which coincided precisely with the heaviest years of Famine immigration. Irish labor contributed heavily to the first transcontinental rail link and dominated most railroad construction east of the Rockies. These men led a dangerous, nomadic life, which took them into untamed wilderness before depositing them in some far away frontier town. Such work, while brutally hard, could provide a welcome escape route from the squalor and overcrowding of the seaboard cities, but wages were sometimes as low as 50 cents a day (although they could be as high as $1.50). Whiskey fueled construction, with daily rations of over a pint commonplace. On paydays workers bought more whiskey from company stores and fights were frequent. Indeed much of their wages were spent in these stores, or on the often extortionate board and lodgings provided by the company. Away from towns and cities, companies enjoyed a natural retail monopoly and they exploited it to the full.

Most railroad and canal workers were single men, but many were married, and by leaving families back East, these labor patterns caused havoc with early immigrant family life. Maximum havoc occurred when the husband failed to return. Removed from the constraints of church and community, some simply abandoned their families and re-settled elsewhere or moved on to the next construction site. Many failed to return because they were killed on the job. Given the appalling conditions and lack of safety regulations of the day, tens of thousands of Irish-Americans were maimed or lost their lives on these construction projects. But Irish lives were cheap in the eyes contractors—far cheaper than slaves, who were deemed too valuable to risk on the most dangerous sites in the South when Irishmen could be used instead. Rock falls, mistimed explosions, and collapsed canal banks were common causes of death—not to mention disease. Dehydrated through heat and whiskey, working from sunrise to sunset (often standing in water all day), and living in dirty shantytowns, laborers were prone to malaria, cholera, yellow fever, and consumption. They were buried where they fell in unmarked graves, often three or four at a time, and there were always more to take their place.

Those Irish men and women who remained in the cities also survived on hard, dirty work, which was increasingly spurned by Anglo-Americans. Some of this was also construction work. The Brooklyn Bridge, one of the greatest feats of nineteenth-century engineering, was built mainly by Irish labor, and by enabling America's most rapidly-growing urban area to expand on to Long Island, it fueled even faster economic and population growth in the city. From 100,000 people in 1810, New York had expanded to nearly a million by 1871. Brooklyn became the third largest Irish settlement in America at this point, with 74,000 out of its population of 376,000 born in Ireland. In this year another great, if tragic, opportunity arose for Irish labor. A fire in Chicago destroyed much of the city center and provided the opportunity for a new type of architecture. The skyscrapers that began to rise in Chicago, and then New York, from the 1880s would not have been possible without Irish muscle power.

On a more mundane level, laboring Irish men and women filled the menial jobs necessary for the smooth running of a nineteenth-century city. In the streets, docksides, warehouses, shops, and stables, Irish men worked as builders, stevedores (cargo handlers), stablemen, barmen, hod carriers, porters, longshoremen, street cleaners, pipe-layers, quarrymen, bricklayers, plasterers, and masons. In 1855, nearly nine out of every ten laborers in New York were Irishmen. They also worked in the new factories, as did thousands of Irish women, who made clothes in cramped, sweltering sweatshops on the newly invented sewing machines from the 1840s.

For hundreds of thousands of Irish women an escape, of sorts, could be found in domestic service, which became the typical occupation of the young, single, female. Because most immigrant groups objected to their young women living under the roof and the control of another man, the Irish (along with Swedes and Germans) had an open field in this market. Living in middle or upper class houses in better areas and better conditions obviously had some advantages. But the very long hours (servants could effectively be on call twenty-four hours a day with no days off in some cases) and the lack of independence, made this work less attractive than it might appear. Especially if the master of the house sexually harassed or tyrannized his employees.

As the century progressed many Irish women preferred the greater "freedom" to be found in a factory. The women and children who filled the woolen and cotton mills of New England had to endure the deafening machinery and choking debris of vast new factories in Lowell, Providence, and Dover. Such employment was often taken by Irish emigrants to Canada who had found their way south (often on foot). Many also came from the teaming tenements of Boston. Initially they too worked from sunrise to sunset, but conditions improved to a standard ten-hour day, six-day week, later in the century.

American economic expansion, while spectacular, was often erratic, and competition for work could be intense. This competition took a number of forms, many of them violent. Irishmen fought with other Irishmen, with other immigrant groups, and with free Blacks to establish and defend their positions in factories, in mines, and on construction sites. It was common for bloody battles to break out between different sets of Irish workers, such as those between workers from Cork and Longford on the Chesapeake and Ohio canal in 1834—when at least six were killed. When Irish workers struck for higher wages, they not only intimidated contractors, they attacked fellow workers from Germany, America, or Britain, who refused to join the strike. These tactics owed much to the practices of Irish secret societies like the Defenders and the Ribbonmen, who had intimidated landlords, agents, and middlemen to set fair rents, tithes, and prices. Strikes often "required" the U.S. military to suppress them. After the Civil War they would inform the emerging trade union movement, which became heavily dominated by Irish-Americans.

Mrs. Thomas McKessy of Limerick, Ireland, upon her arrival in New York on the S.S. Aurania on March 16, 1926. She was joining her husband and four of her children who arrived September 1925. Of her twenty-one children, four were already in the U.S., ten arrived with her, five died, and two stayed at home in Ireland as they were married.

In *How the Irish Became White,* Noel Ignatiev argues that violence between competing workers initially owed less to national or racial allegiances than it did to regional affiliations. In other words, groups would fight any other which threatened their living, even if they were fellow Irishmen. But by the 1850s, he argues, Irish workers had developed a sense of national and racial solidarity—positioning themselves as part of the "white" race in order to push out free Blacks. Certainly, by this point, many jobs which had traditionally been performed by Blacks were the almost exclusive preserve of Irishmen. Longshoremen were a good example of this, and by the 1850s New York's docks were almost entirely Irish, even though free Blacks had commonly worked there previously. Essentially, both groups were in direct competition for the lowest jobs available, and while this competition was only partly to do with developing racial consciousness, becoming "white" made tactical sense for Irishmen.

An additional cause of this growing antipathy was the Irish immigrant's fear of the consequences of a labor market suddenly flooded with freed slaves. These fears usually led to Irish-American opposition to the abolition of slavery. Irish-Americans rationalized anti-abolitionism by claiming that the position of slaves was materially no worse (and often better) than their own. There was some truth in this claim, but its expression also reflected other tensions.

Nativism

Despite the vital role of Irish settlers in performing the menial tasks of the growing republic (or perhaps partly because of it) anti-Irish and anti-Catholic prejudice flourished from the 1820s until well into the twentieth century. The most virulent period of bigotry began in the

1830s and reached a peak during the Famine exodus from the late 1840s to the mid-1850s. "Native" Americans (or rather, established immigrants of British Protestant background) feared cultural contamination from the enormous inflow of poor, ill-educated, and often diseased, immigrants. Workingclass Americans also feared increasing competition in the job market and worried that desperate Irish immigrants would undercut their wages. By the eve of the Famine these Irish Catholics had already established large ghettos in New York, Boston, and Philadelphia, and it was in this period that the term "Scots-Irish" came into common usage as a means for established Protestant Irish-Americans to distance themselves from their fellow Irishmen. Henceforth, the new Catholic immigrants had a monopoly on the label "Irish."

The American Party (or know-nothing party) became the focus of this Nativism. Its goals were to limit immigration and to keep the Irish out of positions of political power. They hoped to exclude those of foreign birth from office and sought twenty-one-year residency requirements for citizenship. One of its leaders, Samuel Morse, likened the Irish influx to mud being thrown into pure water, and as in the British Isles, anti-Catholic prejudice contributed heavily to this anti-Irish sentiment. The Anglo-Protestant American elite, despite constitutional statements to the contrary, had always regarded America as an essentially Protestant country. The seventeenth-century Englishman's fear of despotism and popery had survived remarkably intact in his nineteenth-century transatlantic descendants. For Protestant Americans, Catholicism symbolized superstition, ignorance, and tyrannical political rule. It also equaled disloyalty—for how could a Catholic serve both the Pope and the American Republic. The weary Irish immigrants had merely fled from the callous indifference of British rule to the vocal hostility of American nativism—and the nature of this hostility was depressingly familiar.

Rumors of Catholic plots to infiltrate and destroy Protestant America abounded. The most common being schemes to settle and take control of the Mississippi River valley. Libelous publications alleged all manner of depravity and perversion in the Catholic Church. Violent language led to violent action. In the 1830s and 1840s, anti-Irish and anti-Catholic rioters killed many immigrants, burned down Catholic churches, and destroyed Catholic property. The Irish of New York rallied together under Archbishop John Hughes to defend their churches and homes with armed guards. Hughes warned that if a single Catholic church were desecrated, the Catholics would burn down New York. The threat was taken seriously and violence was averted, as the Irish in New York were by now a considerable force. By the mid-1830s, there were already 40–50,000 Irish immigrants in New York, and by 1860 this increased to around 200,000 out of a population of 800,000. Such growing strength commanded respect, but it also frightened American Protestants and increased support for the nativists.

In terms of electoral politics, the high point of nativism came in 1854-55, when the American Party won elections in Massachusetts, New York, Pennsylvania, Connecticut, Delaware, Maryland, Rhode Island, New Hampshire, Kentucky, and California. In Massachusetts, the new governor actually ordered searches to be carried out on convents in an attempt to confirm the nativists' worst fears of institutionalized depravity. They were, of course, disappointed. Fortunately for Catholics, growing tensions between North and South over states' rights and slavery overshadowed nativism as the key issues of the 1856 presidential election. Otherwise the know-nothing candidate Millard Fillmore might have won, as many expected him to.

Virulent nativism slowly began to subside after this point. Ultimately, Anglo-American Protestants were in a stronger position than Anglo-Irish Protestants and could afford, eventually, to be more accommodating. They were not threatened by an overwhelming Catholic majority in a small island with a long memory of dispossession. Furthermore, "native" Americans still enjoyed an unassailable political and economic hegemony in a fluid, vast, and expanding country. There was plenty of land and plenty of work for all. But nativism only gradually lost its edge. It remained very powerful in the late-nineteenth century, and it lingered in the background until the mid-twentieth.

The Civil War

Nativism diminished slightly with the distraction of the Civil War and the task of reconstruction which followed. This vast conflict, which involved three million combatants (and 620,000 fatalities), provided a theater for Irish-Americans to show their courage and commitment to their new land. By doing so, they strengthened their bond to their new state and strengthened their case for acceptance. But Irish-American participation in the Civil War was complicated. The majority fought for the Union, and in Massachusetts, New York, Ohio, Michigan, Illinois, Indiana, and Iowa, Irish regiments were formed. On some estimates over 150,000 Irishmen donned the blue uniforms of the Union in its struggle to preserve the integrity of the U.S. and (eventually) to abolish slavery.

But Irishmen fought and distinguished themselves in large numbers on both sides, and while many recent Irish immigrants were genuinely committed to the Union, their preponderance in Union armies may have had as much to do with settlement patterns as fundamental allegiances. Around 85,000 Irish-Americans fought for the Confederates, which was probably a proportionally higher figure than for the Union given the larger Irish population in the Northern cities. Indeed, Irish antipathy towards the abolition of slavery—which would have released hundreds of thousands of free Blacks onto the labor market—was a major factor in inhibiting Irish enrolment in Union armies.

Of course, both the Irish and the free Black regiments were often little more than cannon fodder in a brutal war which both groups gained less from than is commonly thought. This is not the place to discuss the problems of the freed slaves in post-Civil War America, but the proportion of Irishmen who lost their lives was certainly higher than their stake in the country might have warranted. Casualty rates in this war were notoriously high, as the destructive power of modern technology had outpaced developments in strategy and tactics. In many instances gullible Irish immigrants who had barely arrived in the U.S. were blown to pieces by their fellow countrymen in a war that was not of either of their making. Induced to fight with offers of citizenship, many emigrants' dreams came to a painful end at Gettysburg, Bull Run, and Antietam.

The fighting qualities of Irish troops were usually recognized, and this did help to elevate their standing, but genuine parity of esteem was out of the question. Bravery in battle was offset by the stereotype of the emotional, whiskey-drinking Irishman who still needed leadership. Half a century earlier, the Duke of Wellington had called his heavily-Irish "British" troops "the scum of the earth"—many Protestant American generals held their Irish troops in similar disdain. Irish-American officers did reach the highest levels. Both Ulysses Grant and "Stonewall" Jackson had Irish ancestry. But this tended to be Protestant and "Scotch-Irish" ancestry rather than recent Catholic.

In the long term, the fact that the majority of the Irish were seen to have supported the winning side did ease some of the prejudices against Irish immigrants in the North, but this first step toward assimilation and acceptance was a costly one.

Climbing the social ladder

Between the end of the Civil War and the onset of the Depression in 1929, Irish-America achieved a remarkable transformation. During the 1870s and 1880s, Irish sons and daughters began to enjoy part of this growth themselves. Life was still hard for the working classes, and it was still precarious for a large minority, but during these years most Irish-Americans emerged from the disadvantages of poverty and prejudice to enjoy some genuine prosperity and a little security.

Apart from the natural process of assimilation and accommodation, which slowly made immigrants better able to function in their new society, this progress also reflects the changing nature of the Irish-American community. Firstly, Irish-America was increasingly American. By 1900 about two-thirds of the five million or so Irish-Americans had been born in the United States. This second generation, raised in urban, English-speaking, commercial America, rather than rural, agrarian Ireland, was much more likely to have the tools needed for success. The second generation was better equipped for skilled, managerial, and even professional, jobs. Among women there was a significant move to white-collar service and bureaucratic employment as they increasingly took jobs as schoolteachers, secretaries, and nurses. For men the big shift was from unskilled to skilled labor. By the turn of the century nearly two-thirds of Irish-American men still worked with their hands, but well over three-quarters of these were skilled workers; fifty years earlier that proportion was reversed. Furthermore, these jobs were usually well paid and unionized. Irish-Americans were still largely working class, but they were increasingly working in the more secure and lucrative segment of that class.

Not all were upwardly mobile, however. Casual labor, domestic service, and the textile industry, were still the common lot of many man and women (especially on the East Coast) and

Group of the Irish Brigade, at Harrison's Landing, Virginia, July 1862.

there were noticeable occupational differences between the Irish-born and the American-born. Indeed one might almost talk of two Irish-Americas: the new immigrants and the second generation. Admittedly, most of the post-1860 emigrants did not leave in a condition of absolute degradation as many had in the Famine era—despite Irish agricultural depressions such as that which led to the Land War of 1879–83. They were also better educated. The National Schools system, established in 1831, had turned Ireland into one of the most literate countries in Europe by the 1870s—with literacy rates of around seventy-five percent. Furthermore, the widespread introduction of steamships ensured that they arrived in better condition. The new vessels cut the journey from four weeks to ten days and better heating and cooking facilities made the crossing far less horrific. Most immigrants also had established social and economic networks to ease their transition. Family and friends in the U.S. could assist in getting work, and these networks increasingly had access to the power and patronage of local politics and the unions.

However, the success of earlier arrivals only went so far in easing the passage of the later ones, and the vast majority of new immigrants came from the least skilled and least educated sections of Irish society (a noticeable divergence from pre-Famine patterns). Hence, hard physical labor and poor housing were still the norm for new arrivals, and often the escape of an established Irish-American family to skilled work and the suburbs merely left a vacant place in the slums for newcomers—whether Irish or non-Irish. For example, in 1900 over half of all Irish-born women were in domestic service compared to one in five of the second generation, and immigrant Irish men were much more likely to be unskilled or casual laborers than second generation Irish-Americans.

These variations also intersected with regional differences. On a sliding scale of opportunity, the West and the Midwest were newer, more open, and more fluid, societies. New York and Pennsylvania were more static in social structure. Puritan Boston and New England were the most rigid ("no Irish need apply" signs were common well into the twentieth century). Hence, in the big Eastern cities of New York and Philadelphia, Irish-American men made up around forty percent of the total unskilled and semi-skilled work force, and in Boston they were nearly two-thirds. By 1900 there was rough occupational parity between Irish-America as a whole and "native" white America (with the exception that fewer Irish-Americans were farmers). This is a remarkable achievement for a group mired in racial and religious contempt less that fifty years earlier, and it implies rapid upward mobility among the American-born Irish in particular.

Given their predominantly urban settlement, Irish-Americans were naturally well positioned to take advantage of the urban and industrial growth around them. They also had advantages of language not enjoyed by most other nationalities, and when the new waves of immigrants from eastern and southern Europe arrived they often took on the most menial physical jobs while Irish-Americans became foremen and union organizers. However, the advantage of English was not universal. Possibly up to half a million Irish immigrants were still using Irish as their primary or only language in the late nineteenth century and up to a million Irish speakers may have emigrated to America before 1880. Half of them went during the Famine exodus of 1846-55, constituting between a quarter and third of all Famine emigrants. Many learned English quickly and became bilingual if they were not already. Few passed their Irish on to future generations. But there were many families and communities that used Irish in America during the late nineteenth century and a few continued to do so in the early twentieth. These tended to be economically or geographically isolated, such as the Point area of Pittsburgh, some communities of miners in the Schuylkill valleys of Pennsylvania, and the settlements on Beaver Island in Lake Michigan.

While many Irish shared a hope to return to their family, friends, and familiar landscape, less than ten percent actually did so. By the turn of the twentieth century most Irish-Americans would have had no personal recollection of Ireland itself, and even the defining moment of the Famine would be a secondhand memory. The sons and daughters of Irish peasant farmers increasingly sought respectability and gentility within the very different norms of urban America. From their jobs as miners, factory workers, and laborers, Irishmen were aspiring to the police force and other local government jobs. Some even made fortunes in business (notably the construction industry) or climbed the greasy pole of state and city politics.

By the early twentieth century a growing number of powerful and wealthy Irish-Americans began to wonder which part of their hyphenated identity was most important, and the distinctive traits of Irish-America were noticeably diverging from those of their homeland. Sentimentality and clannishness remained common to both in popular image, but it was joined by a hardworking, ambitious, and abrasive edge in Irish-Americans which, rightly or wrongly, was not ascribed to the Irish back home.

The shackles of prejudice were further weakened through sport and entertainment. The boxing legend John L. Sullivan, who became World Heavyweight Champion in 1883, did much to enhance that sports' standing and encouraged other young "fighting Irishmen" to follow in his footsteps. Baseball was also full of Irish-Americans around the turn of the century, both as players and managers. Michael Kelly thrilled crowds on the field, John Joseph McGraw led the New York Giants to success for many years, and Charles Comiskey rose from player to owner of the Chicago White Sox. Irish-American actors and songwriters entertained the nation, notably George Cohan with such popular and patriotic ditties as "Over There," "Give My Regards to Broadway," and "I'm a Yankee Doodle Dandy."

Religion

The Catholic Church was a vital unifying institution for the emerging Irish-American communities. It gave Irish emigrants a link with their previous lives and some consolation for hardship, disease, and economic uncertainty. In other words, it provided a social as much as a religious function, and one all the more important because church organization generally proceeded political, cultural, or economic organization. Confronted with the hostility of Anglo-Protestant nativism (based largely on anti-Catholicism) the Irish were frequently alienated from mainstream society. The church was one of the few institutions that could defend their interests, and in doing so it transcended regional and parochial identities imported from Ireland. The Irishness of Irish-America was partly a product of a shared Catholic identity overcoming local loyalties.

In order to create this spiritual and psychological buffer, the church established a parallel social infrastructure outside the state institutions. Typically this began with church building. In Irish areas Catholic churches rose rapidly (helped by the growing Irish-American construction industry) to became the focal point of the community—a place to worship, meet neighbors, and conduct local affairs. Most were simple parish churches, but New York's gothic revival St. Patrick's Cathedral, designed in 1859 by James Renwick and finished in the 1870s, was an impressive demonstration of how growing prosperity was being channeled into church construction.

The church also created its own parochial schools from an early date, funded by private donations, the schools sought to protect the culture and moral values of the Irish communities, but they also provided the education, which enabled entry into the professions by the turn of the century. Ironically, while the parish school cemented neighborhood bonds, the content of their teaching was usually highly Anglicized: very little Irish history, literature, or culture was taught.

Orphanages and hospitals soon followed schools and churches, as Irish Catholic communities became adept at providing for their own needs. These organizations, which flourished under the church's wing, quickly became central to Irish-American life. By providing worthy and responsible employment for thousands of nuns, they also gave many Irish-American women a more fulfilling public life than any other female ethnic group. The fact that Irish immigrants were generally concentrated in urban communities linked by good communications helped the church to establish this central role in their lives.

The usual account of Irish-American Catholicism stresses devout, clannish, urban parishes under the occasionally authoritarian control of the local priest—often recently off the boat from the old country. There is much truth in this image, but the degree of devotion displayed by Irish-Americans did differ markedly—and "displayed" is perhaps the right word here, for Irish-American Catholicism often made a show of its "respectable," moralistic orthodoxy. This tendency was encouraged by the understandable desire to refute Protestant

America's view of their low moral worth and by the importation of the devotional revolution from Ireland. In the third quarter of the nineteenth century, Cardinal Paul Cullen (a close friend of Pius IX) had transformed the traditional, wayward, and folkloristic, church of pattern days and open-air masses into a Romanized, centralized, and orthodox religion of smart, new, gothic revival churches. In areas where the church was in Irish control, these trends led to a disciplined and dedicated flock with high church attendance and deep emotional attachment. When combined with the proximity of an overtly anti-Catholic Protestant population (as in Boston) defensive instincts also reinforced affiliation. But the image of the Irish as a deeply religious people needs some qualification. The huge cosmopolitan cities such as New York often allowed religious laxity to develop in their more secular, anonymous spaces, and German Catholics, for example, often found Irish Catholicism lacking in real piety and learning.

By World War I there were twenty million American Catholics, and Irish-Americans dominated a church which they had built into a powerful, wealthy, and influential institution. Its influence had both positive and negative effects on Irish-American development after the initial stage of community building. Its Puritanism and prudery certainly inhibited generations of guilt-laden Irish-Americans, leading to sexual frustration, late marriage, and stunted emotional growth. The church also encouraged a certain dogmatic rigidity and anti-intellectualism. When combined with the understandable immigrant desire for practical education, this retarded Irish-American intellectual life. Of course, the quality of Catholic schools was widely recognized and Catholic colleges such as Boston College and Notre Dame were efficiently producing an educated, Anglicized, Irish-American middle class. But they produced few national, intellectual leaders in this period. Thus while the church provided psychological protection and spiritual comfort, it could also oppress and stifle intelligent, sensual, and unconventional souls.

Politics

Few groups confirm Aristotle's dictum that man is a political animal better than the Irish in America. In the first half of the nineteenth century very few Irish Catholics rose to political prominence, but by the 1820s the expanding adult male electorate at least meant that their votes were important. Parties began to fight for the support of new immigrants, and the Irish vote became critical in cities like New York. The Irish typically supported the Democratic Party of Andrew Jackson and Martin Van Buren. This coalition of interests included some strange bedfellows. Southern slave owners and Northern workingclass Irish immigrants combined in an anti-Yankee alliance opposing the abolition of slavery. Firm loyalty to the local Democratic Party led to perks of office and patronage, as Irishmen climbed internal party hierarchies in the 1860s and 1870s. Some Irishmen did support the Whigs and, after 1854, the Republicans (notably in Philadelphia) but Republican anti-Catholicism usually discouraged this.

Irish-American political savvy owed much to traditions shaped by Daniel O'Connell back in Ireland in the twenty years prior to the Famine. Through his Catholic Association (which successfully forced Catholic Emancipation from a reluctant British Government in 1829) he gave the Irish an education in political organization and popular political agitation. By encouraging poor Irishmen to become associate members for only one penny a month (the so-called "Catholic Rent") the concept of formal commitment to a political body was familiar to most Irish immigrants. O'Connell's campaign for repeal of the Act of Union in the early 1840s did not succeed, but it generated "Monster Meetings" attended by hundreds of thousands of ordinary Irish men and women. This heritage of political protest against injustice translated easily enough to the subtly different injustices confronting immigrants in America. It was soon producing Irish-American leaders and encouraging widespread political mobilization.

Irish-Americans certainly needed to mobilize their strength in order to gain a measure of control over their harsh environment. The power structures that they developed were a curious mixture of the modern and the traditional. Full use was made of American democracy, which in terms of votes made the poorest Irish-American Catholic as important as the richest Anglo-Saxon Protestant. The leaders of party "machines" realized quickly that numbers counted, and in the strongholds of New York, Chicago, Boston, Philadelphia, Baltimore, St.

Louis, Kansas City, and San Francisco, there were enough Irishmen to seize control of city government for long periods. Within these machines cutting edge party organization merged with the politics of personal fiefdom and patronage.

A hierarchical pyramid of power led up from the voters through block workers to precinct captains and then to ward leaders. At the top sat the local party boss, who was often (but not necessarily) the mayor. He doled out the resources of city government, such as building contracts and jobs in the police, in return for votes and contributions to party coffers. The mechanism was fueled by the local taxes and bribes that electoral victory gave access to, and municipal funds were distributed according to the criteria of loyal service to the party machine and blatant ethnic favoritism. Deference, loyalty, graft, and common interest oiled the wheels of this machine.

Corruption and inefficiency were rife, merit often irrelevant, and fawning obedience to the "boss" the norm. But the system did have its attractions. Problems with debt, rent arrears, or unemployment could be directed to a known figure, within a clearly understood hierarchy, who might help you out if able to do so—in return for future electoral obligations. The system provided jobs for the boys, but then many of the boys needed jobs—especially when poverty and prejudice barred them from certain branches of commerce or the professions.

Americans of Irish birth or extraction played a crucial role in the development and practice of trade unionism. They did not create the movement, nor were they at its forefront in its difficult early years, but they presided over its expansion and maturity in the late nineteenth and early twentieth century. Indeed the scale of their influence is remarkable. In the years leading up to World War I, Irish-Americans headed almost half of the 110 unions in the American Federation of Labor, and this prominence continued into the new industrial unions of the 1930s and beyond.

The newly arrived Irish, as casual or unskilled laborers, lacked the power and the wherewithal to organize independently on a large scale. By the 1850s they were sporadically successful in creating effective, although often short-lived, unions of dock workers (New York's Longshoremen's Society being perhaps the best early example), but the heyday of Irish-American labor came later in the century.

Ironically, Irish-Americans rose to prominence in the labor movement while they actually declined as a proportion of the total workforce. They were also spread throughout the trades in this period and rarely formed a majority of the workers in any one industry, but they increasingly dominated unions in industries where their numbers were significant. Typical activists were second or third generation Irish-Americans whose parents or grandparents had settled in an industrial environment. They were not themselves former members of agrarian secret societies back in Ireland, but they would have inherited some of the mentalities. They merged them with the sober-minded, self-help tradition of the skilled craft unions.

By the turn of the twentieth century, the strong Irish-American influence in the labor unions was generally moderate rather than radical. Most unions focused on collective bargaining to raise wages and piecemeal reform to reduce hours and improve safety. Mainstream trade unionism accepted the capitalist system while seeking to restrain and humanize it. However, there were many genuinely radical Irish activists in the early twentieth century. William Z. Foster, Elizabeth Gurley Flynn, Eugene Dennis, "Big" Bill Hayward, and Ray and Grant Dunne were all notable communists of varying persuasions.

This picture of working class solidarity implies that fewer Irish-Americans aspired to upward mobility through business ownership than is often argued. Hundreds of thousands were more realistic in rejecting bourgeois mentalities for moderate success and security through a fair day's work and loyal participation in their union. They were not always successful, for the giant corporations often ruthlessly suppressed union activity with the support of the state. But if we can pick out one overarching theme between the Civil War and the Depression, it is the slow rise to security and modest success of the majority of Irish-Americans. More of them achieved that success through the collective solidarity of the labor movement than by any other method.

As bitterness towards Britain festered in exile, it combined with nostalgic memories of Ireland to produce an Irish nationalism that was often more Anglophobic than its Irish counterpart. Irish-Americans who were politically radical on domestic American issues were often at the forefront of Irish nationalism. Immigrants had always kept an eye on Irish politics from across the Atlantic, and from the late 1850s onwards Irish-American fundraising was an essential part of any nationalist enterprise, whether constitutional or revolutionary. All of the major expressions of post-Famine Irish nationalism—including Fenianism, the Home Rule party and Sinn Fein—depended on American moral and (more importantly) financial support. This influence has persisted in lesser degree to the present day, with some Irish-Americans funding the republican nationalism of the IRA through NORAID.

The history of Irish-American nationalism begins in earnest with the Repeal movement of Daniel O'Connell in the early 1840s. It received considerable support from Irish-America and it had branches in nearly all states. Mainstream politicians, recognizing that lip-service to Irish nationalism could secure sizeable Irish votes at the polls, also jumped on the bandwagon.

Irish-American influence placed some limits on a generally pro-British U.S. foreign policy, notably by eliciting U.S. condemnation of the Boer War and by preventing U.S. support for Britain in its struggle to contain Russian and German expansion in the Far East. But Irish-Americans provided little ideological leadership and their influence on Irish affairs was not great. The cultural and Gaelic revival which motivated the new nationalism was an entirely Irish affair with more connections to British and European intellectual life than American.

Since the mid-nineteenth century Irish-Americans had tried to secure an anti-British U.S. foreign policy, but while they often won Congressional support they were usually resisted by a succession of pro-British presidents. Wilson was especially impervious to Irish-American influence. He resented their opposition to American entry into World War I, and he had no inclination to browbeat the British into accepting Irish delegates, especially as their support was vital for his dream of a postwar peace guaranteed by a League of Nations. By opposing him, Irish-American inadvertently helped to destabilize the postwar European peace settlement.

As the Anglo-Irish war escalated in 1920, Irish-American influence and American public opinion did persuade the U.S. government to put pressure on the British government. In doing so they contributed in a small way to the truce of July 1921 and the opening of peace negotiations in October. Thus the winning of independence for twenty-six counties was certainly, in part, due to the financial support of Irish-America and the moral pressure of America more generally, but this should not be overstated. The main impetus for peaceful resolution came from Britain and Ireland, whose peoples were thoroughly sick of the war.

Before leaving the relationship of Irish-America to Irish nationalism, we should note one important irony. The strength of American support implied a depletion of Irish resources. For the expansion of the Irish-American community resulted from the constant drain of talent, energy, and youth, from Ireland. In a sense, emigration was a necessary evil for Ireland. Given the intense pressure on the land in areas such Connacht, emigration provided a safety valve for excess population. It also provided an inflow of American money from departed relatives which prevented evictions and supported inefficient agriculture. However, there was a deep and enduring sadness at the ever-present prospect of separation from loved ones. Second and third sons, as well as daughters whose parents could not afford a dowry, were effectively bred for emigration in parts of Connacht and Munster. Their youthful help was needed on the small family farm, but in order to keep that farm intact for the "stem" family, they must either leave or accept the status of unmarried wage laborer on the family holding—many naturally chose to leave. Thus the growth and success of the Irish in America was dependent on their failure to secure a decent life in Ireland.

Sinn Fein recognized this, and while eager to use American money, they were violently opposed to emigration. The new Dail banned immigration and the IRA even raided hotels in Liverpool to confiscate the tickets, money, and passports, of those heading across the Atlantic. To Sinn Fein emigration was the most visible symbol of Irish poverty and political subjugation and was actually hindering independence. They may have been right. Emigration can be seen as a crucial element in the stability of the social and economic system. Indeed the effects of temporary restrictions on emigration on social and political stability could be significant. The years leading up to the Land War and Independence were characterized by low emigration due to economic recession in America and to World War I respectively. This left a surplus of disgruntled young men, with little prospect of work or advancement and few doubts about who was to blame. As Sinn Fein realized, the dissatisfaction that often led to emigration could be channeled into nationalism. Money and moral support from America were invaluable to the long nationalist struggle, but ultimately a truly effective Irish nationalist had to be in Ireland.

The modern era

Paradoxically, mainstream Irish-America came of age, both materially and intellectually, just as the Great Depression hit America. This massive downturn in the economy tends to mask Irish success, but by the late 1920s, Irish-America had achieved rough occupational and educational parity with Anglo-Protestant America. Irish-Americans had become average Americans in most respects; they were the skilled workers, teachers, nurses, clerks, politicians, and lower and middle managers who made urban life tick. Their priests were the spiritual leaders of an increasingly accepted and "respectable" Catholic-America, composed of a kaleidoscopic spectrum of European and Hispanic immigrants. Their nuns educated these immigrants and their local politicians cleverly constructed ethnic coalitions, which gave them some voice in urban government. In short, the Irish occupied a representative cross-section of jobs and income, often acting as intermediaries linking new immigrant groups with the social and financial elite

By the 1970s, with the exception of Jewish-Americans (perhaps an even more remarkable story of triumph in adversity) Irish-Americans had become the best educated and wealthiest of any ethnic group in America—including British-Americans.

The high, if slowly declining, levels of emigration witnessed from the 1840s to the 1920s dropped off considerably in the 1930s. There were modest revivals in the 1950s and 1980s, and emigration was still a common escape from rural poverty and boredom, but the overall trend plummeted. A few figures will show the extent of this change. In the peak decades of the 1850s and the 1880s there were 914,119 and 655,482 direct immigrants from Ireland. In the 1920s there were only 220,591 (itself an increase on the previous decade), and in the 1930s just 13,167. In the forty-year period from 1931 to 1970, the Irish made up less than two percent of all U.S. immigrants, whereas in the forty-year period from 1851 to 1890 they were just less than twenty percent.

CHAPTER 5 # Jews and East Europeans

An engraving of Jewish refugees passing the
Statue of Liberty, 1892.

The pioneers

When Joachim Gaunse, a Jewish metallurgist from Prague, joined the colony at Roanoke, Virginia, in 1585–86, he may well have been the first American Jew. However, since he left for England within a year, the story of American Jewry does not really begin until 1654, when twenty-three Jews landed at Manhattan Island, to make their home in New Amsterdam.

Their story originates in Spain, where for a good part of the Middle Ages, the Jews had prospered in all areas of Spanish life. The end of this "Golden Age" was signaled in 1391, when anti-Jewish riots broke out in Seville, and spread throughout Spain. Synagogues were destroyed, and Jews killed or forced to convert to Christianity. In 1492 the Jews were expelled from Spain by decree. Between May and June 100,000 Jews left, mainly for Portugal, North Africa and Turkey, although they were again expelled from Portugal in 1496–97.

In 1572, the Netherlands rebelled against Spanish rule and their leaders turned to the former Jews of Spain for material help. By 1600, there was a community of Jews from Spain living in Amsterdam. Their ties with other Jews all over Europe and North Africa helped them to prosper, and the community grew in numbers and strength.

It was from this Dutch community that our twenty-three pioneers were drawn. Their journey to New Amsterdam was not direct. Their first resting place in the continent was in Brazil, where the Jewish population had grown between 1630 and 1645 to some 1,500 as a result of the conquest of northeastern Brazil by the Dutch West India Company. However, the local Portuguese rebelled against Dutch rule in 1645, and nine years later the success of the rebellion resulted in the Dutch (including their Jews) being given three months to leave.

It was from here that the twenty-three refugees boarded a French ship, the *Sainte Catherine*, and traveled to New Amsterdam. On arriving in September 1654, they found another Jew, Jacob Barsimon, who had arrived in New Amsterdam in July from Holland. These twenty-four created the first permanent Jewish settlement in North America, and it is their arrival that began American Jewish history.

Peter Stuyvesant, the Governor of New Amsterdam, was hostile. Although they were Dutch subjects, he protested to the Dutch West India Company against their settlement. He called them "a deceitful race" who should not be allowed "to infect and trouble this new colony." The Amsterdam Jewish community, some of whom had investments in the Company, intervened on their behalf. In April, the Company advised Stuyvesant to allow the Jews to remain in New Amsterdam, "provided the poor among them shall not become a burden to the Company or the community, but be supported by their own nation." In June, Stuyvesant was ordered to allow the Jews of New Amsterdam to engage in trade and to own real estate.

Other restrictions continued, however, and Jews were barred from holding civic office and from conducting religious services. They were also barred from doing guard duty, in addition to which they had to pay a special tax. But in 1655 Asser Levy one of the twenty-three pioneers, with the support of Jacob Barsimon, successfully petitioned the Governor against the tax and won the right to do guard duty, a small but important step on the road to equal citizenship.

New Amsterdam to New York

In 1654 the English conquered New Amsterdam and renamed it New York. Fortunately for the Jews, the English guaranteed freedom of conscience to their new subjects. By 1740 the English Parliament had enacted the Plantation Act. This offered naturalization to established residents of the American colonies. Although applicants had to swear allegiance to the Crown "upon the true faith of a Christian," Jews who applied for naturalization could take the oath without those words. Since a naturalized citizen was entitled to all the rights of an Englishman, the Jews of America acquired greater rights than the Jews of England, for whom the naturalization oath still required an oath on the "true faith of a Christian."

Although tolerance was not universal under English rule, the Jews of England and Holland (and later Bordeaux) in particular were attracted by the general message of tolerance that the New World gave out, and many came during the seventeenth and eighteenth centuries. They settled as far afield as South Carolina and Georgia, as well as in Rhode Island, New York and Pennsylvania. An entry in the General Court of Hartford in 1655 notes the arrest of "David the Jew" for peddling, which is the first record of a Jew living in Connecticut, and a tax list reveals that there were two Jews in Boston in 1674.

Many of those who came were of Spanish and Portuguese (Sephardic) origin. In 1720, a renewed Portuguese Inquisition sent 1,500 Jews to London. Many moved on to the New World. What made these people cross the Atlantic? Was the message of religious toleration alone enough to cause them to leave their families and communities in the prosperous cities of Western Europe? For many, it was poverty that pushed them into throwing themselves on the mercy of the ocean and the unknown world that awaited them. For although many of the Jews in London and Amsterdam were wealthy, increasing numbers of them community had become dependent on community welfare schemes.

When Georgia was established by James Oglethorpe in 1733, for example, the London Sephardic community paid for forty-two of their members to go to Savannah. They were

"Their New Jerusalem, Broadway in 1892." A political cartoon depicting fleeing Russian Jews arriving in New York as the older New York families depart for the West. It shows a wealthy Jewish man standing in the center of Broadway, the buildings of which all bear "Jewish" names and occupations, c.1890s.

happy to see Georgia as both a strategic buttress against the Spanish in Florida and a refuge for the poor of their own community.

During the second half of the seventeenth century, many Central European Jews (Ashkenazim) had moved to Holland and England, often escaping economic restrictions and a general economic decline in Germany, which had been exacerbated for German Jews by the arrival of Jews escaping poverty, persecution and war in Poland and Lithuania. But the move to England and Holland rarely alleviated the poverty of the Ashkenazic Jews. Some of whom therefore chanced their luck across the Atlantic.

Not every Jew of central or eastern European origins traveled to escape poverty. Some belonged to families of financiers and merchants that had achieved commercial success in England. These emigrants functioned as commercial representatives of their families. Indeed, this was one motive for emigration, with Ashkenazic mercantile families in England widening their trading sphere by dispatching a son, brother, or cousin to the New World.

Jacob Franks, for example, probably New York's most successful Jewish merchant during the colonial era and a major figure in its synagogue, was the son of a broker in England, who maintained commercial ties with his family in London long after he arrived on Manhattan Island. Similarly, the brothers Barnard and Michael Gratz had left their village in Upper Silesia and joined their cousin Solomon Henry in London. After a few years they moved to Philadelphia, where they believed they would prosper because of their English connection.

This pattern of Jewish migration across Europe and then across the Atlantic can be seen as part of general population shifts within Europe, although the Jewish pattern covered greater distances and began earlier. So seventeenth-century Jews who moved first within Europe and then to America blazed the trail for the larger numbers of non-Jewish central Europeans and British who populated the English colonies in the eighteenth century. But the Jews were different in one important respect. Most American Jews of the time were merchants and traders, while the other immigrants were mainly farmers and artisans.

Newly arrived Jewish exiles from Russia leaving Castle Garden for the emigrants quarters on Ward Island.

Making a living

The earliest immigrants often had no real intention of settling for good, but by the early eighteenth century many had married and begun to raise families. They remained, however, an essentially immigrant community throughout the Colonial period. In 1776 virtually all the leaders of the American Jewish community, which by then numbered about 2,500, were immigrants. They had all come from countries which discriminated by statute against Jews. They wanted in the main to continue to practice their religion, but they also wanted to integrate with the wider community and to cast off the stigma of the European Jew, who had always been a creature apart from his fellows.

It was not easy to strike the balance between becoming American and remaining Jews. The early communities in Savannah and Newport simply disappeared within a few years, although both were reborn by the time of the Revolution. New York remained the strongest community, and it was New Yorkers who established Jewish communities in Philadelphia in the 1740s and in Montreal in the 1760s.

Although Jews achieved a measure of equality in the Colonial period, only Protestant Christians could hold political office, and Jews seemed to avoid an involvement in politics. For the first generation trader, it was enough to have the opportunity to prosper financially and to be allowed to practice his religion free from oppression. The economy was growing, and Jewish businessmen were happy to participate freely in a way that was rare in Europe.

They were mainly shopkeepers, although farmers and planters were not completely unknown, and Jewish silversmiths and other craftsmen were to be found everywhere. The successful shopkeepers became merchants, and the most successful of these were often engaged in transatlantic shipping of foods, forest products and consumer goods. Sometimes they participated in the African slave trade. Jewish merchant-shippers of that day were also industrialists, involved in the manufacture of barrels, the catching and processing of fish and whales, and the manufacture of candles, as well as in the field of army supplies.

It is important to realize that however successful these Jewish businessmen were, the whole Jewish population of America at the time never constituted more than one percent of the total Colonial population, and their overall influence was small.

A Russian Jew arriving at Ellis Island in 1905.

Building Jewish communities

In Europe, the Jews were largely organized in communities based around their synagogues. When they arrived in the New World, they soon established similar communities. The first step was to find land for a cemetery. Then they would find a room, usually rented, in which they would hold services. In due course they would find the money to buy a building, and then later to build their own synagogue.

As they grew and developed their communal activities, they acquired three main communal servants, the *hazzan*, the cantor, who led the chanting of the prayers, the *shohet*, the ritual slaughterer of animals for food, and the *shammash*, the beadle, the general servant of the lay leadership. These ritual professionals were part-timers, generally poorly paid, whose other modest employment often placed them amongst the less well-off within their communities.

Although the majority of the community was Ashkenazic in origin, because the pioneers had generally been Sephardic, the early synagogues adopted the liturgy and customs of the Sephardic world. Religious authority was exercised not by Rabbis, of whom there were none until the early nineteenth century, but by the lay boards of the synagogues, who managed both the ritual and the welfare activities of their communities. They provided pensions for the elderly, medical and nursing care for the sick, loans for new entrepreneurs, and they buried the dead. They also paid for teachers for the children of the poor.

The community in New York established its own Hebrew school during the early part of the eighteenth century, although many of the children of the community were attending non-sectarian schools to obtain their general education. Other communities also created Hebrew schools. Their original purpose was to teach basic practical Judaism, the reading of the Hebrew prayer book and knowledge of Jewish ritual practice. They went on in many cases to provide a more general secular education.

Although most of the immigrants (or at least the men) had a working knowledge of two or more languages as well as knowledge of their trades or businesses, educational aspirations were not high. Very few of the children of the immigrants attended college or aspired to enter the professions.

Outside the Jewish communities there were numerous other communities. The English, Scottish, Irish, Welsh, German, Dutch, Swiss, and Swedish jostled in the marketplaces, and went off to worship in their Catholic, Quaker, Congregationalist, Baptist, Methodist, Anglican, Presbyterian Lutheran, Dutch Reformed and German Reformed places of worship. In a separate category were the African-American and the Native American communities.

This variety made life much easier for the Jew than it had ever been in Europe. Although anti-Semitic behavior was not unknown, the Jew had an opportunity that he never had in Europe. He could mold his own identity, free from a framework imposed by a hostile outside world.

The American-Jewish businessman was a foreigner, but he was a foreigner amongst foreigners. When he did business, he did not do so as an outsider, as he and his father had done in Europe. The air he breathed here smelled very different to the air of the ghettos (official or unofficial) of European Jewry.

Perhaps because there were no Rabbis, the influence of Rabbinic authority was not apparent. He could choose whether or not to be Jew, and he could choose for himself what being a Jew meant to him.

A poster advertising English lessons for Jewish immigrants, c.1895.

The Revolution

The first big choice that the Jews of America had to take was at the onset of the Revolution. They could have kept their heads down to avoid offending one side or the other. Some did, but most of them demonstrated their self-confidence as Americans by declaring openly for one side or the other.

In 1765, the Jewish merchants of Philadelphia joined the protests against English imports in protest against the Stamp Act. In 1770, New York Jews joined the tea protests. In 1775, the Governor of Georgia reported home about the behavior of Mordecai Sheftall, the Chairman of the local patriots group in Savannah, describing his behavior as "most infamous." And in 1775 in South Carolina, Francis Salvador, the first Jew to hold elected office in America, played a leading part in the Provincial Congress, helping to draft South Carolina's state constitution, and sitting in the new state legislature. In 1776 he became the first Jew to die in the American Revolutionary War.

Two years later, Mordecai Sheftall (now a colonel) was taken prisoner during the capture of Savannah by the English. In 1779, Solomon Bush was appointed to the rank of lieutenant colonel, the highest rank by a Jewish officer in the American Revolutionary Army, and Captain Lushington's Company, made up of American Revolutionary War volunteers from Charleston, South Carolina, includes some twenty Jews and was known as the "Jew Company." In New York, Hayyim Salomon, who only arrived from Poland in 1772, advanced over $200,000 for Army provisions. The British arrested him twice on suspicion of espionage, and in 1778, he was sentenced to death but escaped. He died bankrupt in 1785. These were some of the supporters of the American cause—but there were loyalists as well. In Newport, the *hazzan*, Isaac Touro was openly loyal to the Crown, and in 1779 he moved to New York, which was then under British occupation. It seems that in every community there were some who supported the Crown, although they seem to have been in a minority.

When the war ended, the community was full of optimism. In 1784 the first Jew was appointed to a diplomatic post abroad. In 1789, when a public procession and feast was held in Philadelphia to celebrate the new Constitution, the local Rabbi walked arm in arms with the Christian clergy and a special table was laid out with kosher food. The Revolution had been a turning point in American-Jewish pride.

After the war—the battle for rights

The effects of the Revolution were not all beneficial. Communities, and even some families, had been split. Some loyalists left in the aftermath. Many communities moved during the Revolution, notably large numbers of New Yorkers, who moved to Connecticut.

The community of Newport, Rhode Island left and did not return, and the community of Savannah was badly damaged by the war. Although some businessmen prospered, others did not. Some Jews had struggled hard to maintain their ritual observances during the war, but many found the restrictions of the Sabbath and the dietary laws too much to bear. In 1812, one Christian writer expresses concern that American Jews are becoming unbelievers and that their religious laxity might infect their Christian neighbors. If their Jewish observance had weakened, their Jewish pride had been strengthened. They set about campaigning for full political equality, and cited their patriotic endeavors to support their claims. Although the Federal Constitution opened up federal office-holding irrespective of religious belief, the state constitutions generally confined themselves to guaranteeing religious freedom. In the states, it was often only Protestants who could vote and hold office.

Although many non-Jews supported the Jewish claims, others felt that the rights that the Jews had won under the British—to be naturalized, to follow their own religion and to participate fully in business life—were sufficient. Many Protestants wanted to maintain the "establishment" of the Protestant Church, not only against the interests of the Jews, but also against the claims of the dissenters. Even the dissenters, while arguing for religious equality for themselves, were not always willing to extend that to Jews. The Baptist leader, Isaac Backus, for example, while supporting religious freedom, praised the Massachusetts legislature for declaring that "no man can take a seat in our legislature till he solemnly declares, 'I believe in the Christian religion and have a firm persuasion of its truth.'"

By 1830, however, a majority of states had granted Jews full rights. But legislation would not sweep away instantly centuries of popular prejudice. Jews responded to this

A family of English Jews awaiting inspection at Ellis Island before entering the United States. The father may well have come ahead and settled before sending for his family to join him, c.1900.

Jakob Mithelstadt and his family en route to Kuln, North Dakota., May 9, 1905.

prejudice by declaring and demonstrating their good citizenship and patriotism at every opportunity. They organized their synagogues on democratic principles, writing constitutions and even—in one case—a Bill of Rights:

> "Whereas in free states all power originates and is derived from the people, who always retain every right necessary for their well-being individually . . . In a like manner the individuals of every society in such state are entitled to and retain their several rights, which ought to be preserved inviolate. Therefore we, the professors of the Divine Laws, members of this holy congregation of *Shearith Israel*, in the city of New York, conceive it our duty to make this declaration of our rights and privileges."

American Judaism—the first stages

In the Colonial period, synagogues exercised authority over their members. After the Revolution, people increasingly looked for the synagogue to respond to their wishes. As early as 1795, Philadelphia became the first city in America with two different synagogues, when those of Ashkenazic origin established their own synagogue. By 1850, the number of synagogues in New York had risen from one to fifteen, although the population had not grown by anything like this factor. Synagogue leaders knew that in the climate of rights and liberties, laying down the law would be pointless and probably counterproductive. They turned a blind eye to Jews who violated Sabbath laws. They became more relaxed in their response to marriage out of the faith. Some synagogues even started to perform conversions, a rarity in European Jewry.

In European Jewry, the adoption of non-Jewish forms of dress and social customs—had become a taboo. In post-Revolutionary America the desire to become American became the guiding principle.

In the field of religion, this influence is best seen in the development of the role of the Jewish minister of religion. The outstanding Jewish minister of religion in pre-Revolutionary America was Gershom Mendes Seixas, the first native-born *hazzan*, appointed by the Shearith Israel Congregation of New York in 1768. When he was appointed, the principal responsibility of the *hazzan* was to lead the Hebrew prayers and chants during services. Depending on the community and synagogue, the *hazzan* might also circumcise male children, teach and prepare them for *barmitzvah*, and carry out ritual animal slaughter for food.

By 1768, the influence of the Protestant minister as a role model for religious leaders had begun to permeate the American Jewish community. The *hazzan* gradually became more of a pastor, concerning himself with the personal and spiritual welfare of his congregants. Seixas was among the first to concern himself actively with these matters. He provided leadership to the community when epidemics struck. He worked on behalf of the needy by establishing a major charitable organization. When charity became particularly necessary, he would hold a special service, which included a sermon.

The use of sermons became more important than the growing pastoral role. The civil authorities frequently called on the nation's religious leaders for support. When the colonial or state legislatures or the federal government declared days of fasting, penitence, thanks, humiliation, or celebration, they invariably asked the clergy to participate by leading special services or preaching special sermons. The first of such sermons by Seixas of which we have a written record is titled "Prayer for Peace" and was almost certainly delivered during the Revolutionary War. One scholar describes it as follows: "There is virtually nothing in it that would mark it as uniquely Jewish. Rather, it . . . might have been offered by virtually any clergyman supporting the Revolution." By contrast, European rabbis would base their orations on traditional rabbinic texts and would concentrate on details of Jewish observance or on interpretation of holy texts.

In 1825, two developments occurred, which were of profound significance. In Charleston, South Carolina, forty-seven members of the community known as Congregation *Beth Elohim* sought to make reforms in the patterns of worship. When the Board turned them down, they set up the Reformed Society of Israelites. Their reforms were the dominant feature of American Reform Judaism for the rest of the nineteenth century and much of the twentieth. Services were to be shorter and largely in the English language, the sermon was to be a central feature of the service, the payment of synagogue membership fees was to replace voluntary donations and the public auctioning of synagogue honors, and dignity and decorum would be the style of the conduct of worship.

In the same year, rebellion against synagogue traditions appeared in America's first synagogue, the Sephardic Congregation *Shearith Israel* in New York. There were debates about the wearing of the *tallit* (prayer shawl) and about the requirement to make a public charity pledge when called to the reading of the Torah. Younger members, strictly Orthodox in their practices, campaigned for a weekly sermon in English and for early morning services to enable them to attend synagogue on weekday mornings before going to work. They also sought greater democracy in rotation of officers. When their demands were rejected, they formed New York's second congregation the Ashkenazic *B'nai Jeshurun*.

The Civil War

Nothing better illustrates the struggle of the Jews to become a settled part of national life than their story in the Civil War. When it erupted in 1861, it divided Jews in the same way that it did the general population. Jews enlisted in the armies of the North and the South, and set out to become good soldiers.

On the Union side, there were 8 Jewish generals, 21 colonels, 9 lieutenant colonels, 40 majors, 205 captains, 325 lieutenants, 48 adjutants, and 25 surgeons. Six Jews received the Congressional Medal of Honor, the nation's highest honor. General Oliver O. Howard wrote that "there were no braver and patriotic men to be found than those of Hebrew descent."

In the South, Jews loyally supported the Confederate cause. T.N. Waul, who commanded a Southern Legion wrote:

A Jewish immigrant family living as best they could in a New York slum, c.1900.

An immigrant man, wearing a fur-trimmed coat and carrying suitcases, stands in front of a door, c.1900.

"Two of the infantry companies had a large number of Jews in their ranks . . . There were also a number of Jews scattered throughout the command in other companies. They were all volunteers; there was not a Jew conscript in the Legion. As soldiers they were brave, orderly, well-disciplined and in no respect inferior to the gallant body of which they formed a prominent part. Their behavior in camp, as in the field, was exemplary. . . . I never saw or heard of any Jew shrinking or failing to answer any call of duty or danger."

Anti-Semitism did, however, make an appearance, and Jews were accused of using the war to advance their businesses. For example, Jews were already engaged in the clothing industry, and their success in gaining business in the supply of army clothing became a cause of complaints on both sides of the lines.

In April 1862, citizens of Thomasville, Georgia, resolved to ban any new Jews from entering the town and to banish those already there because of the allegedly unpatriotic behavior of Jewish shopkeepers. Jews protested at the "wholesale slander, persecution and denunciation of a people" and claimed that the Thomasville incident had "no parallel except in the barbarities of the inquisition and the persecutions of the Dark Ages."

On the Union side, General Grant issued the infamous Order 11, which expelled Jews "as a class" from the area under his jurisdiction, which included Tennessee, Mississippi and Kentucky. He accused them of "violating every regulation of trade established by the Treasury Department." The thirty families which made up the Jewish community of Paducah, Kentucky, actually had to leave town within twenty-four hours. The Jewish community nationwide was outraged, and protested with passion and intensity.

However, when Grant ran for president on the Republican ticket in 1868, the Jewish community was divided in their response. Isaac M. Wise, a leading Rabbi and acknowledged Democrat was amongst many who urged Jews not to support Grant. He declared that "none in this nineteenth century in civilized countries has abused and outraged the Jew" worse than Grant. "If there are any among us who lick the feet that kick them about and like dogs, run after him who has whipped them . . . we hope their number is small." Others supported Grant, and after he was elected, the prominent New Yorker Simon Wolf acted as adviser to Grant, and persuaded him to mend his fences with the Jewish community by appointing Jews to public offices and to attend Jewish public events. For many, whatever their feelings about Grant's anti-Semitism, the overriding concern was not to provoke further anti-Semitism by allowing a "Jewish vote" to be identified.

So the Civil War experience of the Jews was one of simultaneous participation and rejection. They were proud of their participation, and they did not accept their rejection without vigorous protest. This experience brought to the fore a debate about the role of Jewish identity within the wider society. To some it seemed that the more they asserted their group identity and group interest, the greater the danger of provoking anti-Semitism. To others, the very nature of American liberty demanded that Jews be free to express themselves as Jews and to be protected by right from any resulting discrimination.

The German influence

It was in the 1840s that German Jews began to migrate to America in substantial numbers. The next forty years or so have often been called "the German period." Although Jews came from elsewhere in Europe during this period, the impact of the Jews of German origin was so powerful that a brief examination of their story will shed much light on the creation of the Jewish New World.

The journey from Germany to America was arduous and expensive. When the seventeen-year-old Joseph Seligman came from Bavaria, in 1837, he took eighteen days to reach the port of Bremen. From there he sailed steerage at a cost of forty dollars (which included only one meal a day), and took sixty-six days to cross the Atlantic. He made his way to Pennsylvania, where he worked for a year as an assistant in Asa Packer's store in Mauch Chunk. Then he resigned and traded on his own account as a local peddler.

By the spring of 1839 he had amassed $500 and was joined by his brothers William and James. Before long, Joseph and William opened a small store in Lancaster and James went to Alabama, where he did well enough to encourage four more of their brothers to join them. In 1841 the brothers opened a store in Selma, from where they continued to trade as peddlers. Within two years they had opened four stores—in Selma, Greensboro, Eutaw, and Clinton— each managed by one brother, who continued to trade as a pedler while leaving the store in the care of a manager. Within another few years, there was a Seligman import business in New York and a Seligman clothing business in St. Louis. By this time the last of the eight Seligman brothers had arrived from Bavaria and there was another branch of the new York business in Watertown. In 1850 two of the brothers set up business in San Francisco and a national net- work had been established. By the middle 1860s, the family fortune had probably reached over one and a quarter million dollars, augmented by trading and the flotation of Federal loans dur- ing the Civil War.

The speed of Jewish dispersion across the States can be seen from the fact that the num- ber of synagogues in America increased during the 1850s from thirty-seven to fifty. Jewish communities were now established in California, Illinois, Indiana, Maryland, New Jersey, Wisconsin, and the District of Columbia as well as the places mentioned earlier.

The Seligman pattern was mirrored by many other families, albeit usually on a smaller scale, and in this context, observers of American commercial life will note that the names of Straus, Lehman, Kuhn, Guggenheim, Loeb, and Goldman were prominent during this period. In each case, the first member of the family to arrive in America started his busi- ness life in the 1840s as a peddler in the South or elsewhere away from New York. It was in the 1860s that these names started to make a special mark in the banking and financial world of New York.

Marcus Goldman, who ultimately started Goldman, Sachs, & Co., started as a peddler in Philadelphia in 1848. After two years he opened a men's clothing store. Meyer Guggenheim also arrived in 1848, and peddled domestic bits and pieces in the mining areas of Pennsylvania before opening a wholesale business selling household goods in Philadelphia.

Other German-Jewish financial businesses were established in New York by later arrivals, who arrived with some qualifications in the financial sector.

Many of the major institutions of American Jewry were established or profoundly influenced by these German families, including Reform Judaism, B'nai Brith, the American Jewish Committee, the National Council of Jewish Women, and Hebrew Union College among many others. Although their numbers were small by comparison with the great influx which was to follow at the end of the nineteenth century and the beginning of the twentieth, the frameworks which they established were deeply influential on all that followed.

Western Europe—the Age of Enlightenment

The birth of the United States of America was paralleled by exciting developments in Europe. The ideas of the Enlightenment were abroad, and democratic ideas provided an ideological backdrop for human progress on a broad front.

Emancipation first became a conceivable notion for the Jews. By 1870, with the estab- lishment of religious liberty in Germany, Austria, Hungary, Switzerland, Sweden, and Rome, it seemed that Jewish emancipation had become a reality in all of Western and Central Europe. These developments were followed by the flowering of a new and highly articulate develop- ment of anti-Semitism in Germany, which in 1881, saw an organization called the Anti-Semitic League presenting to the Chancellor Bismarck a petition containing over a quar- ter of a million signatures. It called for the disenfranchisement of the Jews and for the restriction of further immigration.

The new anti-Semitism soon spread to the Dual Monarchy of Austria-Hungary, where it was fanned by a ritual murder trial at Tisza-Eszlar in 1882 (to be followed, not long after, by similar charges at Xanten in the Rhineland and Konitz in West Prussia). Even France, the home of Emancipation, was not immune. In 1886, Edouard Drumont, published *La France Juive* (one of the most widely-circulated books of the century), which declared that every trou ble which had overtaken that country was due to Jewish machinations. In 1894, Alfred Dreyfus, a Jewish captain attached to the French General Staff, was falsely accused and subsequently convicted of passing military secrets to Germany. It was only in 1899, after a massive public campaign and a change of Government, that the Court of Appeal quashed the verdict. Proclaiming his innocence.

In Western Europe, the new anti-Semitism was a worrying force, but it was on the whole unsuccessful in influencing governments to act or to legislate. In Eastern Europe, the ideas of the Enlightenment had not taken root, and the picture was very different.

Eastern Europe—the pressure to assimilate

In the first nineteen centuries of Jewish Diaspora, no exile was harsher than that of the Jews who lived in the territories that came under Russian rule during the eighteenth century. These Jews were perhaps the most narrowly Jewish of all (or the most deeply pious, depending on one's perspective). By and large, they had only their Judaism to sustain their hopes for a better future. The rabbis formed an elite in this society, and from the earliest age, boys were taught that the study of Torah was the highest and best of human endeavors.

In 1791, a decree of Catherine II created the territories known as the Pale of Settlement, the twenty-five provinces of the Tsarist domain in which Jews were generally compelled to live. They were to be found in Poland, Lithuania, White Russia, Ukraine, Bessarabia, and Crimea. Permission to live outside the Pale was granted only to certain groups, such as members of the liberal professions, major entrepreneurs, skilled artisans and former army conscripts.

In 1827, Tsar Nicholas I, implementing a plan to force Jewish children into Christianity, issued an edict forcing Jews into military service for twenty-five years, beginning at the age of eighteen. Children were taken at the age of twelve to be "prepared" for their service. They were placed in special army units, and their lives became a hell on earth. There was no chance of relief or promotion, except by conversion. Many were lost to their Judaism and to their families. Quotas for military recruitment were imposed on the Jewish communities, and to meet the quotas each community had to send what were known as chappers (grabbers) on to the streets to kidnap the children for their service.

Between the 1820s and the 1860s over 600 anti-Jewish decrees were enacted. Hebrew and Yiddish books were censored, and Jewish children were forced into state schools. This program had some success. By the 1870s, large numbers of Russian Jews had acquired a secular education and were ready to continue their studies at the universities and to train for the professions.

Forced military recruitment of Jews lapsed in the 1850s, and after the accession of Tsar Alexander II the regime showed greater tolerance. This did not solve the economic problems in the Pale of Settlement, where the Jewish population continued to rise, enhancing poverty and misery. On the other hand, it did become easier for businessmen and professionals to move to St. Petersburg and Moscow, and by 1880 perhaps ten percent of the Jews were living outside the Pale of Settlement. However, all this poverty and oppression was as nothing compared to the hell which was let loose after the assassination of the Tsar on March 13, 1881, by a group of anarchist revolutionaries—among whom was a Jewish woman.

The age of the pogrom

Six weeks after the death of the Tsar, a riot broke out in a tavern at Elisavetgrad, in the locality of Kherson. The Jews were being blamed for the assassination. For two days, deeds of incredible barbarity were perpetrated under the eyes of local officials, and in some cases even with the cooperation of local soldiers. Five hundred houses and one hundred shops were demolished. Synagogues were destroyed. There was looting, rape, and murder. In May there were two similar major pogroms in Kiev and in Odessa. By the end of the year over 150 similar incidents had taken place all over Southern Russia. In December a series of outbreaks occurred in Warsaw, the capital of Poland, which continued through the first half of 1882 and which was followed by a wave of burnings of Jewish property.

It was said that the new Tsar's principal adviser believed in solving the Jewish problem by securing the conversion of one third, the emigration of another, and the extermination of the remainder. The word *pogrom* (the Russian term for "devastation") entered into every European language, as a synonym for an unprovoked attack upon a defenceless minority.

Instead of taking steps to punish the culprits, the government increased the repression. In May 1882 the infamous "May Laws" were enacted. Jews were to be excluded from all rural areas, even in the Pale of Settlement, outside Poland proper. Towns of as many as 10,000 inhabitants were classed as villages, and their Jewish population expelled.

On the one hand, the regime fiercely resented the refusal of the Jews to assimilate. On the other hand, they imposed fresh restrictions on even those who might have been willing to assimilate. Jews were excluded from the practice of law. The number of students admitted to the secondary schools and Universities was strictly limited. Jewish technical schools were closed. In 1891, thousands of Jews were deported in mid-winter from Moscow and other cities, and in 1898, 7,000 were banished from the Kiev area. Jewish women were allowed to live in the great cities, and to enjoy the benefits of a University education, but only if they acquired the "yellow ticket" of a prostitute.

The Russian example was followed (albeit less brutally) in Romania, where by the middle of the nineteenth century, when Romania attained her independence, there were some two hundred thousand Jews, generally living similar lives to their Russian co-religionists. Although the Treaty of Berlin had made religious toleration a condition for the granting of Romanian independence, this turned out to be meaningless for the Jews. They were declared to be aliens, and therefore not entitled to the rights of citizens. They were subjected to special legislation, deprived of equality of opportunity, and sometimes subjected to physical violence. In 1895 an Anti-Semitic League was organized with the object of making their position intolerable. In Galicia (Austrian Poland) things were little better.

The Russian Liberal movement of 1905 forced a new constitution upon the Tsar, and the Jews gained the franchise. However, all the other discrimination against them continued.

Hester Street, c.1890, in New York's Lower East Side.

A scene in the ghetto, Hester Street, c.1902.

On Easter Sunday 1903 there was a fresh pogrom at Kishinev. It lasted for three days, and forty-seven Jews were killed. Other pogroms followed, and over the next four years, massacres took place in no less than 284 Russian towns, with the total number of casualties estimated at fifty thousand. In the summer of 1910, 1,200 Jewish families were expelled from Kiev on the grounds that they had no legal right of residence.

In 1912–13 the local authority in Kiev charged a young Jew by the name of Mendel Beilis with the gory death of a twelve-year-old boy, whose body had been found in a cave on the outskirts of the city. The allegation was that the crime had been committed for ritual purposes. The prosecutor called "expert" witnesses who would make the case for ritual murder. Judaism and the Jews were to be tried for the alleged crime of ritual barbarism. Beilis spent two years in jail before the flimsiness of the evidence led to his acquittal.

Escape from misery

Over half of the Jewish population of the world was subjected to these miseries. Some prayed daily for the coming of the Messiah. Others were attracted by Marxism or anarchism. Many others became devoted to the idea of a return to the land of Israel and joined the Zionist movement. But for most, the best hope lay in flight. With every fresh pogrom, a new wave of refugees made its way to the frontiers. Between 1881 and the outbreak of World War I in 1914, the exodus continued. Before the end of the century, almost a million Jews in Eastern Europe had left their homes. By 1914 the number had more than doubled. This migration was the biggest and the most important in Jewish history.

The refugees were not welcome in the neighboring countries, although some stayed wherever they arrived, and many settled in Britain. But for most of them there was a country across the ocean whose Declaration of Independence was permeated with the ideals of liberty and equality, which had so eluded them and their parents in Eastern Europe. America became the "*goldener medineh*," the golden state.

The excitement and hope raised by the dream of America was captured by Mary Antin, who came to the United States in 1891 and published her memoirs in 1912. She recalls that back home:

> "America had been in everybody's mouth. Businessmen talked of it over their accounts; the market women made up their quarrels that they might discuss it from stall to stall; people who had relatives in the famous land went around reading their letters for the enlightenment of less fortunate folk. Children played at emigrating; old folks shook sage heads over the evening fire, and prophesied no good for those who braved the terrors of the sea and the foreign goal beyond it; all talked of it, but scarcely anyone knew one fact about this magic land."

From one world to another

The first major exodus began in 1881, when thousands of refugees fled from the first wave of pogroms. Raising the money for the transatlantic crossing was a burdensome challenge. Coping with the practicalities of the journey itself required a desperate kind of heroism. Many did not make it. Taking the decision to leave would have been difficult enough, but the preparations for travel (let alone the journey itself) must have called for enormous tenacity, creativity, and strength of character. These were people whose whole existence had been one of restriction, geographical, political, and cultural. How did you get from Russia, Romania, or Galicia to the other side of the Atlantic?

You could buy a steamship ticket from a Dutch or German port in 1903 for about thirty-five dollars. This must have been in itself a fortune. But how did you get to Hamburg or to Amsterdam from Kiev or Riga? From Russia the usual routes involved an illegal border crossing followed by a train journey to Berlin or Vienna. One traveler's account of his crossing of the Austrian border in 1882 captures some of the flavor of the journey:

> "We were to leave the train at Dubno where we were to take a wagon through the region around Radzivil on our way to the Austrian border. That would be our last city in Russia; across the border was Brody.
>
> "In the evening we followed two young Ukrainian peasants to a small, freshly plastered hut. One of the peasants was tall and barefooted and carried a small cask at his side. In Austria, there was no tax on brandy, so he smuggled it into Russia; on his return trip, he carried tobacco, more expensive in Austria, out of Russia.
>
> "We waited a long time in the hut before realizing we were being held for more money. Having paid, we moved on. We made a strange group going across fields and meadows in the night, halted suddenly every few minutes by the tall peasant holding up his finger and pausing to listen for God-knows what disaster. We stumbled on endlessly. It seemed as if the border were miles away. Then the peasant straightened up and announced we were already well inside Austria."

Getting a passport was a matter of confronting the bureaucracy and the greed of officials who found ways to extract payments from their victims for the most elementary of tasks. The official price of a passport was about ten dollars, but the actual cost was usually much higher. Travel agents provided all sorts of help, some real, some fraudulent. They too required extra fees for their help, and their help often never materialized. Many people sold everything they had, and if they made it at all, they arrived penniless at the other side.

The Jewish community center in Washington, as seen from across the street, c.1920.

The Jews of Western Europe were not unsympathetic to the plight of the refugees, but they were terrified of the effect on their own communities of the arrival of vast numbers of foreign Jews. Eventually they decided that to help the refugees to pass through was the best course of action, and the German community in particular set up information and aid services in Berlin and in the port of Bremen. When their efforts worked out, things could be heart-warming. One group of emigrants before the turn of the century was welcomed in Breslau (in Silesia) "as though for a wedding feast. Rich ladies and gentlemen acted as waiters; even Jewish military officers waited on us. Physicians were also on hand . . . and it goes without saying that they were kept very busy, for is there a time when a Jew is not in need of a doctor?"

However, some measure of the problems that such agencies faced can be gauged from the fact that between 1882 and 1902 the number of emigrants departing from Bremen alone (Jewish and non-Jewish) was over two million.

Medical checks became a regular feature of the procedure at the port of embarkation. Everyone was aware that if you failed the same checks at the American end of the journey, you would in any case be sent back, and the shippers did not want to have to bear the cost of the return journey.

It must be remembered that the Jews probably made up less than ten percent of the emigrants from Europe during this period. The shipping companies equipped themselves for this travel boom by creating a rudimentary style of accommodation known as steerage. This usually involved the fitting of basic bunks into cargo ships for their return journeys westward. Sanitary facilities were less than basic, and supplies of drinking water were limited for a journey that could take between fifteen and twenty-one days.

An Iowa clergyman, Edward Steiner, summed it up:

> "The steerage never changes, neither its location nor its furnishings. It lies over the stirring screws, sleeps to the staccato of trembling steel railings and hawsers. Narrow, steep and slippery stairways lead to it.
>
> "Crowds everywhere, ill smelling bunks, uninviting washrooms—this is steerage. The odors of scattered orange peelings, tobacco, garlic, and disinfectants meeting but not blending. No lounge or chairs for comfort, and a continual Babel of tongues—this is steerage."

The U.S. Immigration Commission tried to impose reforms to improve conditions for the travelers, but enforcement was largely ineffective.

By the turn of the century the Jewish organizations *en route* had acquired some expertise, accommodation on board ship was somewhat improved, and the length of the journey was reduced to between six and ten days. But the ordeal must have remained painful and bewildering.

The Jewish Temple, Cleveland, Ohio, c.1900.

Arrival—the official reception

In spite of all these hardships the numbers crossing the Atlantic in search of a new life continued to rise and the arrival was described by many as "like arriving in heaven." The vast majority of those arriving went through the facilities that had been created at Ellis Island in Upper New York Bay near the New Jersey shore. The Ellis Island complex, built at a cost of $500,000, opened for business on New Year's Day in 1882. Half-a-million immigrants were expected that year.

Ellis Island opened during a period when American opinion on immigration was divided. Strong forces advocated limiting the numbers and kinds of people allowed into the country, and while they did not succeed in ending the nation's official "Open Door" policy until the 1920s, they did manage to impose increasingly severe practical restrictions.

One of the most far-reaching changes was the decision to make shipping companies responsible for inspecting immigrants before bringing them to America and requiring them to pay return passage for any passengers rejected. The ship owners had to prepare information sheets on each passenger—no more than thirty to a sheet—that could be cross-checked when the immigrants were examined at Ellis Island. The list had to include name, age, sex, marital status, occupation, nationality, last residence, destination, whether the immigrant could read and write and a host of other matters.

Five years after it was opened, the Ellis Island complex was destroyed by fire. It took three years to be rebuilt at a cost of $1.5 million. The autobiography of the Commissioner of the Bureau of Immigration appointed after the fire (a former labor leader named Terence Powderly) records the problems he encountered. Immigrants were overcharged for food and cheated in money exchanges. Their relatives were required to pay a fee to get into Ellis Island to greet them. Immigrants who planned to travel to other cities were given false information about the distances involved and overcharged for the tickets. As a result of what he discovered, eleven Ellis Island employees were fired.

Newspapers at the time were full of stories about Ellis Island, and in the summer of 1901, it was discovered that immigration inspectors had been selling forged citizenship papers to immigrants, allowing them to bypass Ellis Island altogether.

When Theodore Roosevelt became president in September 1901, he took immediate steps to put matters right. He fired managerial staff and appointed William Williams, a wealthy Wall Street lawyer, to be commissioner of Ellis Island. Williams moved swiftly and effectively. He posted a notice around the island declaring that immigrants would be treated with kindness and consideration. A number of employees caught cheating immigrants were fired. Other aspects of the administration were cleaned up, and Ellis Island was managed with greater integrity in the coming years.

For all his good points, Williams was not a liberal on immigration policy, and he was critical of the qualities of many of the new immigrants who, in his opinion, did not match up to the standards of the earlier English and German immigrants. In 1909 he decreed unilaterally that any immigrant who did not have $25 would not be allowed entry. He sent back many immigrants who would probably have been allowed in under earlier commissioners. When he retired, the headline of the Yiddish newspaper *Forward* read "The Haman of Ellis Island Resigns."

Ellis Island remained, both during and after Williams, a place of delays, frightening medical examinations, and confusing interviews.

Fiorello LaGuardia, later to serve three terms as Mayor of New York City beginning in 1933, worked as an interpreter at Ellis Island in 1907. He wrote that he saw many cases in which immigrants appeared to be detained unfairly, especially among those classified as mentally deficient. He felt that more than half of those deported for mental problems were wrongly diagnosed, primarily because of a communication failure between doctor and aspiring immigrant. After their long journey, the immigrants were often bewildered, and the trauma of the inspection procedure made things worse. Despite the presence of interpreters, misunderstandings often happened.

A Jewish market on the East Side, New York, c.1890.

Two orthodox Jewish men who emigrated to New York City in the early twentieth century.

In 1907, the peak year of immigration, the inspectors sent 13,064 people back out of 1,285,349 immigrants. The main reasons given were disease or because the inspectors had decided that they were likely to become a charge on the public purse. How many of these decisions arose from poor communications, nobody will ever know.

Arrival—one community response

Helen Barth, a worker for the Hebrew Immigrant Aid Society (HIAS), described how many people left their homes with one name and arrived in America with another:

> "They spoke very badly, were very nervous. The inspector would say, 'Where do you come from?' And they would say, 'Berlin.' The inspector would put the name down 'Berliner.' The name was not Berliner. That's no name.
>
> "All the 'witzs' and 'skis' got their names from their fathers. For example, Myerson is the son of Myer. We knew that and changed the names here because they were spelled so badly. For instance, a Polish name, would be Skyzertski, and they didn't even know how to spell it, so it would be changed to Sanda. It was much easier that way.
>
> "Then there were names like 'Vladimir.' That would be Walter in American, or Willie, some name like that. Vladimir was strictly a Russian name, you know, and they often were very anxious to Americanize quickly.
>
> "And sometimes the children and parents would use first names, and they would call the father 'Adam,' and it became 'Mr. Adam,' and that was the way they went through."

The work which the HIAS was doing became crucial in the lives of many immigrants. On the simplest level, immigrants had no idea how to answer some of the questions that were routinely put to all arrivals at Ellis Island. These were life and death decisions. And yet the average immigrant simply did not know whether to be honest or to lie, whether to admit to having money or not, whether to say that they had a job waiting for them or not, whether to offer a bribe or not. The crude realities of life where they came from gave them one set of answers, but how did that script play in the "land of the free"? A Yiddish paper of the time wrote:

> "Our Jews love to get tangled up with dishonest answers, so that the officials have no choice but to send them to the detention area. A Jew who had money in his pocket decided to lie and said he didn't have a penny . . . A woman with four children and pregnant with a fifth, said her husband had been in America fourteen years . . . The HIAS man learned that her husband had recently arrived, but she thought fourteen years would make a better impression. The officials are sympathetic. They know the Jewish immigrants get 'confused,' and they tell them to sit down and 'remember.' Then they let them in."

Jewish men and women wait for packages of matzo bread and flowers to be delivered in New York City in April 1908.

Especially bewildering to the immigrant was the idea that if you did have a job waiting for you, you were liable to deportation, because the law outlawed the importation of contract labour. The HIAS worker had to advise correctly, and at the same time to gain the trust of the frightened and suspicious new arrival.

Women needed special care, especially if they were accompanied. One such woman was met by her fiancé, who had arrived six months earlier. He was dressed to impress, American-style, complete with Derby hat. The new arrival was so unimpressed that she did not even recognize the man that she had said goodbye to so lovingly only six months earlier. Excited officials were convinced that they had caught one of the many white slave traders who were known to hang around Ellis Island. When the young man removed his Derby, his sweetheart did, at last, recognize him. It was too late. The couple had to go through a legal marriage ceremony at Ellis Island before the officials would release her.

There were HIAS representatives at Ellis Island and at Boston, Philadelphia, and Baltimore. They advised and mediated in all sorts of cases. Some new arrivals were detained for as long as two weeks.

During the peak years of 1904 to 1907, the HIAS representative at Ellis Island was Alexander Harkavy, a scholarly man famous in the world of Jewish letters as the compiler of a Yiddish-English dictionary. On a busy day, there might be over 2,000 immigrants in the main

An elderly Polish Jew telling stories to young Jewish boys before boarding the Warszawa. They were on their way to South America via London in July 1937.

Two Russian Jewish immigrants sitting on a park bench in New York City in January 1910.

detention hall at Ellis Island. Just working out who in the hall most needed his help must have been a daunting task, let alone the challenge of advising and representing those who did need him.

Historian Mark Wischnitzer describes one Harkavy intervention, this time on behalf of a group of fifty-four non-Jewish Russian peasants who arrived in 1905:

> "Having no relatives in the U.S. to act as guarantors, and lacking the $25 required in lieu of a guarantee, the men in the group were detained for deportation. Harkavy remonstrated with Commissioner Williams, pointing out that the Russians were hale and hearty farmers who were not likely to become public charges. When he was unsuccessful in his representations, Harkavy signed a guarantee for the men, who were then found lodgings at HIAS expense. . . . All of the men obtained work after a while, with the exception of one hospitalized in Philadelphia (HIAS met the bill of about $100)."

The Russian government heard of this and offered HIAS an annual subsidy of six thousand rubles to give regular assistance to Russian subjects. The Board of HIAS felt obliged to turn the offer down, on the official grounds that HIAS did not wish to limit its independence by accepting government support. They also had in mind that since immigrants often left Russia illegally, there was a danger that the Russian government might try to get information about them from the Society. Probably their main concern was that Jewish public opinion would profoundly dislike the idea of taking money from the Tsar.

Irving Howe, historian and prominent New York intellectual, describes another instance of HIAS intervention. In 1914 the wife and four children of one Joseph Aronoff followed him to the United States. When they arrived at Baltimore, the decision was taken to return them to Europe because two of the children had contracted a form of ringworm that could take an indefinite period to cure. Joseph had arrived a year earlier. He was earning $10-12 a week. HIAS warded off official attempts to declare the children incurable and thereby deportable. They followed up the case for two years, arranging for prolonged and difficult medical treatment. When the family was clearly unable to pay the hospital bills, HIAS found a private benefactor to cover part of the cost. Eventually, the children were cured and remained in America.

The response of the Jewish community

HIAS was one of many organizations that started up in response to the arrival of the East European immigrants, and was formed in 1909 by the merger of two older organizations. It origins were in a meeting called in an East Side store in 1892 by a group of East European immigrants who wanted to arrange Jewish burial for Jews who died on Ellis Island. From these humble beginnings it grew to become an organization at whose East Broadway information bureau during 1912 there were more than 150,000 callers. In the same year it provided actual shelter to over 3,000 people, naturalisation aid meetings for almost 12,000 people, and Sabbath afternoon classes for 4,000 children.

Its origins were in the East European immigrant community itself, and it remained rooted in that community despite its dramatic growth. From its success it gained public and official respect, as a result of which it learned to function successfully as a pressure group within a network of other Jewish welfare and pressure groups. When in 1911 a committee of the New York State Legislature proposed to deport immigrants deemed to be suffering from mental disorder, HIAS and others persuaded them to drop the idea. In 1913 HIAS was among those who fought successfully against a proposal to establish a literacy test for immigrants.

For a long time, however, the public voice of the Jewish community was articulated through the persons and organizations of the German-Jewish community. They were, after all, well-established before the East European influx, with a well-organized network of representative and welfare organizations, and many of its leading members were well-known and respected in the wider American community.

But the German community was ambivalent towards the East European immigration. Even before 1881, the United Hebrew Charities of New York and the newspaper *American Hebrew* were advocating the introduction of restrictive immigration laws.

As the influx grew, the Jewish Press frequently reported that immigration was not popular in the community. The Union of American Hebrew Congregations, which represented Reform Judaism, declared that it could no longer accept responsibility for material aid for the immigrants, motivated apparently by a fear that Western European Jewry was "dumping" the refugees on America.

When 415 Russian Jewish refugees arrived in Boston in June 1882, the local Jews promptly shipped them back to New York. In New York the Russian Emigrant Relief Fund, wrote to a European Jewish charity: "Please bear constantly in mind that the position of the Jews is not such that they can afford to run any risk of incurring the ill-feeling of their fellow citizens."

There was certainly some fear among the German community about the financial burden that the immigrants represented. However, when a representative of the United Hebrew Charities of Rochester warned that the "enviable reputation" German Jews had earned in the United States was being "undermined by the influx of thousands who are not ripe for the enjoyment of liberty," he was expressing something deeper than mere economic concerns.

Rabbi Jacob Voorsanger of San Francisco was not alone in thinking that Jewish immigration should be stopped completely and that "not a single sensation of sympathy nor any sentiment of affection generated by kinship or religious affiliation should prevent us from appreciating the justice of this ultimate procedure."

Financially, German Jews were generous toward their Eastern co-religionists, but socially they were embarrassed by them. One of the elite German Jewish social clubs had an unofficial slogan, which was "More polish and less Polish." There was much distressed talk of the criminal activities among the immigrants, of political radicalism, of religious Orthodoxy, and of their "strange ways and speech."

Interior view of the Jacob Birder home, Park River, North Dakota, in 1899.

A Jewish store in Colchester, Connecticut

photographed by Jack Delano, November 1940.

There was a real fear that these factors would stimulate the anti-Semitism that kept bubbling to the surface in the wider community. The 1890s in particular were a period of economic uncertainty, with many business failures and high unemployment. Politicians and journalists frequently resorted to anti-Semitic allusions, and there was real social discrimination against even the most assimilated of the German community.

"If there should grow up in our midst a class of people abnormal and objectionable to our fellow citizens," declared the Union of American Hebrew Congregations, "all of us will suffer. The question is largely one of self-preservation."

Despite all these feelings, there was a great deal of generous philanthropic activity. In 1895, in the midst of a depression, the budget of the United Hebrew Charities of New York, was $116,000. One important group was the National Council of Jewish Women, which met immigrant girls at the New York port, provided them with addresses where they could apply in case of need, offered them advice, and helped them to find accommodation. Other projects such as the Clara de Hirsch Home for immigrant girls, the Hebrew Technical Institute for Boys, the "model" tenement built by Isaac Seligman (whose family history we touched on earlier) and Felix Adler's pioneering kindergarten (among many others) all made a real difference to the lives of the immigrants.

Lobbying for justice

It would be very unfair, however, to characterize the German community as just salving their conscience by helping out financially. Once the pogroms of 1881 had occurred, there were key members of the German community who did not waver in their political efforts to keep the gates open to immigrants. By 1905 or thereabouts the horrors of the pogroms had touched the hearts of virtually all in the community. One member of the Goldman banking family wrote frankly in a letter that although he had found "much indifference and unwarranted dislike" among his own community towards the new immigrants, he had not met a single one who was prepared to close the ports to them.

Their political work was extremely effective. It demanded both skill and persistence. From the early eighties to the start of World War I, there was a constant struggle between those who wanted to restrict immigration and those who wanted to keep the gates open.

The restrictionists were powerful. Here is a summary of what they achieved in just over two decades:

1882   an Act to exclude "lunatics, idiots, any person unable to take care of himself or herself without becoming a public charge."

1885   an Act to outlaw the hiring of cheap labour from abroad.

1891   an Act to exclude "paupers, polygamists, persons suffering from a loathsome or dangerous contagious disease, and persons whose tickets had been paid for by someone else, unless it was shown that they were not otherwise objectionable."

1891   an Act empowering the authorities to deport those who had become a charge on the public purse, forbidding advertising which might encourage immigration, and centralising in the Federal government all powers in respect of the inspection of immigrants.

1903   an Act to exclude "believers in anarchistic principles and all persons who are of a low moral tendency or of unsavory reputation."

At the same time, the campaign to impose a literacy test on immigrants never relented. Three presidents, Cleveland, Taft, and Wilson had to veto such laws after they had passed through Congress.

Without lobbying from the German-Jewish community, the vetoes would never have happened. Their lobbying style was deliberately quiet. The American Jewish Committee, founded in 1906 to "prevent the infraction of the civil and religious rights of Jews in any part of the world" was led for many years by Louis Marshall, widely regarded as a brilliant campaigner. 1905 he explained his approach to the issue of the moment: "I consider a public discussion of the (immigration) question at this time by any Jewish organization, an extremely unfortunate step. It serves to attract the attention of Congress and of the various labor unions, to the fact that we expect a large influx of Jewish immigrants from Russia. It is a subject which can only be handled with the greatest delicacy."

To the immigrants themselves, especially the many socialists among them, Marshall's attitude was at best incomprehensible, at worst contemptible. They favored greater stridency, with the use of public demonstrations and mass protest, and they did not trust what was being said behind closed doors and out of their earshot. Even if they trusted the integrity of leaders such as Louis Marshall, they could not put out of their minds the uncomfortable suspicion that to Marshall and his friends, the real reason for the soft tactics was that they were embarrassed to be reminded that the newcomers were their kinsfolk.

Education or transformation?

Another area of philanthropy for the German community towards the new arrivals was in the field of education. In this field as in the field of politics, the two communities viewed each other from starkly different cultural starting points.

Perhaps the biggest single project in this field was the Educational Alliance. Housed in a five-floor building on East Broadway and headed up by business leaders like Isidor Straus of Macy's department store and Jacob Schiff of the investment house Kuhn Loeb, it was intended by its founders to be a "center of sweetness and light, an oasis in the desert of degradation."

The project has been described as "a curious mixture of night school, settlement house, daycare center, gymnasium, and public forum". The intentions of its leader were undoubtedly the betterment of the lot of their fellow-Jews. The problem was that the instrument for such betterment was seen to be something that was known as "Americanization."

One of the beneficiaries of this process described it like this: "We were 'Americanized' about as gently as horses are broken in. In the whole crude process, we sensed a disrespect for the alien traditions in our homes." If that judgment sounds unbalanced, the editorial views of the weekly journal of the German community, the *Jewish Messenger*, will show that it is well founded. It declared that the newcomers "must be Americanized in spite of themselves, in the mode prescribed by their friends and benefactors," and described them as "slovenly in dress, loud in manners, and vulgar in discourse."

Fortunately, a new director was appointed in 1898, David Blaustein, who was both Harvard-educated and East European in origin. Although as a result the pressures to Americanize were softened somewhat, a protest meeting was called in 1903 to protest at the Americanization program of the Center. It attracted no fewer than 2,000 people.

It is fair to say that although this turnout demonstrates the anger of the immigrant community, it also reflects the importance of the services that the Center was providing. Here is just a small selection of the social, cultural, and educational activities presented at the Center: vocational training for young people, healthy lunches, free medical examinations, free vacations in summer camps, courses in English and English literature, in religion, Zionism, American history, ancient history, hygiene, gymnastics, music and art, as well as flag-waving exercises on the national holidays. In many ways it matched its founders' ambitious dreams.

It is also fair to say that what the host Jewish community was attempting to do was not an exclusive invention of a group of German-Jewish snobs. To a large degree it reflected a national consensus. The Roman Catholic Church was trying to do much the same thing with its Irish, Italian, and Polish immigrants. The whole project was summed up in popular talk by the notion of America as "the melting pot." President Woodrow Wyatt no doubt thought that he was merely stating the obvious when he said in 1915 that "America does not consist of groups. A man in America who thinks of himself as belonging to a particular national group in America has not yet become an American."

Louis Marshall himself admitted in a letter to a friend that the German Jews had "held themselves aloof . . . bringing gifts to people who did not seek (them) . . . The work was done in such a manner as not only to give offense, but to arouse suspicion of the motives." This admission is a token of the intelligence and sensitivity of the German leadership as they

Jewish farmers and their families, Hightstown cooperative farm, New Jersey photographed by Dorothea Lange in June 1936.

Carpenter on the Hightstown project

photographed by Dorothea Lange in June 1936.

struggled to fulfil their responsibilities as they saw them. In due course, the Educational Alliance lifted its earlier ban on the use of the Yiddish language in the Center and offered many activities conducted in Yiddish, which proved to be a popular move.

Dispersal

The other major way in which the German community tried to solve the perceived problem was to disperse the population across the country. Like the other newcomers between 1880 and 1920, East European Jews huddled together in urban ghettos, principally New York's Lower East Side, but also Chicago's West Side, Boston's North End, and South Philadelphia. Of over one million Jews who arrived in New York between 1881 and 1911, more than seventy-three percent remained there.

Even before the mass influx, as early as 1869, Rabbi Bernard Felsenthal of Chicago had proposed that Russian and Polish Jews be settled in Kansas, Iowa, and Nebraska. Simon Wolf, later to become President of Bnai Brith, added the Shenandoah Valley and Washington Territory, which was administered by Edward S. Solomon, a fellow German Jew.

By 1882, 2,000 immigrants had been sent to nearly 170 different locations all over the country. In 1890 the Jewish Alliance of America was created to help the process of dispersal.

In 1900, the Baron de Hirsch Fund brought the Jewish Colonisation Association's ideas to America from Europe, with the specific social engineering aim of creating a class of Jewish farmers. They established the Jewish Agricultural and Industrial Aid Society, which helped finance more than 160 agricultural settlements. In 1901, the society also created the Industrial Removal Office, with the aim of relocating individual Jews across the country. It operated mainly through local voluntary committees, often linked with Bnai Brith Lodges. They usually established monthly target figures for the absorption of immigrants into their areas, and liaised with the Industrial Removal Office itself with information about specific job vacancies. By 1917, over 75,000 people had been dispersed to 1,670 different communities in every one of the forty-eight states as well as in Canada.

But these 75,000 were only six percent of the Jewish newcomers to America. For the overwhelming majority of the immigrants, dispersal was an adventure too far. In the ghettos they had synagogues, kosher meat, cultural networks, friends and family. Very few of the new-comers were prepared to add a new journey into the unknown to the traumas they had already suffered. Nevertheless, the German leadership had a dream. Jacob Schiff spoke of taking every one of "our persecuted people out of Russia" and relocating them in America. In his eyes this could not be done without substantial dispersal over the whole of the United States.

In 1906, working with Oscar Straus, Secretary for Commerce and Labor (and a member of the Macy department store family) he secured the passage of a bill to establish an entry station for immigrants at Galveston, Texas. The plan was that immigrants should be sent straight to Galveston from Europe by European Jewish organizations. From Galveston, their fate would be in the hands of the Industrial Removal Office. Schiff made a personal pledge of half a million dollars to the project. However, by 1914, the project had only processed 10,000 immigrants.

Hopes of creating a class of Jewish farmers also failed to make any substantial numerical progress. At the peak in 1909, there were about 15,000 people in the Jewish farming communities, less than one percent of the Jewish population. Although some of the Baron de Hirsch Fund projects lasted for a few decades, the majority failed sooner. There were other groups of immigrants who came with a specifically socialist agricultural dream, such as the *Am Olam* ("people of the world") group. In 1882 they settled at Sicily Island, Louisiana. After they suffered a flood disaster there, they set up two colonies in South Dakota, but both of these collapsed within a few years. Other similar projects fared no better.

What we have seen so far have been some of the communal efforts to greet the massive wave of new arrivals. We shall now turn to look at how the immigrants themselves created their new lives, and how they faced up to the realities of the *goldener medineh*.

From East European ghettos to New World slums

Almost all East European Jewish immigrants who arrived in New York after 1880 began their stay in the Lower East Side. In 1892, seventy-five percent of the city's Jews lived there. Although this percentage declined over time, the absolute numbers increased steadily. In 1910 the number had risen to 542,000, and it was said that nowhere else in the world were so many crowded together in one square mile. David Blaustein surveyed the area in 1903 and reported in an address:

> "Ladies and gentlemen, I took a census of the Lower East Side which takes in about 32 streets south of Houston Street and east of the Bowery . . . I will simply give you an idea of what is to be found in this square mile. There are 5,000 tenements, with 64,268 families. Of these 6,499 persons have 84 different occupations . . . There are in this particular section of this city as many as 306 synagogues. There are 22 churches and a Mission House, which are closed all the time. On May 13, 1903, there were 72 pleasure places, clubs of the people, literary and social."

Jewish farmer at Hightstown photographed by Dorothea Lange in June 1936.

In the standard tenement buildings of the late nineteenth century, there would be four apartments to a floor. In each apartment there would only be one room that received natural light. Most families took in boarders. Water, light and air were all in short supply and of poor quality. Less than one in five of the people of Manhattan lived in the Lower East Side, but over one in three of the fatal deaths by fire occurred there. If housing conditions were all that mattered, many of the immigrants might have wondered what they had gained from their long journey. But for a community that prided itself on the quality of its family life, however, the social problem that hurt most was the rate of family breakdown. Often the husband had arrived months or years before the rest of his family. By the time they were reunited, they had often grown apart. Sometimes the man had already formed a relationship with a local woman, and the arrival of his "foreign" family did not break the bonds of the new relationship. In other cases, men became weighed down by the burden of feeding and clothing their families and just ran away from those responsibilities.

By 1911 Jewish charities were spending so much money on family support for deserted families that they found it necessary to set up a National Desertion Bureau to trace and charge deserting husbands. Some of the children of these families ended up in municipal institutions. Even in families which had remained physically united, the stresses of poverty and relocation often made the home a very unhappy place in which to grow up. In these circumstances, some children became criminals, either in childhood or when they became adults.

In 1908, New York City Police Commissioner Theodore A. Bingham claimed that Jews made up fifty percent of the city's criminals. Although he was forced to withdraw the claim, there was a real crime problem in the Jewish ghettos.

At first the official response of the Jewish community was defensive, often concentrating on showing that the level of crime in their community was proportionately lower than in other slum communities. But within the community itself there was concern about the activities of a number of prominent criminals. There were Jewish figures who operated prominently as brothel-keepers, fences, arsonists, and in leading positions within the gambling fraternity. The madams and pimps even established their own traditional mutual aid society, called the Independent Benevolent Association.

Some of the criminal statistics produced to condemn the community were exaggerated by the inclusion of barely criminal offences. Kosher animal slaughterers could hardly avoid breaking some regulation or other. Orthodox Jews who obtained rabbinical divorces (but not civil ones) did not intend to offend against the criminal law. People brought up under the shadow of the tsarist regime had a suspicion of police which often meant that they instinctively lied to the police even when they had nothing to hide. Most Jewish crime was petty, and little of it was violent. But some Jews rode to the top in this field as in many others, and Arnold Rothstein, who was a major figure in the gambling world, was immortalized by F. Scott Fitzgerald in *The Great Gatsby* as Meyer Wolfsheim, the man who fixed the World Series.

The Jewish home in the ghetto

There were, of course, many faces to ghetto life. The sculpture Jacob Epstein, one of the best known former students of the art classes at the Educational Alliance, provided a number of glimpses in his memoirs:

> "Saturday in the synagogue was a place of ennui for me, and the wailing prayers would get on my nerves; my one desire would be to make excuses to get away . . . The picturesque prayer shawls with the strange faces underneath held my attention only for a short while, then the tedium of the interminable services would drown every other emotion . . . . The earnestness and simplicity of the old Polish-Jewish manner of living has much beauty in it, and an artist could make it the theme of very fine works. This life is fast disappearing on contact with American habits, and it is a pity that there is no Rembrandt of today to draw his inspiration from it before it is too late."

The "old manner of living" often centered on eating; the rules about Kosher and non-kosher food, the traditional East European dishes, the family meals on Sabbath and festivals.

Out in the street, many gave up the stricter traditional ways very quickly. But it was in the home that the traditions hung on. At the center of it all was the Jewish mother and house-wife. One autobiographer, summed it up: "The kitchen gave a special character to our lives: my mother's character. All my memories of that kitchen are dominated by the nearness of my mother sitting all day long at her sewing machine . . . The kitchen was her life. Year by year, as I began to take in her fantastic capacity for labor and her anxious zeal, I realized it was our-selves she kept stitching together." It was their instinct for the old ways that helped them to create sanctuaries of traditional values at home whilst the husbands struggled against the forces of Babel outside. And it was the same instinct for tradition that kept the man as the nominal head of each household to whom respect was due.

Below: Joseph and Mary Bosh's house, sod barn, and blacksmith shop. Born in Bechyne, Czechoslovakia in 1858, he came to the United States with his parents in 1870. This 1880s photograph was taken while they were raising their thirteen children.

Opposite: Jewish postwar emigration evinced by three new Americans on November 11, 1954.

In these circumstances the phenomenon of the American Jewish matriarch was born, the power behind the throne, who never challenged for the right to occupy the throne itself. In addition to keeping the flag of Jewish tradition flying at home, she often looked for ways to bring some American style to the family. She started to keep her eyes open for ways to improve the family's image in the eyes of their neighbors. Whether it was by music lessons for the children or potted plants for the home, she would apply great energy to stretching the family budget to attain the new objects of her desire—and the family learned to appreciate her efforts.

Perhaps the least well-known achievement of the Jewish mother was the relatively high standards of health displayed by the Jewish community. Despite poor living and working conditions, Jewish mortality rates for childbirth, tuberculosis, measles, and scarlet fever were the lowest in New York. The general Jewish mortality rate has been estimated at half that of the Italian immigrant community. This is particularly surprising since the Jews of the time were generally thought to be poor physical specimens.

Matriarchal militants

It would be a mistake, however, to interpret the superficial symbolism of the Jewish mother figure as some kind of unthinking bastion of conservative values. Many of these women, especially as time went on, had spent the years before marriage in the working environment. Although the synagogues paid little attention to teaching the finer points of Jewish religious culture, the younger immigrant girls did attend public schools, and were able to benefit from other educational programmes.

So in many cases, the new Jewish mother was a much more sophisticated person than those who had married in Europe. Even for the older women, the pressure to Americanize made them very aware of the world around them. They knew the rhetoric of America. They absorbed the concept of rights in a way that in Europe would have been classed as revolutionary. So when in May 1902 the retail price of kosher meat soared from twelve to eighteen cents

a pound, Jewish women organized the Ladies Anti-Beef Trust Association and took to the streets. They raised a fighting fund of eighty dollars and organized a successful boycott of kosher meat shops throughout the Lower East Side and in other parts of New York. They broke butcher shop windows and poured kerosene over the meat. They went to the labor movement and to the synagogues, and they won the support both of the socialist and the Orthodox religious daily newspapers. This organizational ability came to the fore again in 1907, when Lower East Side women were at the head of a rent strike movement. Kosher meat strikes were also held in Cleveland in 1906 and in Detroit in 1910.

Yom Kippur ball

For many of those who came from Eastern Europe, there was a more radical agenda. Some declared war against God and did everything conceivable to deride Judaism and all its observances. To the anarchists, for example, all religions were allies of capitalism and the state.

In 1889, a group of anarchists started to circulate a series of propaganda sheets parodying the prayers and practices of *Yom Kippur*, the most solemn day in the Jewish religious year. They hired a hall on Thirteenth Street for the eve of *Yom Kippur*, the night on which virtually every Jew would attend synagogue. They distributed thousands of leaflets calling on Jewish workers to come and enjoy a pleasant evening at a ball instead of going to the synagogues to ask forgiveness for sins and transgressions which not they but their "bosses" had committed.

The Orthodox community was furious, and they prevailed on the police to persuade the owner of the hall to break his contract with the anarchists and to close the hall to them.

On the night itself, thousands of people crowded the streets, but the anarchists had struck the wrong chord with the Jewish masses, and anarchism as a political creed made little headway within the Jewish community. The most famous of the Jewish anarchists, a woman by the name of Emma Goldman, was heard more readily outside the Jewish world than inside it. In 1919, she was deported to Europe with a boatload of other radicals, victims of a First World War law empowering the deportation of aliens who preached revolution.

Socialism—the new religion?

If anarchism did not capture the imagination of the Jewish masses, then socialism often did, particularly among the clothing workers of New York. By the 1890s the clothing industry was expanding rapidly, particularly in New York. Since many of the immigrants had relevant skills, the mass immigration came at a good time for the industry. Most of New York's clothing industry was in Lower Manhattan, and ninety percent of the employers were German Jews, who would be willing to allow their staff a day of rest on the Sabbath as well as the other Jewish Holydays. By 1897, seventy percent of the clothing workers in New York were Jewish, but the benevolence of the employers was often limited to the granting of Sabbath and holy-day leave. The system of working, which became known as the sweatshop system, led almost inevitably to the rise of labor activism. One labor activist described the birth of the Knee Pants Makers Union:

> "In 1890, there were about 1,000 knee pants makers employed in New York, all 'green' (immigrant) and most of them illiterate. It was a sweatshop industry *par excellence*. A contractor employed about ten workers and usually operated his shop in his livingroom. . . . The operator provided his own machine, needles, and thread. The workday was endless, and the average earnings . . . from six to seven dollars per week. Often the contractor would abscond with a week's pay; often the worker would be discharged because he was not fast enough, and often he would be compelled to quit because of maltreatment or intolerable working conditions . . . Every time . . . he was compelled to put his sewing machine on his back and carry it to his new place of employment. In early 1890, they struck. The movement was spontaneous, without program, leadership, or organization. It was a blind outbreak of revolt and was destined to collapse if left to itself."

It was not left to itself. The United Hebrew Trades, a labor union federation created by Jewish socialists in 1888, stepped in. Although the language of these Russian intellectuals was Russian, they learned Yiddish in order to be able to communicate with those whose lot they were committed to improve.

Unlike the anarchists, they learned to refrain from directly Judaism. They tried to give the Jewish socialism an idealistic flavor that might appeal to the Jewish ethical sentiments of the workers. In 1890, Abe Cahan started a column in the *Arbeiter Tseitung* (Workers Times) in which he linked the traditional weekly Torah reading with the ideals of socialism. Jewish workers were attracted to socialism. The left-wing Yiddish daily, *Forwertz*, was the largest circulating non-English newspaper in the country, and its ideas clearly struck a chord with many. By 1917, the votes of the New York Jewish districts for socialism were strong enough to elect ten Socialist state assemblymen, seven Socialist aldermen, and a Socialist municipal judge.

This peak in political success for the socialists coincided roughly with a dramatic increase in the strength of the unions. In the early years there was no shortage of unions. By 1907, there was even an International Beigel Bakers Union. And on November 29, 1909, something happened which was to be a turning point in the American labor movement, and a milestone in the history of women and politics.

On that day, 20,000 shirtwaist (blouse) makers, mostly women between the ages of sixteen and twenty-five (mostly Jewish but a large number also Italian)—went on strike. They were protesting against long hours and generally oppressive management practices, but more importantly they were protesting against sex discrimination in pay levels, sexual harassment, and exploitation by bosses and other male workers, who recruited girl workers at three or four dollars a week calling them "learners," and keeping them as learners when there was nothing left to learn. More than twenty percent of the work force were "learners." The strike dragged on until February 1920. The outcome fell somewhat short of the demands made by the workers. In particular, they failed to achieve full union recognition, but the membership of the local branch of ILGWU rose to 10,000, and the immigrant community had gained a whole new sense of what was possible. "The uprising of the 20,000," as it became known, inspired the cloak makers' strike of 1910. In July 1910, 65,000 workers in the cloak and suit trade walked out. The employers were intransigent. In particular, they would not contemplate the demand being made for a "closed shop." Leading members of the Jewish community, such as Jacob Schiff, Louis Marshall, and Louis Brandeis, became involved in mediation efforts. What eventually emerged, the "Protocol of Peace," provided for a number of improvements in working conditions, including a fifty hour working week, higher wages and a "preferential shop" scheme that fell short of the full closed shop demand but gave a real recognition to unions for the first time. Three boards were set up to create a stable framework for the future, Boards of Arbitration, Grievances, and Sanitary Control.

These two strikes and the Protocol of Peace provided signposts for the future resolution of disputes. The workers were left with a sense of the value of collective action, women with a sense that they could take a lead, and the Jewish community with a belief that it was possible for the community itself to find solutions to the social problems that arose within it. All of these beliefs held more than a grain of truth. This was not the end of labor unrest in America. The Protocol itself was abrogated by the employers a few years later and there was strife between different unions. In addition, bitter feelings between workers and employers did not decrease as some Russian immigrants became employers themselves.

There is one more milestone event which touched the hearts and moved the minds of Jews far beyond the Lower East Side. In 1911 a fire broke out in the factory of the Triangle Shirtwaist Company. More than 140 women died. American Jewish class-consciousness would never be the same again.

The years leading to World War I saw increased working class and socialist militancy among both Jews and non-Jews. The Garment Union's membership increased by sixty-eight percent in four years. During the War, some of the more radical aims of the socialists, particularly its pacifist tendencies were modified or put on a back burner. At the same time, the Progressive Party (Protestant in origin but supported by Jews such as Lillian Wald) started to develop a broad appeal, stressing a liberal social philosophy without a class analysis of political events.

Two Czechoslovak immigrants at Ellis Island, August 9, 1920.

The Jewish socialist and labor movements served the Jewish community well. They built the first power base for East European Jews in America. They helped to establish a strong general union movement. For many immigrants, the main tool of Americanization was their membership of some part of that movement.

Education for advancement

If the labor movement offered one way to self-confidence and fulfillment, the most cherished way was through education. Back in Eastern Europe, scholarship was one of the important communal and personal values. The objects of the scholarship were generally religious texts – and only for men. But study was a *mitzvah*, God's will for each individual, and to be acknowledged as a scholar brought universal esteem. When the opportunity came to translate this love of learning into the American environment, the response was enthusiastic. Night school became the secular temple of learning. There were 100,000 students enrolled at night school in New York in 1906, the majority of whom were Jews.

From night school, their educational ambitions developed, and by 1920, the Jewish enrolment at the Washington Square campus of New York University was ninety-three percent, even higher than at City College of New York, which was a tuition-free institution. By the 1930s, Jews, who comprised 3.5 percent of the population, provided ten percent of the student population. By the middle of the 1930s fifty percent of the applicants to medical schools were Jewish. And all this was against a background where a number of the institutions of higher learning were trying to restrict Jewish entry.

No doubt some of the motivation for this level of attainment was connected with the esteem for learning mentioned earlier. But the main motivation must have been the simple drive for upward economic mobility. Entering one of the professions provided at a stroke both a better income and a higher social status. The community that had at the beginning of the century supplied the workers for the sweatshops of the Lower East Side became within two generations the most middle class ethnic group in the country.

The drive for higher education was in the early years largely for the men. For women,

the highest ambition was to get an office job while waiting for the right marriage, but this did not last long. By the early 1930s over half of New York's teachers were Jewish women. In this respect the German Jewish elite provided useful role models. The two daughters of the Supreme Court Justice Louis Brandeis, born in the 1890s, both had distinguished careers in the law. One of their classmates, also a daughter of a Judge from the German community, graduated in medicine and went to Vienna to study under Freud. Another classmate, Estelle Frankfurter, whose brother became a Judge of the Supreme Court, did post-graduate work at the London School of Economics, and had a distinguished career in the Civil Service.

Generations in conflict

For the first generation immigrants, the changes they had to endure were challenging enough, but the changes that happened to their children were often too much to bear. Lincoln Steffens, a Christian journalist, observed the Lower East Side at the turn of the century with great affection:

> "The tales of the New York ghetto were heartbreaking comedies of the tragic conflict between the old and the new . . . We saw it everywhere all the time . . . We would pass a synagogue where a score or more of boys were sitting hatless in their old clothes, smoking cigarettes on the steps outside, and their fathers, all dressed in black, with their high hats, uncut beards, and side curls, were going into the synagogues, tearing their hair and rending their garments. . . . They wept tears, real tears . . . Their sons were rebels against the Law of Moses; they were lost souls . .. Two, three thousand years of continuous devotion, courage, and suffering for a cause lost in a generation."

The newspaper *Forvertz* illustrated another aspect of the stress between the generations:

> "There is no question but that a piano in the front room is preferable to a boarder. It gives spiritual pleasure to exhausted workers. But in most cases the piano is not for pleasure but to make martyrs of little children, and make them mentally ill. A little girl comes home, does

A concert at Ellis Island by Ukrainian immigrants, June 4, 1916.

her homework, and then is forced to practice under the supervision of her well-meaning father. He is never pleased with her progress, and feels he is paying fifty cents a lesson for nothing. The session ends with his yelling and her crying. These children have not a single free minute for themselves. They have no time to play."

The story of Golda Meir (later to become Prime Minister of Israel) is another example. Golda's family left Russia in 1906. They settled in Milwaukee, where Golda's father, a skilled carpenter, was frequently unemployed. Her mother ran a grocery store. Golda's sister refused to help out in the store, and Golda had to spend long hours at the grocery counter before and after school from the age of eight. Her sister had contracted tuberculosis, and left Milwaukee for Denver, to seek treatment at the Denver Jewish Sanatorium. Shortly afterwards, Golda's parents decided that she should leave school. "Men don't like smart girls," her father told her. "It doesn't pay to be too clever." In addition, her mother planned to marry her off to a local man more than twice her age. When her sister got married and invited Golda to join them in Denver, she did not hesitate. She ran away from home and did not return until, two years later, her parents had agreed to her starting a teachers' training course.

However, if there was one woman whose story encapsulated the East European immigrants' story it was the singer Sophie Tucker. Her mother, Jennie Abuza, (later to become immortalized as Sophie's "My Yiddisher Momma") was seventeen when she gave birth to Sophie en route from Russia to America in 1884. She was on her way to join her husband, who had left Russia to avoid conscription. By the time Sophie was eight years old the family had established a restaurant in Hartford, Connecticut. Her autobiography describes a traditional family attached to the Orthodox way of life. Her father was a quiet man. Her mother was the powerhouse that ran the business, leaving her husband to sit at the cash till. Many show business visitors to the restaurant complimented the little girl who was always ready to break into song for the customers. But Sophie's parents plans were clear: "After you are through school," her mother told her, "you must look around for a good, steady young man and get married."

So Sophie did what she was told—although not quite as mother intended. One week after graduating from high school, she eloped with a neighbor by the name of Louis Tuck. She became pregnant almost immediately, and the couple returned home. The Tucks moved in with the Abuzas, and Sophie was back in the kitchen, chopping vegetables and washing dishes.

It was not long before Sophie ran off to New York to try her luck as a singer, having adopted the stage name of "Tucker," leaving her mother to care for the child. When she returned for her first visit two years later, her mother's hair had turned white and her son barely recognized her. Sophie vowed not to return to Hartford until she had become a star, and remained away for more than five years. She played the Greenwich Village restaurants and the small-time vaudeville circuit. She sent much of her pay home. For six years from 1906 she was a blackface performer (like Eddie Cantor and Al Jolson, two other iconic Jewish Vaudeville performers). Eventually the opportunity arose to move on from the blackface act, and the persona of Sophie Tucker comedienne and all-round entertainer was born, vulgar, unloved, lovable. Her song—"Nobody Loves a Fat Girl But How a Fat Girl Can Love"—characterized her story.

As she rose to stardom, she returned home from time to time: "No matter how set up I was with myself, the minute I set foot in Ma's house I had to fall in line with the rules of an old-fashioned, religious household . . . and remember I was just a daughter."

When her mother died, she had a nervous breakdown and was unable to perform for several months. Soon after, in 1925, she gave her first performance of "My Yiddisher Momma," a song which became an anthem for a generation or two of Jews who clung with sentimental fervor to aspects of their past whilst battling to make it in the New World. She became a leading social activist, and in 1938 she was elected president of the 15,000-member American Federation of Actors. Under her leadership, the Federation called several successful strike actions and became the fastest growing of all the entertainers' unions.

In her mother's image she became "just a Yiddisher Momma, begging, pleading and weeping, like Mother Rachel for her children," when she set out to raise money for her favorite charities. "I ran away," she declared in a fund-raising speech in Hartford towards the end of her life, "but I've been running back ever since."

Entertaining for success

If Sophie Tucker's story illustrates the individual and family struggles of her generation, the story of the movie industry epitomizes the commercial story. Although the earliest movies were made by non-Jews, Hollywood itself was largely a Jewish creation, and the vast majority of the people in power were Jews. Samuel Goldwyn, the Warner brothers, Louis Mayer and other lesser names dominated the film industry in their time, and by the late 1920s the eight major studios were owned or controlled by Jews. More recently, at the turn of the 21st century, the most exciting prospects appear to be in store for a relatively new enterprise called Dreamworks SKG, which was created by Stephen Spielberg, Jeffrey Katzenberg, and David Geffen, who have been described as "the most powerful threesome in the entertainment business" (and who are all Jewish).

Although history identifies the early movie pioneers as Jewish, their personal objectives were assimilation, and Jewish performers were encouraged to adopt "neutral" names. The major Jewish stars of the 1930s and 1940s, such as Edward G Robinson, Betty Hutton, and Lauren Bacall all jettisoned their Jewish surnames and played primarily or exclusively non-Jewish roles. In 1937, a film was made on the life of the French writer Emile Zola which dealt with the famous anti-Semitic scandal known as the Dreyfus affair without even mentioning that Dreyfus was Jewish.

However, films with a specifically Jewish content were being made even in the early years, perhaps the most significant being *The Jazz Singer*, which starred Al Jolson in an autobiographical role as a young Jewish singer who forsakes the family tradition of synagogue cantor for the more exciting world of jazz. And following World War II, there was a conscious effort to encourage Jewish themes and to promote positive Jewish images in movies. By the sixties, it was possible for Barbra Streisand to rise to the top in Hollywood without losing her Jewish name, nose, or persona, and for Woody Allen to cultivate a style of writing and performing that often focused on the neuroses of the typical middleclass (Jewish) New Yorker. By 1998, Woody Allen had collected a record thirteen Academy Award nominations for best screenplay.

Of course, Jewish prominence in the movie business did act as a focal point for the anti-Semitism which was never far from the surface in American society. When Groucho Marx

Opposite, Above: Russian Orthodox church built by a colony of fifty White Russians near Lakewood, New Jersey. The immigrants were helped so the original caption identifies by the New Deal's Rural Rehabilitation, 1937.

Opposite, Below: Russian exiles in NYC—the first day in New York from an undated sketch by S. F. Yeager.

Right: Male Russian immigrant on the deck of the Leviathan.

Below: Slav immigrants board with a tenement family in New York City, photographed by Lewis Hine, c.1905.

joked about not wanting to join a club that would have him as a member, he struck a chord with all those Jews who knew that however successful they or their families might be in business or the professions, membership of the best country clubs would be denied to them (as well as to Catholics and African-Americans).

The People of the Book

As we have already noticed, the drive for self-improvement through education was a key feature of the East European immigrant generation and their children. In a short period, the results were becoming clear.

Between 1930 and 1995 over sixty American Jews won Nobel Prizes as against a handful before then. Half of the Nobel Prizes in medicine and physiology went to Jews in the ten years starting 1975. By 1970, when Jews constituted less than three percent of the U.S. population, they held twenty percent of the teaching positions at the private universities (many of whom had previously been prominent in resisting the influx of Jews) and twelve percent of all college teaching positions.

American writing, whether poetry, prose, or drama has had a massive following in the Jewish community, and many of its leading creative and entrepreneurial figures were Jewish. These include Nobel prize-winners for Literature Saul Bellow, the novelist (born in 1915 to Russian immigrants), Joseph Brodsky, the poet (a refugee from the Soviet Union in 1972) and Isaac Bashevis Singer, the Yiddish novelist, who came to the United States in 1935 at the age of 31. Playwrights, Clifford Odets, Lillian Hellman, George S. Kaufman and Arthur Miller, novelists Bernard Malamud, Philip Roth, Edna Ferber and Isaac Asimov, poets Gertrude Stein, Allen Ginsberg and Karl Shapiro are a selection of names which represent the Jewish input into American literature. Some of these writers drew heavily on their ethnic experience, some not at all. Some wrote with an intense social conscience which could perhaps be identified as a Jewish contribution to their work, others (such as the poet and short story writer Dorothy Parker) betray not an atom of their ethnic origins in their work.

Polish immigrants in line at the immigration office waiting to have their passports checked and their luggage examined before leaving. 1927.

The Jewish identity

In assessing the story of Jewish immigration to America, the predominant influence of the East Europeans has become clear. But it is equally clear that those who were there before them had laid all kinds of foundations, social, cultural and organizational, from which the subsequent Jewish community derived much benefit. There were in fact two waves of immigration which came later on in the twentieth century.. Around 200,000 came during the 1930s and 1940s as a result of the Nazi persecution in Europe, and a further 80,000 or so came during the late 1980s as a result of the dissolution of the Soviet Union.

The total American-Jewish community now numbers perhaps around five to six million, depending on how one chooses to judge affiliation. Its presence in selected aspects of national life has been described. There have been prominent Jews in sport, politics, and the professions. The early Jewish prominence in the mercantile and financial fields of business have now spread to all aspects of the commercial world. There are Jewish artists, architects and photographers, but the works of Mark Rothko, Robert A. M. Stern, and Richard are American even though their creators are Jewish.

Over half a million Jews served in the armed forces in World War II. 10,000 died and 25,000 were wounded, captured, or missing. There were six Jewish major generals, thirteen brigadier generals, one admiral, two rear admirals, and a commodore.

The precise details of such Jewish participation in American life tend to be of interest mainly to Jews and anti-Semites, for different reasons. The kind of anti-Semitism, which in 1945 led three out of the five sponsors to withdraw their sponsorship because a Jewish woman, Bess Myerson, had been selected, has largely disappeared. When Senator Joseph Lieberman, an observant orthodox Jew, was selected as a vice-presidential candidate on the Democratic ticket in 2000, the immediate effect on opinion polls was positive.

The history of the Jewish experience in America has been partly one of assimilation, in which Jews became absorbed into the wider society by giving up some or all of their Jewish identifying features, in particular their religious affiliation.

A major feature of assimilation is intermarriage with people from different ethnic backgrounds. Concern over the numbers of intermarriages has been a focus for the concerns of those within Jewry who sought to strengthen Jewish continuity. By 1990 the figure for marriages by Jews to non-Jewish partners had risen to fifty-two percent. Jewish leaders spoke of "the forces of attrition and hemorrhaging."

At the same time as the numbers looked alarming, there were three major forces which have strengthened the sense of Jewish identity, and no account of the story of American Jewry would be complete without referring to them: the first is the memory of the Nazi Holocaust, the second is the creation of the State of Israel, and the third is the increasingly effective network of community organizations, both religious and social which provide, for some, a positive reason for affiliating to the official Jewish community.

In the aftermath of World War II, religious faith was powerfully challenged by the sheer horror of what had actually happened in Europe. But many who had abandoned all interest in religion began nevertheless to recognize and to articulate feelings about their Jewishness which, in the words of one leading New York intellectual, were "rarely in accord with what we wrote or thought." The defining experience of their identity as human beings became that sense of Jewishness, which they were given by the Holocaust. Neither religious Jews nor Zionist Jews, they were unable to abandon being Jewish. Questions were asked. Did American Jews do enough to help European Jewry? Did the assimilationist culture of many German Jews actually contribute to their own destruction?

Above: A young Polish immigrant carries a trunk aboard the President Grant *at Ellis Island, New York, 1907.*

Right: Two Polish peasants, now successful young Americans, about to leave Ellis Island, c.1910.

For many, therefore, being a Jew became not a matter of religious belief but of group association linked to a vibrant sense of responsibility—if not guilt—for some aspect or other of the Holocaust. One way of translating that sense of group association was by identifying with the new State of Israel and its survival. Giving money to Israel was made easy by the efficient and sophisticated fund-raising organizations which developed out of the pre-State Zionist struggle.

Lobbying for Israel was an honorable way of participating in the democratic process, and politicians, particularly in the main centers of Jewish population soon saw the electoral value of wooing the Jewish vote by expressing support for Israel's survival and development. In the fifties, American official support was limited, and in the 1956 Israel-Egypt War, the U.S. government was hostile to the Israeli case. However, by 1961 President Kennedy had approved the supply of antiaircraft weapons to Israel, and in 1956, President Johnson approved the sale of airplanes to Israel. In 1956, Adlai Stephenson got sixty percent of the Jewish vote, and in 1964, Johnson got ninety percent.

At the time of the 1967 Six Day War, France was the main supplier of military equipment to Israel. When that supply was withdrawn, the United States stepped in. U.S. aid to Israel grew from $13.1 million to $600 million in 1971, and has been growing ever since. As the Soviet Union became hostile to Israel, the politics of the Cold War placed Israel in the Western camp. Supporting Israel became a good American enterprise for Jews. And the campaign for religious freedom for Soviet Jews, which had begun in 1964 as a student campaign, became a central feature both of Jewish community life and of the American human rights stance within the world community.

Organization of American-Jewish Community

Through the first half of the twentieth century, the three main religious groupings, Orthodox, Conservative, and Reform were busy developing their organizations and their rabbinical training colleges. By 1937 there were 4,771,00 Jews and 3,728 congregations. In the thirties a new grouping known as the Reconstructionists began to develop. Their key idea was the presentation of Judaism as a civilization rather than a theistic religion. Rituals from the religion were adapted to this new concept, and by 1968 that movement had its own rabbinical college.

These synagogue-centered organizations were admirably placed to tap into the Jewish sense of identity described above and to build on it. Support for the African American civil rights movement in the fifties and early sixties became a feature of the leadership of many Rabbis.

The drama of the 1967 Six Day War and the tensions of seeing Israel change from vulnerable victim to military superstar in just one week set off powerful new currents within the community including a rightward shift in both religious and Zionist-political stances for many Jews. Evangelical outreach groups (principally the Chasidic Lubavitch movement) stepped in to work with young people in particular, and within a short time new qualities of professionalism and dynamism were showing in all sectors of the Jewish community.

Jewish children of all denominations were now often attending Jewish Day Schools (previously thought to be a socially divisive phenomenon and supported only by the Orthodox). The Reform, Reconstructionist and Conservative movements (and to a much lesser extent the moderates in the Orthodox camp) were responding to the demands of Jewish feminists, and by the end of the century, women had gained equal rights in all but the Orthodox movements. For many women, the chance fully to express their spirituality, was an opportunity to which they were ready to respond, and they have provided much new vitality within the non-Orthodox religious communities.

Whether the positive developments described here will be enough to maintain the survival of the American Jewish community in a recognizable form through the twenty-first century is a matter of intense debate within the community. "Will we have Jewish grandchildren?", is the question often asked. This is not the place to answer that question, but it is fair to say that the right questions have been asked and a plethora of solutions offered. The future will provide the answer.

The S.S. Marine Flasher *brought 549 displaced persons to America on December 21, 1945. Among the passengers were Antoni Bar and Audycha Kristyna, both two years old, from Poland, and on their way to Detroit.*

CHAPTER 6 # Italians

CHAPTER 6 Italians

Opposite: Newly arrived Italian immigrants on

Ellis Island in 1905.

Although Italian sailors and explorers, most notably of course Christoforo Colombus and Amerigo Vespucci, pioneered the discovery of the Americas by the Mediterranean world at the end of the fifteenth century, the then divided states of the Italian peninsular played no part in the colonization that followed over the next three centuries. Even in the nineteenth-century Italians were comparative latecomers in the great river of mass immigration that flowed into the United States in the 100 years between the 1820s and the 1920s. As late as the 1860s there were less than 5,000 people of Italian origin throughout the entire country. Yet a hundred years later, in the census of 1990, Americans of all or partly Italian descent made up the sixth largest group in the nation, amounting to 14,664,550 individuals.

The key to this transformation was an extraordinary burst of Italian immigration which saw over four million migrants from the region arrive in the United States in the brief period between 1880 and 1920. Contrary to the negative stereotypes promoted to stir up prejudice and hostility by American nativist opponents of immigration keen to encourage rivalry with other ethnic groups, these Italian migrants brought with them both the inheritance of their rich cultural and artistic legacy and a diversity of regional and local traditions which were to play a part in the development of Italian-American communities within the wider sphere of American life in the twentieth century. Although a significant minority of the migrants came from the relatively well-developed northern regions of Italy, the majority were victims of the oppressive and exploitative system of government and land-ownership that had developed in the south under centuries of foreign rule. But these immigrants were not generally the most marginal and poverty-stricken villagers unable to survive at home—rather it has become clear that most migrants were precisely those individuals who had sufficient initiative and industry to obtain the necessary fare and the courage to venture what was then a virtually incredible distance into the almost unknown, in pursuit of a better life for themselves and their families.

At first glance it seems paradoxical that the massive movement of emigration from Italy, involving huge flows of people not just to the United States, but also to Argentina, and in lesser numbers to Brazil, should take places in the decades just after the long-held dream of Italian unification was finally achieved in the 1860s. Italy was still a fragmented backwater ruled by repressive and reactionary foreign governments and still hardly touched by the spreading Industrial Revolution. However it has been argued that it was precisely the failure of the new united Italian government to meet the hopes for progress and the relief of endemic rural poverty raised by the thrilling events of the Risorgimento (literally "Revival") that helped to stimulate the huge exodus that followed. Underlying these factors was the continued growth of a rural population unable to sustain itself on the largely impoverished land to which it was restricted by semi-feudal land ownership patterns.

A divided people

Until the mid-nineteenth century the area that makes up modern Italy was a patchwork of rival mini-states whose borders fluctuated with the rise and fall of military and economic power in an ever shifting kaleidoscope of alliances and hostilities. Rome and an expanse of the center of the peninsular made up the Papal States, with the Kingdom of Naples ruling most of the main-

land to the south. Sicily was a separate kingdom, while both Sicily and Naples came under Austrian rule early in the eighteenth century before falling to the Spanish crown in 1735. North of the Papal States the principal political entities were the Republics of Venice, Genoa, and Lucca, and the Duchies of Tuscany, Savoy, Milan, Parma, Massa, Mantua, and Modena.

Opposite: An Italian immigrant family on board a ferry at the docks to Ellis Island, 1905.

The cities of northern Italy had been both the cradles of the Renaissance and key economic centers combining urban artisanal industries and important early banking families with great wealth derived from international trade. As early as the fourteenth century, Venice, Milan, Genoa, and Florence, had populations in the vicinity of 100,000, making them, along with Paris, the largest cities in Europe at the time. Economic success was not however accompanied by strong political leadership, as struggles between the leading families and factions cut across external alliances with rival papal and imperial interests.

By the end of the sixteenth century the military forces that could be mustered by the wealthy but fractious city states of northern Italy were becoming increasingly ill-matched with those of the more powerful centralized monarchies that were establishing themselves in France and Spain. The territorial gains of the Habsburg emperor Charles V after he inherited control of Naples, Sicily, and Sardinia, in 1519 allowed him to dictate terms leading to the establishment of the hereditary duchies listed above in the mosaic of small weak states that remained largely in place over the next 200 years.

It was at this time of military weakness at the start of the sixteenth century however that the idea of an Italian nation began to gain currency among humanist scholars. The Venetian scholar Pietro Bembo (1470–1547) promoted the spread of the vernacular dialect of Tuscany as the major literary language throughout the peninsular. Although this was only adopted by an educated minority it was a first step away from the extraordinary linguistic diversity of the peninsular and in the nineteenth and twentieth century Tuscan became the basis for the linguistic unity of modern Italy

The nineteenth century

Between 1796 and 1806 the political map of the Italian peninsular was drastically altered after a series of military conquests by Napoleon Bonaparte. However, Napoleonic rule failed to follow through on the overdue reforms it introduced. The abolition of feudalism had little impact in the more economically advanced areas of the North, but in the South the measures led to the displacement of the landed nobility by a new urban middle class of merchants, doctors, and others who frequently took over and enclosed the common lands vital to the poor. With few exceptions these new landowners proved as uninterested in the development of the land and the welfare of their tenants as the old nobility.

Life only got worse for the poor—many small peasant farmers were obliged to become day laborers, while other rural workers migrated to the cities where they survived only by begging, occasional work, and petty crime. Banditry increased throughout the peninsular. Population growth throughout rural areas only added to these problems. The tendency of day laborers to produce large families so that the number of workers available to bring income into the family was increased and helped push up the population of Italy from 18 million in 1800 to around twenty-two million by 1840. In the cities recurrent epidemics kept down the numbers of urban poor so almost all the increase was due to the countryside, which became increasingly overpopulated. Over the following years governments came to see emigration as a vital safety valve drawing off some of the surplus population from overcrowded rural areas so reducing the danger of riots and insurrection.

The Risorgimento

Three figures were key to the mid-nineteenth-century reform and the revolt known as the Risorgimento—Guiseppe Mazzini, Count Camillo Cavour, and the revolutionary leader Guiseppe Garibaldi.

Finally, after battles the length and breadth of the peninsular, in an historic encounter, Victor Emmanuel and Garibaldi's forces met north of Naples, where Garibaldi loyally surrendered the territory he held to the authority of Victor Emmanuel as King of a united Italy. The final, unconquered areas were brought under the control of the new nation in the following decades.

The post-revolution regime was essentially a government of and for the new middle class of predominantly northern bankers, professionals, and industrialists, proving a bitter disappointment to Garibaldi, Mazzini, and many of their followers. It was primarily the failure of the new liberal regime to implement reforms that would allow a significant improvement in the situation of the rural and urban poor throughout Italy that stimulated growing emigration in the second half of the nineteenth century, at first to Brazil and Argentina, then to the United States.

Taxes rose sharply as the regime struggled to pay off a high level of public debt. The burden of taxes fell disproportionally on the already hard pressed rural dwellers, with an 1868 tax known as *macinato* imposed on the milling of wheat a particularly resented measure that provoked widespread rioting. The government also raised revenue by confiscating and selling both church and communal land totaling some two million hectares. The result was that the sell-off only added yet more land to the existing under-utilized estates of big landowners, while at the same time depriving the peasants in many more areas of their traditional access to common land. Far from improving the economic circumstances of the rural poor actually worsened significantly.

Faced with the implacable opposition of the still powerful Catholic Church, and the regular outbreaks of social unrest and banditry, in the South in particular, the new regime was unable to reform economically and socially as it desired. Measures that might actually improve the situation of the poor were consistently blocked by the opposition of large landowners. The inheritors of the radical tradition of the Risorgimento were increasingly turning towards socialism and even anarchism. The embattled regime resorted to harsh repressive measures against any signs of unrest repeatedly sending in the army to deal with the riots and inevitably provoking still further opposition.

In spite of an increasing population, nearly two-thirds of Italians were dependent on agriculture—widely agreed to be in an appalling state—with conditions for the rural population said to be the worst in Europe. Small proprietors and tenant farmers were constantly at risk of dispossession of their land and the growing numbers of day laborers lucky to find work at all for much of the year. To the ill effects of an inadequate diet, were added those of bad housing conditions, with the inevitable result of widespread sickness and disease. In many areas most rural families lived in a single-room house with a beaten earth floor, often sharing the space with a mule or ox. A report in 1881 found that tens of thousands throughout the South were living in caves and the remnants of ancient tombs. In the North the reliance on maize resulted in vitamin deficiency leading to the disease pellagra, which resulted in dementia and eventually death. In the South malaria was a major killer, while throughout the country tuberculosis was widespread. Imports of cheap grain from America, combined with reduced demand in the U.S. for Italian citrus fruits after production increases in California and Florida were, along with French measures to cut off imports of Italian wine, further blows to the impoverished agricultural sector in Italy in the 1880s that did much to contribute to the exodus.

Since so many Italians were dependent on agriculture and their income was insufficient to meet their basic requirements there was no surplus available to be spent on the products of industry. Indeed little money was used at all outside of the main cities, with peasants relying on barter or using salt as a currency.

Economic hardship in itself is rarely sufficient to prompt people to emigrate. Other aspects such as the technology that produced steamships and made cheap mass transport across the Atlantic accessible to more people are also important. Many people of course chose to remain at home or lacked the means and initiative to leave. Underlying these abstract conditions were the actual decisions and personal initiatives of thousands of men, women, and often children, who left behind families and homes to improve their lot in life in the Americas. Of course even in the era of mass migration only a modest percentage of the Italian population made the decision to leave.

The pioneers

Among the Italians who played a crucial role in the discovery and initial exploration of the Americas were Christoforo Columbus, John Cabot (Giovanni Caboto), Amerigo Vespucci, and Giovanni da Verrazzano. These pioneer Italians in the New World were a reflection of the important role played in maritime commerce by the wealthy Italian city states of their day, but the failure of their voyages to leave any more lasting Italian legacy on the continents of North and South America also reflected the weakness and political fragmentation of their homeland which would be left behind by its neighbors when Spain, Portugal, Britain, and France went on to establish colonies in the Americas. However, other less well known adventurers and missionaries from the Italian peninsular followed in the colonial period .

Francesco Vigo, a soldier and fur trader, served as a colonel and intelligence officer during the Revolution, and is generally recognized to have been the first Italian to become an American citizen. However probably the most significant Italian contribution to the founding of the Republic was that made by the agronomist and philosopher Filippo Mazzei. Mazzei decided to continue his agricultural experiments in Virginia after meeting Thomas Adams and Benjamin Franklin in England where he was importing Italian foods. In the colony he became an enthusiastic supporter of secession from England, publishing a series of pseudonymous articles translated by Thomas Jefferson in the *Virginia Gazette*, one of which included the words "All men are by nature equally free and independent," a form of words which was incorporated into the Virginia Bill of Rights and later redrafted by Jefferson as "all men are created equal" in the 1776 Declaration of Independence.

Interesting and inspirational though these pioneer Italians were, their contribution to the actual formation of an Italian-American community in the U.S. was perhaps less signifi-

A group of relieved and happy Italian immigrants in a railroad waiting hall on Ellis Island, 1905.

An Italian market on Mulberry Street, New York, c.1905.

cant than that made by a larger number of mostly anonymous ordinary men and a few women who came to America in the years before the 1870s. Between the founding of the Republic in 1783 and the start of the 1870s, some 12,000 people, most of them men, but also significant numbers of women and children, from the lands that make up the state of Italy settled in the United States. This total, of course, was swamped by the huge flows of immigrants from Ireland, Germany, Britain, and parts of northern Europe in the first half of the nineteenth century and the presence of Italians in the nation elicited little public comment. Many of these early arrivals were from the relatively prosperous North of Italy, and were political refugees, artists, or musicians.

Garibaldi is only the best known of many refugees from the political turmoil preceding the Risorgimento who saw the democratic United States as an ideal refuge from persecution at home. There was considerable sympathy for cause of Italian liberation in liberal circles in the United States and on occasions American consuls in Italy actively intervened to assist in the escape of activists. In return many refugees supported the Northern cause during the Civil War, with one of two regiments of Italian and other nationals formed during the early part of the war becoming known as the Garibaldi Guard. Not all Americans were impressed by the political agenda of the refugees however and considerable concern was expressed by the (mostly Irish) hierarchy of the Catholic Church over the strongly anti-clerical tone of their writings.

Among educated and cultured nineteenth-century Americans there was a general interest in Italian art and in Italy as the home of the Renaissance, with Italy as perhaps the most important destination on the Grand Tour of Europe which was still regarded as an essential component of a full education for the sons of the wealthy. A number of Italian artists took advantage of this interest to forge moderately successful careers for themselves as painters and art teachers in cities such as New York and Philadelphia. Some of them became influential figures on the local art scene, although none achieved any lasting recognition. Numerous Italian artists and sculptors, and on a less exalted level, stone cutters and marble workers, found work on the public buildings, many of them in a classical style, which were being erected across the nation. At the bottom of the scale, numerous itinerant Italian men hawked plaster sculptures door-to-door.

Italian musicians were also well represented in polite circles, with a number of violinists and piano instructors making a living from teaching and the occasional public recital. The majority of Americans got their first exposure to a public music show, and had their first contact with Italians, in the form not of the traveling musician—the majority of whom were organ grinders. This last group attracted some of the first public expressions of anti-Italian feeling because of concern that young boys were being bought from their families back home in Italy and forced to work as street players by unscrupulous bosses known as *padroni*.

Of all the Italians who took up residence in America before the 1870s it was the small businessmen, the often struggling entrepreneurs, and the small number of ordinary working men and women who did most to set the pattern of what was to follow and to lay down the roots of an Italian-American community. At first they were almost isolated individuals, often with shops selling imported Italian goods. Although the evidence is sketchy detailed examination of contemporary records such as church registers, naturalization documents, newspapers, and court records, has allowed historians to piece together a glimpse of the lives of some of these early migrants. Some achieved considerable success leaving estates valued in the thousands of dollars, while others died in relative poverty and obscurity. The requirement to state the country of former allegiance when taking an oath of naturalization to become an American citizen allows us to establish that, not unexpectedly, the majority of migrants at this period were from the relatively prosperous regions of northern Italy. Interestingly, in most cases the witnesses who vouched for the good character of the applicants to become citizens were themselves locally born Americans.

As the eighteenth century progressed a growing number of prominent naturalized Italian-Americans stood as witnesses for their fellow countrymen, this can be seen as an indicator of the early stages of the formation of a community. However the sample was small, as between 1801 and 1860, a total of only 155 Italians petitioned for citizenship throughout the entire country. Of necessity, since there were very few Italian women among the early migrants, marriages to women of non-Italian origin were a regular occurrence, increasing the integration of the migrants into the mainstream of American life.

In the seventeenth and early eighteenth century the handful of Italian residents in each city were scattered geographically, by mid-century the beginnings of Italian-American settlement in those areas which were soon to become "Little Italies" could be traced. There were also early signs of the arrival of a number of migrants from the same family or village—a process known as chain migration—which became a key feature of the emergence of the far larger Italian-American community in the decades ahead.

The United States had already been welcoming tens of thousands of immigrants each year since the 1830s—some 600,000 in total arrived in the ten years from 1831–40, rising sharply to over 1.7 million in the following decade, jumping again to 2.6 million between 1851 and 1860, before falling back in the decade of the Civil War to a still massive 2.3 million. By the end start of the 1870s America was changing from a mostly rural nation to a predominantly urban one. Industrialization had far overtaken the settlement of new territories as the leading factor in soaking up the flow of migrants, drawing ever increasing numbers of people from Europe as urbanization pushed ahead at a dramatic rate. New railroads and canals were being constructed, factories were opening almost daily, and the demand for labor seemed unending.

Wage levels were relatively high compared with incomes available to workers in impoverished parts of Europe. Even such migrant groups as the Swedes, who at first settled in rural areas of the northern central states such as Minnesota, Nebraska, and North and South Dakota, were being drawn to the greater opportunities in the expanding cities by the end of the decade. The Italians migrants too were to become overwhelmingly an urban population, despite their predominantly rural origins in the Italian South.

The social world of rural Italy

It has been estimated that in 1860 only 2.5 percent of the population of the Italian peninsula understood Italian, which as already mentioned, was derived from fourteenth-century literary Tuscan. Even some of the ruling classes were more comfortable speaking in French. For the uneducated majority there was a huge range of dialects, many of which were, in effect, separate languages. Elements of archaic Latin were retained in some areas, while in others there were small Greek, Albanian and even, in Sicily, a Catalan-speaking community. This extreme linguistic diversity was a reflection of the reality that, even in the aftermath of unification, Italy as a nation existed almost in name only.

People derived their identities not from an abstract sense of nationhood, but from direct personal experience of their own local village or town and of the position of their extended family within it. For many it was only in America that the migrants would receive a sense that they were Italians, and even there local identities were still an important factor in determining residence patterns. It is then a considerable oversimplification to talk of Italian migrants en masse. Perhaps the main thing that united the migrants to America was precisely that shared experience of leaving behind home, and often family, and enduring the hardships of traveling in usually grim conditions to a new and little understood land half a world away.

Some generalizations can, however, be made. Unlike the earlier immigrants who had helped to establish nascent Italian-American communities in the cities of America, the vast majority of those who came to America in the 1880s and the decades that followed came from the South. If parts of northern Italy were beginning to draw near to their European neighbors in terms of modernization and industrial development as the nineteenth century drew to a close, the same could not be said for the South. The most basic infrastructure to join isolated communities to the urban world was lacking in many areas—it has been estimated that in 1890 almost 90 percent of all southern communes were unconnected by road, forcing travelers to rely on ancient tracks and paths. Mules were the main means of transportation. The most remarked consequence of this isolation was the development of a particularly intense feeling of attachment to the family and beyond that to a very localized community, with a corresponding hostility towards, and suspicion of, outsiders. This was reflected in the early years of settlement in America, where it became common for migrants from a particular village or region to set up home in the same street even in the largest of cities.

Village life revolved around the piazza (or chiazza as the main square was called in parts of the South), where the men would meet to stroll, chat, and pass the evenings telling stories in the café, while women mostly entertained their friends on home visits. Religious festivals, in particular Christmas and the festival devoted to the town's patron saint, were the main occasions of communal celebration, when there would be music, a procession, and as elaborate a feast as could be afforded. Landowners and other local gentry were treated with a grudging respect but rarely played an active role in peasant life. Artisans such as smiths, masons, and tailors, and the few shopkeepers jealously guarded their slender claims to a higher status than the small farmers and laborers. Land was scarce and often infertile, with a trek of several hours each day back and forth to the common fields.

The Catholic Church was the only outside institution that penetrated with any success into the parochial world of the rural South. Taking an almost missionary approach in an area where often unorthodox folk religious traditions mingled with a reverence for the personal intervention of the saints, the church managed to succeed by compromising with local beliefs and social divisions rather than combating them. It promoted the cults of local saints and recognized numerous miracles, organizing guilds whose leadership provided status markers for landowners and other local elites, while also making an effort to ease the hardships of the sick and elderly.

In contrast the State made very little progress in its attempts to extend its authority beyond the confines of the main towns. After centuries of isolation and of resistance to the excessive demands of absentee landlords and their corrupt overseers, it was not surprising that a state which demanded taxes and conscripts for its armies, but seemed to offer no tangible benefits in return, should be met with passivity at best, and with regular if mostly short-lived outbreaks of armed opposition. The mountainous terrain and inadequate roads made central control almost impossible to enforce and banditry was a continued problem into the twentieth century. More serious unrest was met by savage repression by foreign soldiers, or after unification by the northern-dominated army of the new state. In some cases, such as the brutal suppression of the unusually well organized and radical revolt of the Sicilian fasci (mutual benefit societies) in 1893, when the shooting dead of twenty-two unarmed demonstrators was

followed by mass arrests, these acts of repression acted as a major factor in stimulating large numbers of people to join the growing tide of emigrants.

The Italian headquarters, Madison Street, New

Orleans, Louisiana, c.1906.

Leaving

By the 1860s letters home from members of the nascent Italian-American communities in cities such as New York and Chicago were beginning to exert their effect. More and more people across Italy—especially in the South—were starting to recognize the opportunities emigrating to the U.S. offered to escape from the poverty and hardship of life in Italy. It was generally not the very poorest and most desperate who were compelled to emigrate as an alternative to starvation, since they were usually too apathetic to make the move and in any case lacked the necessary money to purchase a ticket or the relatives in America to provide assistance. Rather it was those who had just sufficient resources and the necessary courage and initiative who joined the exodus. Unlike the artists, musicians, and aspiring entrepreneurs who preceded them from the North, most were small farmers or tenants, agricultural laborers, fishermen, artisans such as masons, carpenters, blacksmiths, cobblers, tailors, and other petty tradesmen.

Joining them, although in far smaller numbers, were the would-be businessmen and professionals such as doctors, lawyers, and teachers. It was rare for families to leave together; far more commonly a father or son would set off alone, with all involved hoping that either he would return wealthy, or as more usually happened, would gradually send sufficient money for his immediate family to be able to purchase tickets to join him one by one. Such hopes were usually realized eventually, but the unexpected hardships many were to meet with in America combined with the general uncertainties of life made these anticipated reunions a chancy prospect. For many of the women left behind America came to be seen as a cursed land that brought them only tears, suffering, and years of uncertainty.

Italian bread peddlers, Mulberry Street, New York, c.1900.

The departure of any member of a tight-knit rural family, particularly of a husband and primary breadwinner, was more than just a cause of great sadness, it also raised considerable economic problems for the already struggling family left behind. Many women had to labor in the fields themselves while they waited hopefully for a prepaid ticket to arrive. Even when it came, a journey alone or with young children beyond the familiar confines of the village to a distant port, was often a terrifying prospect. Both for the men who lead the way and their families left back at home deciding to go to America was not a step to be taken lightly.

Helping or hindering people in making these choices were the reports they received of the prospects and opportunities available in the U.S. for those prepared for hard work. Some heard about America first hand in their villages from migrants who had returned to Italy—as many of them did for reasons that ranged from ill-health to love of their home village, to retirement on the land they had purchased with their American earnings. The number of these returnees was remarkably large, totaling about 1.5 million between 1900 and 1914, and many men in particular made the difficult voyage two or three times before finally settling. Of course most of these returnees made the best of their experiences and few passed on accurate details of the difficulties they had encountered.

The vast number of letters home also tended in most cases to paint the most favorable view possible to their loved ones. Even where men wrote of the squalid housing, backbreaking labor, and cheating bosses they had endured, the money that accompanied their letters told a different story. The flow of remittances from America brought evidence of the most tangible of rewards from migration into the remotest villages of the South, enticing thousands more to follow. Historians have noted that it was no coincidence that the states where migrants sent back the largest amounts of remittances continued to attract the biggest flows of new migrants. Added to these inducements were the activities of the steamship companies and the notorious padroni (frequently unscrupulous labor agents) who had an obvious interest in advertising the prospects of emigration and exaggerating the ease with which would-be migrants could strike it rich.

For those who decided to migrate their problems began almost straight away. Naples and Genoa were the two main ports used by the shipping lines operating to America, with Palermo third in importance once large numbers of Sicilians began to leave. Many made the long distance from their village to the port on foot accompanied by donkeys or carts laden with whatever belongings their family could spare them, sleeping rough by the roadside each night. Others were crowded into dirty and uncomfortable trains, or coastal vessels, to be unloaded at the dockside to await departure. The port authorities made little effort to cater for the migrants, leaving them to be cheated and robbed in slum hostels in the port areas, despite government legislation in 1901 providing for official hostels to be established.

Once on the ships the vast majority of migrants who booked the cheapest passage available in steerage class found themselves herded together below decks in cramped, insanitary, and often dangerous conditions. The Genoese shipowners (who dominated the transport of Italian migrants) were later than those of other European countries in switching to steam navigation, leaving some wooden sailing vessels still in service into the 1870s. When steamships were introduced they were generally slower and less well equipped than the already poor standards set by the vessels that carried migrants of other nations—a minimum speed of 11mph for ships carrying migrants was set by the 1901 legislation, for example, compared with the norm of around 20mph for ships operated by the British Cunard line.

Called steerage class because it was literally beside the ships mechanics well below the waterline, the passengers were packed into hot, ill-ventilated rooms holding as many as 200–300 people. Men and women were separated, with tiny cubicles available for families, and each migrant was allotted a cramped berth for use as both bed and store for their luggage. Access to the deck and its fresh air was restricted, with groups of the passengers having to take turns on the small area open to them. Washing and toilet facilities were extremely limited and food always poor and often far from fresh. Complaints of brutality by the crew and of the abuse of women were frequent. Attempts to improve conditions after adverse publicity in both Europe and America were made with Italian legislation in 1901 and the passage by the U.S. Congress of the Passenger Act in 1902, but it seems many of the new regulations were frequently ignored.

Not surprisingly outbreaks of disease on board ship were a regular occurrence despite the medical checks imposed by authorities at ports of embarkation. All too many of the migrants failed to live to reach their destination, while many more failed health checks on arrival in America and faced the grim prospect of returning home. Despite these often horrendous conditions however, the vast majority of migrants, totaling many millions, did endure the Atlantic crossing and disembarked in the ports of the East coast to begin a new life as Americans.

Arriving

Although the overall numbers of Italian migrants arriving in the United States before the 1920s were remarkably high, even more astonishing is the speed and intensity of this huge migration, almost all of which was compressed into forty years between 1880 and 1920. Before that there were notably few Italians in North America.

The U.S. census of 1850 recorded only 3,645 persons born in Italy. Italians were spread across all the states and territories with the exception of Delaware and New Hampshire, with the largest concentration in New Orleans and some 200 around San Francisco. Forty years later in the census of 1890, that number had risen massively to 182,000. In total from the time records began in 1820 to the ending of the century of mass European immigration in 1920, the figure of 4,195,880 Italian immigrants were recorded entering the United States. Not all of them remained in America. For a variety of reasons a substantial minority, estimated at between one in three and one in two, went back to Italy, although many of these *ritornati* may have returned to the U.S. to settle permanently and been counted twice in the overall figure. In any event more than four million of that total were packed into the last forty years, making Italians the largest group of new immigrants during most years of that period, overtaking the Germans and Irish who had dominated in previous decades.

Italian migrants came to America with an intense sense of family and of often rival local identities and with little awareness of any common nationality as Italians. There is a real sense in which it is over simplistic to generalize about Italians as a group, however necessary it may be in an account of this length. Their history is really no more than an aggregate of the history of the many far smaller village groups, families, and even individuals, who made up the migration, each with their distinctive stories and experiences.

New York was the main point of entry for migrants into the United States by the second half of the nineteenth century. The joy and excitement immigrants felt on sighting the harbor, and after 1885 the iconic sight of the upraised arm of the Statue of Liberty, were mixed with fear and apprehension at what was awaiting them once they landed. Although the unknown troubles of the future were perhaps more daunting, especially for those who had no relatives in America to meet them at the port side, it was the receiving station and the medical examination they would be subjected to there that were most feared. Everyone knew that an incorrect answer or a previously unnoticed symptom could cause the disaster of rejection and a long and humiliating voyage back home.

The famous receiving center at Ellis Island was not opened until January 1, 1892. Before that, migrants were processed in an old fort at Castle Gardens in the Battery district of Manhattan, which soon developed an extremely dubious reputation. Its staff were accused of extortion and theft from migrants, and scandal increased to an unacceptable level when it was learned that corpses of migrants who died in the hospital were being sold for dissection. Such was the outcry that Congress was forced to step in and legislate to assume control of immigration processing at the federal level, setting up the facilities at Ellis Island. After a fire in 1897 when the wooden buildings were destroyed, the process of expanding the island and building fire proof structures got under way. Eventually the original 3.5 acres of the island was extended to twenty-seven acres holding thirty-five buildings, including a respected hospital.

Arriving ships did not go directly to Ellis Island since its wharf could not handle large ocean-going vessels. Moreover new arrivals soon learnt that in America too the rich were treated differently—when the ship was placed in quarantine at the Lower Bay dock the first- and secondclass passengers were allowed ashore to meet their waiting relatives after just a brief interview. The steerage passengers were then assigned identification numbers and loaded onto barges for transport to Ellis Island. Once there, the immigrants lined up in long queues in a huge chamber known as the Registry Room, awaiting their turn for the medical check. Passing eventually after a wait of one to up to six or more hours into the room called the Judgement Hall they would each be briskly examined by one of a group of uniformed Marine Corps doctors.

More than 5,000 immigrants could be examined in a single day at busy periods, so inevitably there was little time for niceties. The examiners judgement of each applicant was simply marked in chalk on his or her clothing, with those receiving a mark sent into a room assigned for a second, more detailed, examination (see the Introduction for more on the chalk marks). The majority who were judged by the second examiner to be quickly curable were transferred to the hospital, while the unfortunate remainder were detained pending deportation.

Trachoma was a particularly widespread cause for rejection and the eye examination came to be especially feared. As Fiorello La Guardia noted when he worked as an interpreter on Ellis Island from 1907–10, the judgement of mental deficiency or illness was also particularly difficult for examiners who didn't understand the language or cultural background of their subjects. Rejection of migrants often lead to the enforced separation of families and always to the dashing of hopes in which so much had been invested, causing Ellis Island to become known to generations of Italians as an Island of Tears.

After they had passed the medical checks, migrants were questioned about their prospects and intentions in the United States. Each person had to show that he or she had sufficient funds and contacts to organize employment, so that they would not become a public charge. At the same time however, under legislation intended to limit the exploitation of immigrants as contract laborers by *padroni*, those who were suspected of having arrived at the instigation of a labor boss could be excluded. In a hasty interview conducted through an interpreter it was not always easy for a nervous migrant to give the right answers to these questions, and on occasions inspectors seem to have deliberately trapped people into getting themselves

The Italian neighborhood, Mulberry Street, New York, c.1905.

deported. Among those detained pending deportation suicides were not uncommon, and a number of others drowned in the treacherous currents while attempting to escape to the shore.

Perhaps the most humiliating of the trials on Ellis Island was the treatment sometimes meted out to single women and young widows traveling alone. Concerned that they might be or become prostitutes, the authorities subjected them to detailed inquiries and often detained them for long periods if they could not produce acceptable sponsors to assure officials of their good character. They were also particularly vulnerable to the abuse and corruption that were a sporadic occurrence, with money or sexual favors being extorted in return for a promise that the certificate of entry would be issued. Such incidents seem, however, to have been comparatively rare and the authorities to have made serious efforts to combat them. Finally Ellis Island was also the place where many migrants made a start, usually involuntarily, on a process of modifying and Americanizing their names, with the complexities of Italian spelling often being drastically simplified and shortened as the officials hurriedly completed their documentation.

In 1901 Gino Speranza, an attorney brought up in the United States, founded the Society for the Protection of Italian Immigrants to help as many as possible of his compatriots in a situation where there was clearly widespread exploitation of new arrivals of all nationalities. With the help of American patrons it set up a shelter in New York City to house homeless migrants and offer them assistance and advice with obtaining housing and employment. It also funded investigations into some of the worst abuses of migrants. Similar work was performed by the Catholic Church via the San Raffaele Society and other organizations.

Despite such good efforts, however, many newly disembarked immigrants found themselves at risk from a variety of con artists, slum landlords, and other swindlers. Those who arrived alone with no relatives or friends to greet them were particularly vulnerable and were often tricked out of what little money they possessed by unscrupulous cab drivers before they even found a place to stay for the first night. Sadly all too often a few Italians living in the immigrant areas were also willing to collude with other locals in defrauding their compatriots by posing as benefactors. Traveling on from New York to other destinations throughout the

The Mulberry Bend area was at the heart of
New York's Little Italy, c.1890.

United States exposed migrants to further problems, with railroad companies in particular regularly overcharging for their poorest trains and often deliberately sending migrants by more expensive indirect routes that added hours or days to their journey. When they finally reached their destination, in New York City or any of the thousands of other cities and towns where Italians congregated, the migrants had then to begin the difficult task of remaking their lives in a new land and of remaking themselves as Americans. They were assisted in this process by the aid and example of countless compatriots in the rapidly expanding communities of the Little Italies which sprung up across America in the decades after 1880.

Building "Little Italy"

The Italian enclave that developed in the Mulberry District, a few blocks from City Hall not far north of the landing point at Battery Park, was the earliest major community of Italian-

Americans to form and the birthplace of the seventy or so "Little Italies" that grew up by the 1920s in the New York metropolitan area. Well before the Italians moved in during the 1870s and 1880s, the Mulberry District was a notorious slum in which the law-abiding rarely ventured. The Italian migrants, brought in often by labor agents, were crammed in at first into the worst rooms in squalid overcrowded tenements, gradually displacing the Irish and African-Americans who had previously dominated the area. Whole families lived in tiny windowless, poorly heated rooms, spilling out into the narrow alleyways and cobbled streets during the daytime. The area became a focus of outraged comments by journalists and social reformers, with even the municipal authorities obliged to take action and order the demolition of the worst section in the early 1890s.

Yet the appalling conditions were fairly typical of those suffered by urban working people of the day, and despite its hardships the Mulberry District did serve its purpose as a transitional community where huge numbers of Italian migrants lived and worked . While many new migrants were obliged to take the poorest sorts of labor available, working as junkmen and rag pickers, others managed to establish themselves in the district in a wide range of occupations from manual workers to professionals. As early as 1881, when there were some 20,000 Italians in Manhattan, an article in *Harper's Magazine* noted the wide range of occupations they pursued and commented that already New York City possessed two Italian-language newspapers, *L'Eco d'Italia* and *Il Republicano*, as well as three Italian mutual aid societies.

From their base in the Mulberry District Italians moved on to establish enclaves elsewhere in Manhattan, uptown in the district that became known as Italian Harlem, south of Washington Square in Greenwich Village, and on the West Side. Larger numbers settled in South Brooklyn, others in areas of Staten Island, the Bronx, and Queens. By the 1920s Italian-Americans had became one of the largest ethnic groups in the New York metropolitan area.

The first Italian national parish anywhere in the United States was St. Mary Magdalen de Pazzi, established in Philadelphia in August 1852. Clearly the numbers of Italians in Philadelphia had to reach a certain threshold before these developments occurred. In 1850 no ward in the city had more than fifteen Italian residents, but by 1860 there were 299 Italians living just below South Street in the Second, Third, and Fourth wards. Although this enclave was the earliest sign of the substantial Italian community that later grew up in south Philadelphia, by this stage it was still predominantly made up from northern Italians, predominantly from the vicinity of Genoa, with a smaller number of Tuscans. In the origins of these people it is possible to identify early instances of a process known as "chain migration," which was to be a key feature of the subsequent formation of Italian-American communities across America. Essentially chain migration occurs when one man (or more rarely woman) from a community migrates successfully, and is then followed by others from his own family and from nearby families, so that a small but ever-growing number of migrants from the same village or town end up living in close proximity in their new country. Reflecting the intensely parochial nature of the Italian South, this was very much the pattern of their immigration experience, with clusters of migrants from the same Sicilian village living side by side for many years on a street in New York or Philadelphia.

The first mutual aid society for Italians in the city was founded in 1867. The Societe di Unione e Fratellanza Italiana, organized by prominent members of the Italian community, lasted for some sixty years, holding annual balls and providing charitable assistance to Italian -Americans and others. The concentration of Italians apparent in 1860, had expanded slightly a decade later, although there were still only just over 500 Italians in the city. Yet when the real expansion began in the later part of the 1870s it was this diverse community of Italian-Americans in South Philadelphia that acted as a magnet, helping to socialize the new arrivals and providing an established set of community leaders.

In Chicago there were at least sixteen distinct Italian enclaves. The first was a district of some 1,000 Genoese established on the Near North Side by the 1890s. Southern Italians were generally not welcomed there, although some did attend the first Italian church in the city, the Church of the Assumption, which was established in 1881. A short-lived but important Little Italy formed on the South Side, in a vice area known as Polk Depot, as a flood of new migrants from the Italian South settled in the cheapest available accommodation. When this area was subject to commercial redevelopment most moved on to the Near West Side in the face of often violent opposition from the predominantly Irish residents. Stretching from Polk Street south to Taylor Street, and from Halsted Street in the West across to Canal Street this became the largest of Chicago's Italian enclaves with a third of the city's Italians, totaling 25,000 people, living there by 1910. All the southern districts were represented, with groups from Naples, Salerno, Bari, Basilicata, Abruzi, Calabria, Messina, and Palermo, particularly notable.

Chain migration has also been shown to be important in the residential composition of other significant Italian-American communities in Chicago. From the town of Ricigliano in Salerno province (which was said to have seen half its population migrate), several hundred families settled in the Armor Square district. Here it became the norm to marry within the village group, even among second generation migrants. Next to, but distinct from them, were a community of Sicilians, also divided between migrants from the small towns of Termini and Nicosia. Most of the Nicosia men were laborers, while the Terminesi were predominantly fruit peddlers. Similar groups formed elsewhere in the city, driving out the earlier migrants from Ireland, Germany, or Scandinavia. The Italian born population of Chicago surged to 16,000 by 1900, reaching 59,215 by 1920.

On the West Coast the city of San Francisco attracted the largest number of Italian residents with the first significant numbers arriving during the Gold Rush era of the 1850s. Like thousands of other foreigners, several hundred Italians were drawn by exaggerated rumors of gold lying on the ground ready to be picked up by the first man to come along. With these hopes soon dashed most settled in San Francisco, opening boarding houses, groceries, or restaurants in the Telegraph Hill district and, slightly later, in North Beach. The fishing industry in the Bay area was gradually taken over by Genoese, displacing earlier arrivals from Greece and Slovakia. Other Italian fishermen, particularly Sicilians, were prevented by the Genoese from operating in San Francisco, but were an important factor in towns such as Monterey.

Italians also played a significant part in the establishment of the Californian wine industry, with a notable contribution being made by Italian Jesuits at the Noviciate of the Sacred Heart of Los Gatos. Unlike in almost all other areas of the United States, northern Italians continued to make up a majority of the Italian community of California in general, and of San Francisco in particular.

Despite the rural Southern roots of most of the Italian migrants, their settlement in America was overwhelmingly an urban phenomenon, with the vast majority being drawn to the work opportunities available in the expanding industrial cities. Work was the key to settlement patterns everywhere. Some work was well away from the major conurbations, but much of this was contract labor that left little permanent settlement. There were, however, isolated cases of Italian farming and mining communities developing. First though we will look briefly at the popular response to the rapid growth of Italian immigrants.

Hostility

The first men or families into a district frequently had to suffer abuse, harassment, and even physical attacks, from the street gangs of existing residents, usually the Irish as they were the last nationality to arrive in U.S. cities in large numbers. Gradually Italian presence became grudgingly accepted as their numbers grew, previous residents moved out to a slightly better area as they became more established in the labor market, and the streets took on an increasingly Italian character. Racial prejudice against Italians was widespread and almost invariably people would refer to the Little Italy as "Wop Town" or "Dago Town."

Away from the streets prejudice grew as well and nativist sentiments (which were ultimately to result in the imposition of restrictions on immigration in the 1920s) began to find expression in polite circles. As the Italian population in particular increased, it was noticeable that the formerly positive attitude to them as artists and musicians expressed in the newspapers began to be more mixed. As the period of mass immigration got underway attitudes changed as Americans came into more frequent contact with ever greater numbers of poor immigrant Italians. American cities were expanding at an apparently alarming rate as the labor demands of industrialization grew, and it became easy for local opinion formers to put the blame for

Opposite: Three children from the same Italian town having arrived in New York on the S.S. Regina de Italia will separate and go to three different cities with their parents. From left to right: Linda Scholi, Flielina Scholi and Vincent Lanlani. January 7, 1920.

At Bleecher Street School, Southington, Connecticut, the student body consisted of fifty percent Americans of Italian descent and fifty percent Americans of Polish descent. May 1942.

many of the urban problems that emerged on the ever more visible population of new immigrants. At its least bad, this new approach was patronizing and offensive. At its worst, however, anti-Italian sentiment could lead to atrocities such as the notorious New Orleans lynching of eleven Italians in 1891.

It was at this period that enduring prejudicial stereotypes associating Italians with crime and violence began to become widely accepted. Even by the 1880s the corrupt police force and local papers in cities such as New Orleans were already showing a tendency to blame crimes of violence on Italians. In New Orleans the Italian community at the time, which numbered some 20,000, was made up mostly of Sicilians from Corleone and Palermo. Unsolved murders were frequently attributed by the police to "unknown Sicilians" and cases have been noted where newspaper reports of arrested Frenchmen or Spaniards deliberately Italianized their names. When the corrupt Chief of Police David Hennessy was shot dead on the night of October 9, 1890, it was quickly assumed that there was a connection to his intervention in a violent dispute between two rival Italian families involved in unloading fruit at the docks. The Mayor ordered the police to arrest "every Italian you come across," pronouncing the killers to be Sicilians before any charges were even laid. Despite efforts to mislead the jury and daily press attacks on Sicilian bandits and Mafiosi, the nine Italians put on trial were all acquitted. Instead of being freed the men were returned to prison and two days later the jail was stormed by a mob whipped up by an assistant to the mayor. The nine accused, together with two other Italians in the prison were shot repeatedly, with several victims hung from street lamps and trees. The following day even the *New York Times* noted the attack was justified, headlining its article "Chief Hennessy Avenged." When President Harrison, concerned by protests from Italy, called the lynchings "an offence against law and humanity," there was talk of impeachment. Although this was an exceptional and tragic incident it was also a reflection of the wider prejudices that were being stirred up in the face of mass immigration.

Work and family

Italians in America made a living in almost all spheres of life with at least a few of them finding work in every state of the union. For all of them, whether they had brought their immediate family with them, or as so many of the early migrants were obliged to do, left them behind for years in their home village, family remained vitally important. Family and locality were the links that allowed many migrants to gain a place on American soil, and they were also key factors in determining occupational prospects.

Any discussion of the working lives of Italian-Americans has to consider the notorious *padrone*, labor agents who recruited workers in Italy, at the dockside in America, or in the cheap boarding houses that accommodated impoverished new arrivals. Traditionally they have been blamed for exploiting and corrupting their fellow immigrants. More recently though, some writers have argued that without minimizing the hardships which they inflicted on their victims, *padrone* were an inevitable feature of the migration process and played an important role in facilitating the movement of such a huge number of immigrants in so brief a period. There is a sense in which *padrone* can be seen as an alternative, darker version, of the family link, providing men who lacked real ties there with a connection to America, albeit one that left them very vulnerable to deception and abuse.

The first *padrone* seem to have operated well before the 1880s. For many mid-nineteenth-century Americans the first Italians they encountered were the numerous itinerant musicians, organ grinders, and strolling players that reached even the remotest of towns. The controversy that surrounded the recruitment practices of at least some of these street musicians was to be repeated on a far larger scale in the era of mass migration. In a case that provides early evidence of the so-called padrone system, historian Richard N. Juliani recorded that in a Philadelphia court in 1867 two Italians disputed custody of an eight year old boy that one of the men had brought from Naples. He testified that he had agreed to pay the boy's mother $20 a year for the use of her son as a street musician, but the boy had fled to the second man complaining of ill treatment. The publicity such cases received in the press of the day helped to tarnish the image of Italians generally just as the period of large-scale migration was getting underway, and prompted legal measures to outlaw a practice that seemed uncomfortably reminiscent of slavery.

Despite this, the involvement of *padrone* expanded from the small-scale recruitment of a few musicians to take in the supply of contract laborers to the major construction projects, especially railroad work gangs across America. To a large extent their success was a consequence of earlier policies of the federal government which, in legislation passed in 1864 in a period of increasing labor demand after the Civil War, had given manufacturers and other businessmen the right to import foreign laborers under contract. As the authorities recognized in an industrial commission report in 1901, this had opened the way for speculation in cheap labor for which uneducated and often illiterate rural Italians had proved the easiest victims. The report noted that in 1900 54.5 percent of immigrants from the Italian South were illiterate, compared with a level of 24.2 percent for all migrants, and a low 11.8 percent for northern Italians. Moreover, even among the literate, few could read English. Their lack of knowledge about conditions in America made them relatively easy prey for the unscrupulous although there was little but the specific details that was unique about the experience of the victims of the worst *padrone*. Many other workers, both American-born and immigrants, also suffered badly in the process of building up American industry, mines, and railroads in the late nineteenth century.

At first *padrone* played an important part in stimulating the flow of migrants in Italy itself. They would act as agents for a manufacturer or other labor contractor and tour a region of Italy signing up workers. A majority of the workers signed up by *padrone* were men, but there was also demand for women and children for factory work. In return for the cost of their passage they would sign an agreement binding them to work for the contractor for a period of one to three or more years. As well as collecting a commission from the contractor, and generally a bribe from the men recruited, the *padrone* continued to profit once the workers reached America. They were responsible for accommodating the recruits on arrival, transporting them to the place of work, and often furnishing them with food and a place to live for the duration of the contract. All these costs plus a substantial mark-up could be recovered directly from the workers' earnings by the *padrone* who would often act as an interpreter and go-between. There was also a profit to be made in commissions and other payments from remittances he would assist in sending back to Italy, and often a further payment for arranging a passage for any who wished to return to Italy after the contract expired.

Usually the *padrone* worked with another dubious type found in most large Italian-American communities who was known as a "banker." This man —generally a prominent and often respected individual—acted to finance the activities of one or more *padrone*, taking a share of their profits and handling aspects such as the sending of money back home, when considerable "shrinkage" could occur. Over the years the role of *padrone* changed. Often he became a kind of employment contractor in his own right, recruiting workers and bringing them to America at his own risk, then hiring them out to employers as needed. Frequently the workers' wages would be paid directly to the *padrone* who could deduct as much as he wished for board and lodging. By the 1890s the flow of migrants was so great that there was rarely any need to recruit in Italy. Legislation also restricted the scope of contract immigration. Instead sufficient penniless new immigrants could be signed up at the dockside or in the cheap boarding houses of Little Italy, easily lured by misleading promises of regular pay in a town not too far away.

If the actions of many of the *padrone* and their bankers showed the willingness of some Italian-Americans to profit from the misfortunes of their countrymen, others in the same community worked to expose and improve conditions in the labor camps and factories. Gino Speranza of the Society for the Protection of Italian Immigrants investigated working conditions in many parts of the U.S., publishing numerous articles and reports. The controversy this publicity generated was an important factor in improving conditions in the early years of the twentieth century.

The hardship and brutality experienced by migrants in the labor camps across America was merely one aspect of an especially bleak phase in the history of confrontation between American capitalism and a developing organized labor movement. Strikes were seen as challenges to the rule of law and even national security, that could be forcibly suppressed by the militia, backed up if necessary by armed Pinkerton agents. Italians, along with other recent migrants, were on the front-line of these conflicts, often as strikers and union activists, more rarely driven by hunger to work as scab laborers in place of the strikers. Two Italian women and ten children were among those who died in one of the most notorious incidents in this conflict, known as the Ludlow Massacre. On April 20, 1914, a detachment of troops opened fire with machine guns on a camp housing striking miners and their families during a dispute between the United Mine Workers and John D. Rockefeller Jr.'s Colorado Fuel & Iron Company Works. The shooting set the canvas tents ablaze and fire swept across the camp, killing more than forty-five people, most of them women and children trapped in holes dug for protection against gunfire.

Among the Italian migrants were many activists with experience of clandestine struggle on behalf of Socialist and even anarchist groups back home, with veterans of the Sicilian fasci particularly important. Some of these men and women, together with others who were radicalized by their experiences in America, played an important part in the early history of the labor movement. The more established unions, such as the American Federation of Labor, were reluctant at this time to recruit immigrants, driving them instead towards more radical groups. Among the areas where Italian workers participated in major periods of labor unrest in the early decades of the twentieth century were miners strikes in Utah in 1903, stonecutters in Barre, Vermont, in 1908, and major textile workers strikes in Lawrence, Massachusetts in 1912 and again in 1919.

Italian immigrants, Nicola Sacco and Bartolomeo Vanzetti, became the most notorious victims of the repression that followed when the widespread climate of paranoia and hostility to radicalism that marked American life in this period was heightened by the country's entry into World War I and by the Bolshevik Revolution in Russia in 1917. Relatively small groups of workers interested in anarchism had been formed in many of the urban centers, attracting support among Germans, Poles, Spaniards, and Jews as well as Italians. Prominent Italian anarchists included the intellectuals Guiseppe Ciancabilla and Errico Malatesta, and the more activist Carlo Tresca. The latter was an important organizer for the IWW who was himself acquitted of a murder charge after the death of a striker in a mining dispute in Minnesota. Nicola Sacco, who was age seventeen when he came to America from the town of Torremaggiore in 1908, was a quiet family man who worked as an edge trimmer in a shoe factory. Bartolomeo Vanzetti, from Vallefalletto in Piedmont, had worked as a laborer on construction sites, but at the time of his arrest in 1920 was a fish peddler. Both were self-educated men who saw in anarchism the support for a human dignity and freedom that had eluded them in working life. The two men were arrested while distributing anarchist literature, then charged with two murders committed during a robbery the previous month. Despite demonstrations in their favor across Europe and America, and a lack of evidence against them, the judge was clearly hostile and both were convicted. They were executed on June 1, 1927 after nearly seven years on death row.

The death of Sacco and Vanzetti marked something of a turning point for Italian-American radicalism. In the years that followed Italian workers tended to find wider acceptance within mainstream unions and the community as a whole began to take on more conservative politics. Nevertheless Italian-American men and women continued to play significant roles in the union movement. A notable example was that of Angela and Maria Bambace who were important organizers of Local 89 of the International Ladies Garment Workers Union in New York, which with 40,000 members was the largest local in the United States by 1934.

Women and the family

Rather than seeking greater independence from their husband and/or family, most Italian women worked to contribute to the family budget and sustain their families in the face of high living costs and inadequate wages. In places where there was a high demand for female labor, such as the garment district of New York, or the cigar industry in Florida, a substantial proportion of Italian-American women were employed. Often women began to work as young as 14, continuing to take on paid work outside the home at least until marriage. In some areas, such as the shoe-factories of Endicott, in upstate New York, many married women continued

to do factory work, but it seems to have been more common elsewhere for them to switch to other sources of income, such as taking in lodgers or doing piecework. Piecework was, however, notably badly paid, and even by drawing on the help of young children after school, income from such occupations as making rag rugs could be as low as fifty cents a day.

Italian immigrant settlers Mr. and Mrs. John Forgone at Cerri Ranch in Paradise Valley, Nevada.

Occupations available to Italian-American women changed only slowly as the century progressed. Over three-quarters of all working Italian-American women were still employed in the textile industries in 1950, a proportion that didn't decline below a quarter until after 1970. Over the same period the percentage of clerical workers rose from eight to 40 percent, managers from two to nine percent, and professionals such as teachers, nurses, and lawyers, from two to nine percent.

Many first generation women lived and worked largely among their fellow Italians in the urban enclaves and consequently had little opportunity to learn English. Frequently they had to live in their new surroundings within the tight strictures that had governed appropriate female behavior in the very different circumstances of an Italian village. While most no doubt shared the ideas of duty and respect they had been brought up with, that did not prevent some from feeling and expressing resentment at their lot. Conflict with their children was inevitable as a second generation grew up speaking English and educated into very different ideas and norms. On the other end of these conflicts many younger women reported feeling a sense of turmoil and guilt about moving away from their parents. For many Italian–Americans the family remained both a still powerful reality and a tiresome cliché as individuals struggled to frame their responses to a changing world in ways that reflected their unique personalities and opportunities.

Crime

The ultimate cliché of the family in the context of Italian-American life is of course, the distorted image of Italian participation in organized crime. Virtually from the start of any substantial Italian immigrant community in America, exaggerated and misleading accounts of the extent of their involvement in criminal activity have been a major source of prejudice against them, and a useful instrument in the hands of those who wished to promote such anti-Italian feeling for ends of their own. Such has been the success of these stereotypes that they have become part of the popular culture of America, promoted and recycled in countless movies and novels, ironically often in recent decades the work of Italian-American filmmakers and authors.

In fact the evidence behind the sensationalized accounts suggests that organized crime was largely an indigenous development in the United States, in which a tiny minority drawn from both earlier arrivals in America such as the English, African-Americans, and Scots-Irish, and virtually all immigrant groups participated as and when opportunities occurred in their areas. Contacts between organized crime groups in America and the Mafia in southern Italy seem to have been minimal, at least before the quite recent development of large-scale drug smuggling.

An Italian family arriving at Ellis Island,

September 9, 1920.

The roots of the stereotype lie back in Italy, with an equally distorted image of a supposed natural tendency towards criminal activity among southerners in general and Sicilians in particular, that was perpetuated by the northern-dominated government in the decades after unification as a justification for the failure of their social policies in the region. Although crime in Sicily seems to have been no higher than elsewhere in the 1870s, the complaints became something of a self-fulfilling prophecy as continued neglect and official corruption in the South created a climate in which older traditions of banditry could be transformed into a wider pattern of criminal activity in cities such as Naples and Palermo.

In the crowded enclaves of "Little Italy" in New York and other American cities, crimes such as burglary, blackmail, street robbery, and extortion were widespread, but crime had been rampant in poor and squalid areas such as the Mulberry District long before the Italians had arrived, and was equally common in districts housing Irish, Jews, or African-Americans. Frequently the police, (often not beyond corruption themselves) made little effort to enforce the law in these districts. Newspapers, as always quick to promote and exaggerate any sensational event, seized on a few incidents in which extortionists operating in New York used the name "mano nero" or Black Hand, turning what appears to have been the activities of individuals or small gangs into a vast conspiracy. With the extortion of more prosperous immigrants a favored offence, criminals within the Italian community quickly realized that attributing their actions to a mysterious "mano nero" by leaving an imprint of a hand in coal dust both intimidated their victims into paying faster and muddied the waters of any police investigation. By 1910 this mysterious and, in fact, nonexistent organization was widely held to be responsible for a vast range of offences right across America.

It is no coincidence that the New Orleans lynching took place at a time when the reality of a new wave of mass immigration was becoming apparent and anti-immigrant sentiment was rampant. The Black Hand became the focus of attention after the turn of the century and, perhaps surprisingly, little more was heard about the Mafia until after World War II. In the intervening period, crime in general and organized crime in particular, were certainly a seri-

ous problem in urban centers throughout America, reaching a peak in the Prohibition era. There is no doubt that Italian-Americans played a prominent part in some of these activities but the press and politicians spoke of "gangsters," "syndicates," or the "Mob," rather than of any specifically Italian organization. What seems to have occurred is a gradual expansion of existing types of street-based gangs with the collusion of corrupt city politicians and police. At the end of the 1890s the Neapolitan, Paolo Vaccarelli, headed one of these street gangs in New York, but the gang was made up of Jews and Irishmen as much as Italians, and its leader had Americanized his name to Frank Kelly.

The next generation of criminal figures grew up in the United States and their involvement reflected their experience growing up in poverty in America, and the patterns of criminal activity—from prostitution to labor racketeering to liquor smuggling—already there. Among these men were Frank Costello, "Lucky" Luciano, and Al Capone, but also such members of other immigrant nationalities as Meyer Lansky, Bugsy Siegal, and Arthur Rothstein.

If all the main figures in organized crime became the subject of exaggeration and myth making in the media, few have attracted quite so much attention or remained the subject of so much speculation as Charles "Lucky" Luciano. Born Salvatore Lucani in Sicily in 1897, Luciano started out as a small time hustler along with Lansky, Siegal, and others in gangs around 14th Street and Second Avenue. He came to public attention in 1931 following the killing of two leading gangland figures. Partly as a result of statements made during Congressional hearings into organized crime, the Press transformed these killings into an episode known as the "Americanization of the Mob" in which as many as ninety Sicilian gangsters were supposedly wiped out across the whole country. More sober assessments indicate that this alleged massacre never took place.

Luciano's subsequent activities as a gangster became bound up in ways that have yet to become fully clear with the activities of the prosecutor Thomas Dewey, who built his career on a campaign against organized crime. After Luciano was arrested in 1936 and subsequently sentenced to thirty to fifty years, an extraordinary deal was struck by Dewey, under which he was allowed to retire to Sicily at the end of the war. By this time Dewey had become Governor of New York, allegedly with the assistance of large campaign donations from Lansky and Costello, and the mob-controlled union vote. To provide cover for this odd arrangement the totally false story was spread that Luciano had used his supposed connections with the Sicilian Mafia to assist in the Allied invasion of Sicily.

If, as seems to have been the case, what we might call real "Mafiosi" were too busy making money in Italy to emigrate to America, why did the image of "the Mafia" become so pervasive? Firstly of course truth is often duller than fiction and doesn't sell nearly so many newspapers or movie tickets. Moreover as Dewey demonstrated, politicians and police officials could transform their careers by sensationalizing a story that would guaranteed public attention.

Much of the vocabulary we associate today with the Mafia emerged from witnesses to a U.S. Senate investigation chaired by Senator Estes Kefauver in 1950-51. According to one of the reports it issued, "there is a sinister criminal organization known as the Mafia operating throughout the country with ties in other nations. The Mafia is a direct descendant of a criminal organization of the same name originating in the Island of Sicily." Although almost all the Italian-Americans called as witnesses before the committee denied the existence of any such organization, these denials were attributed to a supposed ancient Sicilian code of silence. Everyone else seemed to "know" about it so the denials came to seem a further confirmation of its mysterious power.

A second enquiry ten years later drew on the plea bargaining testimony of a minor gangster Joseph Valachi from whose often confused and rambling answers a then new but now familiar vocabulary emerged. He talked of the "Cosa Nostra," the family, of button men, etc. Valachi's information was of course exactly what the enquiry and the media wanted to hear and received extensive publicity worldwide. The impact of this was then to be multiplied a hundred fold with the publication in 1969 of Mario Puzo's *The Godfather*. The book's success launched an entire industry of Mafia fiction, sensational "true crime" exposes, and of course numerous movies in which the Italian-American gangster and his pasta-cooking mother became a worldwide cliché. Although much of the focus of media anxiety has since moved on to the perceived threats posed by other sources of foreign conspiracy against the American way, such as Colombian drug cartels and the so-called Russian Mafia (and it is no coincidence that this has coincided with increased immigration from these areas in turn) the stereotyped denigration of Italian-Americans is still never far below the surface.

Religion and identity

Although the migrants who came to America from Italy in such large numbers in the decades after 1880 were classified by immigration authorities as Italians, even this identity had very little meaning for most of them in a country which had only been formed a few years earlier. Very few even spoke Italian. Instead most were attached to other extremely local identities, to their village or town, settling in America wherever possible side-by-side with people they knew from their village. Many no doubt began to become aware of what they shared with their fellow Italians during the common ordeal of their transatlantic voyage, but for most it was only in America living in the urban enclaves of the major cities that a more effective perception of a national identity emerged.

This awareness of being Italian, and subsequently of being Italian-American, was a continually evolving sense of identity, which despite the weaknesses of the "melting pot" approach did involve an increasing degree of assimilation to mainstream American life. For a majority of Italian-Americans religion played a significant role in this changing sense of identity, both in providing transitional mechanisms in the process of assimilation, and through events such as festivals, providing a continuing focus for markers of ethnicity that remain important today.

It was not until the end of the nineteenth century, after a period of considerable struggle, that national parishes became the norm. Other than the notable exception of Philadelphia (due in part to a sympathetic bishop, himself an immigrant from Bohemia), elsewhere in America the small but growing number of Italian migrants worshipped alongside other Catholics, most of whom were from Ireland or Germany. They seem to have been welcomed as co-religionists worshipping on equal terms, with records indicating a number of marriages taking place between Italian men and Irish women. Even when Italians opened churches, such as St. Anthony's established on Sullivan Street in New York by Italian Franciscans in 1866, the congregation was mixed. Irish and Italian Catholics, with lesser numbers of French and Germans, worshipped side by side on friendly terms in churches across the main cities of America.

However, as in other areas of American life, a marked change in attitudes occurred in the 1880s when the flow of immigration increased and the balance of new arrivals shifted towards poorer, less well-educated migrants from the South. Partly this was due to the sudden arrival of large numbers of migrants in new areas as groups of laborers were sent by *padrone* and other labor contractors to work on railroads and mines in remote regions. Men who often walked miles into the nearest towns on a Sunday morning frequently found that they received a hostile reception from local churches. Many were forced to sit at the back or even in the basement. However, even in the cities where Italians had previously been accepted as part of congregations, prejudices developed and once receptive neighborhood churches began to discriminate against Italians.

Much of this reaction was due to the fear and hostility aroused by the relatively sudden appearance in American cities of huge numbers of new and strange immigrants competing for jobs and living space in the same districts and it found expression in naked prejudice against Italians in general. Slightly more reasoned opposition focused on two complaints, namely that the newcomers were not true Catholics, but believers in an idolatrous folk religion, and that many were dangerously anticlerical.

It was certainly the case that many of the migrants from the South brought with them a version of Catholicism that was very different from the worship of the Irish, and especially of the Germans. Over the centuries of hardship and isolation ancient folk traditions had lived on under a veneer of Catholic orthodoxy, with pragmatic priests frequently compromising on strict details of doctrine for the sake of their congregations. There was a strong belief in the direct patronage and intercession of the saints, with each village dedicated to its patron or patroness who was called on regularly to work miracles for the benefit of her flock. There was often a deeply personal belief in the powers of the Madonna and in the reality of the Holy Family, but set against this in the eyes of many American Catholics was an inappropriate approach to the church itself and, in their view at least, a pervasive ignorance of Catholic orthodoxy. In reality of course it was more a matter of different styles of worship, and of relatively unimportant details of behavior, but in the climate of the day these nuances were magnified.

Accompanying these concerns was a general suspicion in the American Church hierarchy that the attitude of many Italians towards their priests was not the one of unquestioning obedience expected by the Irish. Instead Italians in the South had tended to assess each priest on their merits. Some came from similar backgrounds of rural poverty and did what they could to ease the plight of their parishioners and to meet their interest in local festivals. Others, particularly outsiders from the north, tended to view their rural posting as a bitter exile among ignorant peasants and exact what they could in the way of gifts and food from already hard pressed villagers. Many of these priests were regarded as parasites and were both feared and resented. Overlaying these local concerns was a more general anticlericalism resulting from the church in Italy's long established support for a series of repressive foreign regimes and its fierce opposition to the Risorgimento and the reformist state. This anticlerical feeling was however largely confined to the more literate of northern Italians and their journals and newspapers, although there were instances of radical workers such as the stonemasons of Barre in Vermont driving away a priest.

Since they were now being made to feel unwelcome and ignorant in the established Catholic churches across America, Italian immigrants in the 1880s began to worship together

New Haven, Connecticut. Mr. and Mrs. Andrew Amarone and their fifteen children were the largest family in town. They lived on the combined earnings of Mr. Amarone and two daughters, amounting to between $25–$30 a week, April 22, 1938.

with the support of sympathetic priests. At first they were denied the chance to establish churches of their own but were, often reluctantly, given permission to hold masses in the basement rooms of existing churches. Some supported their demands for national parishes on segregationist and racist grounds—one Irish pastor in New York is reported to have told Archbishop Corrigan in 1889 that Italians "cannot well be mixed with other nationalities on account of their filthy condition and habits." The Archbishop was sympathetic to the Italian-Americans demands and expressed his support for Italian national parishes to authorities in Rome, but the plan was opposed by other American bishops despite the precedent set by the authorization of German parishes in the 1870s.

Although the Church in America did not really agree to the formation of national parishes with Vatican approval until the final decade of the century, many had already emerged on a de facto basis somewhat earlier as the influx of new migrants into old German or Irish neighborhoods displaced existing residents leaving their churches serving all-Italian congregations. Often this involved the local Italian-American community and its representatives in a long struggle with the bishop to gain recognition and approval for their activities. Depending on where their sympathies lay some bishops gave tacit support and did their best to assist in obtaining premises, while others deliberately obstructed efforts by such measures as refusing to appoint Italian-speaking priests.

Everywhere that Italian-American communities established mutual aid societies one of their first goals was to organize an Italian parish, but many had to wait until approval was finally given by Pope Leo XIII in 1899. After that the number of Italian parishes grew rapidly, with more than five hundred established across the nation in the following two decades. No longer able to block the appointment of Italian priests, hostile members of the Irish-dominated church hierarchy continued to intervene by insisting on the selection of northern Italians that they saw as being more likely to resist the supposed excesses of their southern flocks.

The intensity with which many Italian-American communities fought to establish their own churches and national parishes reflected the central role which the church had played in the communal life of their villages and towns back home. Whatever their attitude towards the local priest and even to church attendance the whole population would assemble to celebrate the annual festival of their patron saint. Months of hardship and sacrifice went into assembling the resources for days of music, feasting and parades. In the early decades in America, when clusters of villagers had formed living side by side along the streets of the Little Italies, each group of any size continued to celebrate its own saints day fiesta as elaborately as they could. Where there was a church they insisted that it find room for a plaster statue of their saint to be prominently displayed along with all the others, often a cause of disputes when there was an Irish or a northern Italian priest. In many areas these local festivals and folk customs continued to be celebrated at late as the 1940s but over time as regional loyalties waned and a new American-born generation came of age, there was a general tendency in each district to consolidate celebrations around the festivals of the Madonna and a small number of other major saints days.

New, distinctively Italian-American, festive occasions emerged over the years, attended and enjoyed by all regardless of their ancestral homes. Yet the form of these festivals retained many Italian elements. Women still processed barefoot behind the saint's statue. Votive offerings were still made, children were held high by their parents to pin dollar bills to the robes of the statue as the procession passed along the street. Music from marching bands filled the streets heralding an evening of fireworks, feasting and dancing. Other Americans were drawn to these celebrations which were widely reported in the newspapers and later on television and they came to be regarded as a distinctive and important part of what it meant to be Italian-American.

However, there were, and still are, a significant number of Italian-American Protestants and Jews. People of the Jewish faith had formed a small, but mostly wealthy and respected, minority in Italy for many centuries. The anti-Semitism and occasional pogroms that were a feature of the treatment of Jews in most other parts of Europe had been comparatively rare. In the early part of the fascist era during the 1920s little action was taken against them, but the situation changed as Mussolini's alliance with the Germans grew closer. In the 1930s a number of Italians were among the many Jews who fled to America to escape increasing persecution in Europe. Many of these migrants were educated professionals who found little difficulty in adapting to life in America.

An immigration officer checks the names of some of the thousand refugees who have just arrived from Italy escaping Fascist persecution, August 4, 1944.

Some of the earliest Italian immigrants to America were Protestants. In 1657 a group of 150 Waldensians, French-speaking Protestants from what is now northern Italy, landed in the Dutch colony of New Amsterdam, seeking a place where they could worship freely. Some settled at Stony Brook on Long Island, the remainder in Delaware. A second influx of Waldensians occurred in the period of mass immigration, with a community of some 400 people arriving in the 1890s and forming the town of Valdese in North Carolina. A sense of origins is still very important in Valdese, where Italian festivals and some of the buildings of the original settlers continue to prove a major tourists attraction.

Other Italian-American Protestants were mostly converted as a result of missionary programs run by American Baptists, Methodists, and Presbyterians both in Italy and among newly arrived migrants. American Protestants, who had already began attempts to evangelize in Italy, albeit with little success, were quick to recognize that the hostility of the Catholic Church in America towards southern Italians offered them an excellent opportunity to attract converts. They made particular efforts to provide much needed social services, such as schools, nurseries, and other assistance to converts, and were quick to offer them national churches and services in Italian. By 1917 there were a surprisingly high total of 107 Presbyterian churches and missions for Italians, eighty-two run by the Baptists, and sixty by the Methodists, almost all of them run by Italian pastors. However most churches had only tiny congregations and despite the expense and energy devoted to this missionary project there were only some 17,000 Italian-American converts. In the following decades it appears that barriers between Italian immigrants and mainstream American Protestants were minimal as intermarriage became common and the occupational and residential mobility of this minority was far higher than their Catholic countrymen. By the end of the 1930s the ethnic identity of the surviving churches had almost disappeared, with services mostly held in English for integrated congregations, and the descendants of the early converts blending in to the general body of American Protestantism.

Italian-Americans in public life

In general the majority of Italian immigrants were at first confined by a combination of their poor language skills and by the prejudice that confronted them to industrial jobs that were often dangerous and were almost always the worst paid. Children were obliged to labor from the age of fourteen or even younger. Surveys conducted in the early decades of the twentieth century showed average incomes of Italian-American families to be the lowest of any ethnic group apart from African-Americans. For most the success story in America was to be only an extremely gradual one, extending often over several generations as educational attainment rose and median incomes increased nearer to the national norms.

Yet among even the earliest migrant communities there were individual success stories of a different scale. Some few of these resulted in considerable wealth and in lasting business achievements, although no others were on the scale of A.P. Giannini who founded Bank of America. Amadeo Pietro Giannini was born in Genoa in 1870 and began working in San Francisco as one among many Italian fruit peddlers. After borrowing some money from his stepfather and a few friends he opened his own bank in 1904, calling it with some exaggeration the Bank of Italy. He started off like many other "bankers' to his local community, going door to door taking deposits and making loans to his Italian neighbors. His success was remarkable, since it is reported that in the San Francisco earthquake of 1906, only two years after he began, he had some $2 million in gold and securities to rescue from looters. Legend has it that it was his achievement in opening for business as soon as the fires were put out that made his name and sparked a dramatic expansion—by 1945 his renamed Bank of America was the world's largest privately owned bank. Giannini died in 1949.

There were quite a large number of other successful Italian-American entrepreneurs although operating on a smaller scale and without such far reaching success, but more significant for the general life of the immigrant communities were the men, and a few women, who achieved only local renown within their own urban communities. These people, who were known as *prominenti*, middle-class migrants who often had some small wealth amassed as a shopkeeper, restaurateur, or other trade, usually became known as a leader of their local community through their activities as a "banker" and notary. Unfortunately, most were exploiting their fellow countrymen and women as much if not more than assisting them, although at least some of them did become communal benefactors. By writing letters for the illiterate, assisting with small loans or with finding employment, helping people to arrange passage for family members left behind, negotiating with the police when someone was in trouble—all these services gained them respect and trust from those they helped.

The other side of the coin however was that to the less scrupulous all these activities offered prospects for money making, often including the recruitment of labor in collaboration with *padrone*. Immigrants were vulnerable to deception by those who assumed the title of "notary," some of them Italian lawyers unable to practice in the U.S., who became known for extracting fees and commissions for a huge variety of swindles. So-called "bankers" were able to collect deposits without offering interest and invest or speculate with the funds in ventures of their own, many of which collapsed in the recession of 1907. Perhaps because so many succumbed to the temptation to exploit their position, those *prominenti* who were regarded as honest attracted an extraordinary degree of respect and support.

Closely interconnected with the activities and careers of many *prominenti* in the early decades of the Italian-American presence in the United States was the establishment of a wide variety of mutual aid associations and societies. Some scholars have argued that the traditional attachment of Italians to the family made them relatively slow to participate in communal organizations in America, and consequently delayed the emergence of Italian-American involvement in the political process compared to other contemporary immigrant peoples. Nevertheless it is still the case that numerous such societies were established in the 1880s and 1890s, and there can be no doubt that they played a crucial role in mediating the involvement of the new Italian migrants with wider American civil society. To some extent these societies

A special Piedmontese dinner in the Boggio household during May 1981. The feast included pig's feet, zucchini flowers stuffed with sausage and spinach, focaccia, and grissini.

were able to fill in gaps in the social support network that would have been the responsibility of the extended family back home, such as paying benefits to those who were prevented by sickness from earning money to feed their family, and providing for funeral expenses. In the early years virtually all the societies brought together men and women from the same village or region, so their meetings also provided a forum for nostalgic discussions and for passing the latest news and gossip from back home. Even later when the close knit local residential patterns of the original enclaves had begun to disperse many still supported these societies as a forum where often increasingly fragile ties with their home community could be sustained. In Baltimore, for example, there were eight societies by 1902, with a combined membership in the region of one thousand.

Frequently these institutions were started up by the local *prominenti* who had sufficient support to be able to mobilize followers and clients to participate, and who found the societies a useful means of both acknowledging their achievements and legitimizing them as men of influence to outsiders. But, however powerful and respected they became in their own communities virtually all Italian-American *prominenti* remained marginal figures in the wider world, useful when votes were needed at elections, but never fully accepted at the centers of power and influence in local or national politics.

The heavy reliance which the New Deal coalition of President Franklin Delano Roosevelt in the 1930s placed on the ethnic vote made community leaders and spokesmen such as the *prominenti* increasingly influential in national politics. Although most of the *prominenti* did not attempt to translate their local support into an elected political office their control over key blocks of Italian-American voters gave them an entry into the political mainstream for the first time. In the period leading up to the U.S. entry into World War II the political life and public representation of the Italian-American community became increasingly divided by conflict between the largely pro-Mussolini *prominenti* and the antifascists. Although most ordinary Italians stood aside from the details of this dispute, apart from sharing an understandable sense of national pride in what was widely perceived to be a resurgence of Italy, it was to be vitally important in deciding where the loyalties of the community lay when hostilities between Italy and America finally broke out.

Across most of the country Italians were widely dispersed occupationally by this time, and although there were many Italians among the unions in occupations such as mining, construction, clothing, fur processing, and other industries they were only sufficiently concentrated to elect powerful Italian-American leaders in New York City. Pearl Harbor prompted the *prominenti* to finally make a public break with fascism and express their loyalty as citizens of America. Leading *prominenti* organized rallies and patriotic banquets that did much to convince the public and media of the loyalty of Italian-Americans. These efforts paid off the following month when the Attorney General agreed to remove all 600,000 or so non-naturalized Italian-Americans from the list of so-called "enemy aliens." Of course many thousands of Italian-Americans went on to serve with distinction in the armed forces, mostly in the Pacific theater. For both the men and women that enlisted and those they left behind the war was a key event in speeding up their assimilation into American society.

Beginning in the early decades of the twentieth century a few significant figures did attain elected political office, marking the early stages of the acceptance of Italian-Americans into the mainstream of political life. Fiorello La Guardia, perhaps the best known Italian-American political figure, was born in New York in 1882. Son of a musician who had come to America to work as an arranger before joining the U.S. Army as a bandmaster. La Guardia had a varied career before going into politics including serving in the American Consular Service in Budapest, Hungary, and in Trieste, Austria 1901–04 followed by a period spent as consular agent at Fiume, Hungary, 1904–06. His long political career culminated in six terms as a Republican Congressman and starting in 1933 served three terms as a vigorous reforming mayor of New York working in particular to root out political corruption as well as promoting slum clearance programs.

The gradual rightward drift in Italian American political representation continued as the community became more prosperous. Italian-Americans did not switch their vote en masse from the Democrats to the Republicans, but over time the balance of their votes tended to become more even and in line with general American voting patterns. Thus between the early 1930s and early 1940s the percentage of Italian-American votes cast for Republicans rose from twenty-six percent to a more even forty-four percent. This shift allowed Republicans to take control of previously solid Democrat boroughs in the major cities of the East Coast and marked a further stage in the gradual assimilation of the community. In the decades that followed numerous more Italian-American politicians achieved office at a variety of levels across the nation.

In the arts and entertainment world many Italian-Americans have gained prominence, among them figures such as Rudolph Valentino, Frank Cappa, Frank Sinatra, or more recently, Madonna, and Leonardo di Caprio. Italian-Americans have also been notable successful in the field of sports, where we can mention such legendary figures as Joe DiMaggio and Vince Lombardi.

Italian-Americans today

In the earliest days of mass emigration life was undeniably hard. Then, as the immigrants settled and began to prosper and become accepted Italian-Americans in common with other communities of immigrant origin, social mobility became closely linked to residential mobility. As soon as they had gained sufficiently rewarding employment, Italians began to move out from the inner city enclaves to residential suburbs, participating in the wider move away from inner cities by the more affluent sectors of American society. This lead over time to the dissolution of many of the close knit communities of Italian speakers. In the suburbs residence patterns became far more diffuse, putting a strain on the contacts that had maintained the closeness of communal institutions. Italian-Americans are now an accepted and generally unremarked part of the patchwork of peoples of diverse origins that make up modern America, competing on an equal basis for opportunities in education and employment.

After a century or more of adaptation and assimilation to life in America, the evidence suggests that while Italian-Americans today are generally well within the range of parameters of other well integrated ethnic groups socioeconomic distinctions from the average can still be observed.

The changing nature of Italian-American identity today is reflected in and at least in part constituted by the changing position of the Catholic religion in the life of the community. As in American society generally, church attendance has fallen and surveys indicate that the hold of the church over even its continuing nominal adherents as indicated in such sensitive issues as attitudes to divorce and contraception is becoming increasingly tenuous. For those that remain regular churchgoers Catholicism has offered itself as an alternative pole of cultural identity which can become more important than ethnic origin in certain contexts. National parishes mostly disappeared with the movement out of the ethnic enclaves and Italian-Americans are fully integrated into the mainstream of Catholic church life and playing an increasing role in the church hierarchy throughout America.

Despite falling church attendance's the religious festivals remain crucial to what it means to be Italian-American today. However these festivals have themselves participated in the processes of change over the past century. As the early patterns of settlement in village groupings brought about by chain migrations broke up and the need to appeal beyond the commemoration of local patron saints became apparent the marking of many minor saints days in each area became subsumed under a smaller number of major festivals. These provided important occasions on which all the organizations, associations and informal groups could work together, mobilizing community resources to provide the best possible celebration. Italians from all regions of the home country were drawn to events that had previously been focused on regional patrons, while over the years the colorful parades, music, and feasting drew ever bigger crowds of non-Italians as well. From about the mid-1970s many of them were renamed as generic Italian citywide events with titles such as Italian Heritage Festival or Festa Italiana, although some of the more important ones still retain a link to the saints day of a local parish. At the same time the form of the events underwent similar processes of change in order to appeal to a wider audience, which today usually includes both local and national TV coverage.

CHAPTER 7 # Chinese and Japanese

The Pacific seaboard Immigration Station was at Angel Island, California; seen here in c.1915.

Immigrants from China and Japan were in many ways similar to the majority of migrants coming to America from Europe in the nineteenth century, men and women taking considerable personal risks in the hope of securing a better economic future for themselves and their families. Yet they were frequently seen as posing unique and sinister threat to the American way of life and in consequence were subjected to both legal discrimination and public hostility that went well beyond the usual nativist opposition to other immigrant groups. The Naturalization Act of 1870 restricted rights to acquire American citizenship to "white persons and persons of African descent," making Asian migrants ineligible to become Americans until the provision was lifted in 1943, and providing a legal basis for much of the discrimination that followed. Moreover the passage of the Chinese Exclusion Act of 1882 made the Chinese for almost forty years the only people in the world denied free entry into the United States. Only Japanese military might prevented a similar legal exclusion of further Japanese migrants, although an informal agreement with the Japanese government imposed de facto limits there too. Until the 1970s many scholars also tended to perpetuate this essentially racist distinction disregarding Asians in histories of immigration, often treating them as simply temporary working visitors. In fact however much of the significant differences between Asian and European immigrant communities may be accounted for largely by the discrimination itself rather than by more fundamental distinctions.

Chinese

The first Chinese arrived in the Americas as sailors and servants aboard Spanish galleons in the sixteenth century, with the beginnings of a Chinese enclave in Mexico City dating to as early as 1635. Some of these may have visited California, while later Chinese sailors on European vessels are recorded on the East Coast at Baltimore in 1785 and in the Northwest at

an English settlement on Vancouver Island in 1788. Others, including the occasional merchant or other traveler will have arrived unrecorded in the first half of the nineteenth century. By mid-century the Chinese empire was weakening internally and opening up to the wider world after an unprecedented defeat at the hands of British traders in the Opium War (1849–52). Economic dislocation and a series of rebellions contributed towards a substantial exodus of people from the southeastern provinces of the empire. The migration to America, which was recorded as totaling over 332,000 Chinese predominantly from the coastal provinces of Fukien and Kwantung, was merely a part of a larger exodus of some 2.4 million people to neighboring countries in Southeast Asia, Hawaii, Peru, and the Caribbean Islands in the years before 1900. It was the California Gold Rush of 1848 that diverted part of this migrant flow toward America and first brought Chinese immigrants to the United States in significant numbers. So strong was this association that the characters that came to stand for California in Cantonese may be read as "gold mountain."

A few Chinese were among the earliest to stake out claims but by 1850 they numbered only 500 out of the almost 60,000 miners in California. After that though as news spread back home the number of Chinese miners grew extremely rapidly, prompting attempts to exclude them from several mining camps and the first state anti-Chinese discrimination in the form of a tax on foreign miners first directed against Mexicans. Despite this Chinese miners followed the series of gold strikes over the following decade, in Nevada, Oregon, and British Columbia in the 1850s, the Columbia River basin, northeast Oregon, and Montana in the 1860s, and in Colorado and South Dakota during the 1870s.

Employment

In the popular imagination, stoked by countless hostile press reports, Chinese immigrants to America were indissolubly linked with the image of "coolies" laboring unpaid on the railroad construction gangs. In fact, although Chinese laborers did help build the western sections of the transcontinental railroads they were certainly not connected with the so-called "coolie trade." This was an organized exploitation of indentured Chinese laborers exported to the Caribbean and Latin America by European and Chinese entrepreneurs as a substitute labor force following the abolition of the transatlantic trade in African slaves. Anti-Slavery legislation after the Civil War made such contracts of indenture unenforceable in the United States (although they differed only in degree from the earlier indentures under which thousands of Europeans had reached America) and there is no evidence that "coolies" were brought here at all. Instead some Chinese financed the $50 dollars or so cost of their voyage via family resources or rotating credit associations, while others relied on Chinese moneylenders. Undoubtedly some of them were obliged to work in degrading conditions to repay their loans but the same was true of countless other migrants of the era. Moreover it is now clear that Chinese railroad construction workers, although often paid less than Europeans, were able to save up to $20 a month from their $35 salary, which was by no means a poverty wage by

View of an early Chinese immigrant community in California, c.1900.

contemporary standards. In all some 10,000 Chinese laborers were employed on the western sections of the Central Pacific, Southern Pacific, and Northern Pacific railroads. Some of them settled in town along the routes as far afield as Utah and Texas.

Of course even in the early years not all Chinese migrants in California were gold prospectors or railroad builders. Despite the frequent hostility towards Chinese immigrants American officials recognized that they supplied cheap labor essential to the development of the West in general and California in particular. During the 1870s more than 12,000 arrived each year, and taking into account a quite high number of returnees and multiple voyages the Chinese population in America by the end of the decade was around 105,000, most of whom lived in California. They brought with them agricultural skills that transformed large expanses of the state, whether as field laborers, sharecroppers, small holders, or truck farmers supplying vegetables and citrus fruits to the rapidly expanding towns. Many more Chinese were employed as cooks or household servants. Thousands of others supplied much of the labor force in the early phase of Californian industrialization that centered on San Francisco, dominating employment in the city's garment, shoe making, woolen mills and cigar factories during the 1870s. Chinese labor contractors, like the "padrone" of the Italians, frequently acted as middlemen, paid by the employer to supply a number of laborers for a set wage and period. Exploitation certainly occurred but there is no particular reason to believe that it was more prevalent or more severe than that suffered by inexperienced new immigrants from any other ethnic group at the same period. There were occasional outbreaks of labor unrest, such as a failed attempt in 1867 by Chinese railroad construction workers to gain equal wages with Caucasian laborers, but on the whole attempts to improve their lot by organized disputes were unsuccessful. Using the 1880 census research by Ping Chiu has detailed the employment of about three quarters of the male Chinese; about a fifth were miners, a fifth laborers, a seventh involved at some level in agriculture, a seventh in manufacturing industry, a seventh in domestic service, and only a tenth in laundering. They could be paid less than white workers but employers, whatever their personal prejudices, mostly also regarded the Chinese as being dependable and quick to learn new skills. A small but important minority of Chinese immigrants were themselves entrepreneurs and employers of other Chinese workers in both agriculture and industry. In addition to numerous garment and shoe factories, truck farms, and other enterprises, Chinese businessmen developed the Californian shrimp and abalone fishing industries. Later in the century, as we will see, these employment patterns were significantly modified under the pressure of anti-Chinese discrimination.

The historian of Chinese immigration Roger Daniels has argued persuasively that the major differences between Asian and European migrants were differences of degree rather than of kind. One area where these differences of degree were most marked was in the gender balance of the Chinese immigrant community. In almost all immigrant groups in the early years there were significantly more males than females but in the case of the Chinese this imbalance was hugely greater than the norm. The censuses of 1880 and 1890 showed that males outnumbered females by an extraordinary twenty to one. Most of the Chinese, like many other migrants, came intending to spend only a brief period in the United States to earn enough money to improve life for themselves and their families back home. Many of them were married but except for a small minority of wealthy merchants, they sent remittances and made occasional home visits rather than bringing their wives with them. The male dominated nature of Chinese society of the day made it virtually impossible for single women other than servants and prostitutes to travel. Once a more stable immigrant community with long term residents was established in America it might have been expected that the imbalance would ease as more wives joined their husbands and unmarried men brought brides from the home country, but the passage of the Chinese Exclusion Act made this impossible, freezing the skewed initial position for many years. Families were of course one of the main means by which immigrants became assimilated into American life, so it was ironic that nativists failed to recognize that the lack of assimilation by the Chinese that so alarmed them was to a large extent a consequence of their own discriminatory laws.

Anti-Chinese discrimination

Virtually all immigrant groups met with a greater or lesser degree of hostility and prejudice in nineteenth-century America, with anti-Catholicism a frequent cover for nativist protest. However it was only in the case of the Chinese that the nativist lobby was able to transform federal immigration policy with far reaching consequences for the future development of a Chinese-American community.

The growing Chinese presence in California had coincided with an upsurge of racism in European thought in the later decades of the nineteenth century. Prejudices that had already been evoked in support of the slave trade and the ongoing suppression of the Native Americans were given new respectability by pseudoscientific theories of Caucasian superiority. The hostility that had been directed against Chinese in California from the first mining camps became stronger and more organized as their numbers grew. Although more informed sources recognized that this influx of Chinese labor was vital to the Californian economy, to many white laborers, shopkeepers, and small farmers they seemed to pose a direct threat, working for lower wages and apparently resisting pressure to assimilate American working practices. Racially based antagonism that pictured the Chinese as a uniquely sinister and alien, almost non-human group then provided a convenient and widely acceptable cover for anxieties about economic competition. One of the few contemporary critics of this overt racism was the author Robert Louis Stevenson, who, in his book *The Amateur Emigrant*, described his experiences on a train packed with migrants to the West: "Of all stupid ill-feeling, the sentiment of my fellow-Caucasians towards our companions in the Chinese car was the most stupid and the worst . . . their forefathers watched the stars before mine had begun to keep pigs."

Labor unions blamed the Chinese for unemployment and low wages, leading a campaign of discrimination and pressing for restrictions on further immigration. The visibility of the Chinese in their tightly bounded urban enclaves, with their exotic dress and appearance left them vulnerable. From 1854 a ruling by the California Supreme Court made Chinese testimony against whites inadmissible (the Civil Rights Bill of 1870 made this discrimination, which was also in effect against African and Native Americans, unlawful, but this had little practical impact.) The State legislature passed numerous taxes and restrictions on further Chinese immigration and effectively segregated the public school system. Anti-Chinese demonstrations and opportunist attacks on individual Chinese were frequent. In one of the most violent incidents

Chinese arriving in San Francisco, being inspected by custom officers. Woodcut, 1877.

nineteen Chinese men were killed in a riot in San Francisco in 1871. Although the railroads and big corporations often defended their Chinese workers out of self-interest they found it easy to give in to pressure to dismiss them when the economy worsened in the 1870s. The ten thousand Chinese laid off in May 1869 when the Union-Central Pacific Railroad was completed helped depress wages throughout the western states. The Californian Workingmen's Party began campaigning with the slogan "The Chinese must go." The supposed excesses of the "coolie trade" were cited as a reason to ban all Chinese immigration, while the California legislature started to petition Congress to impose national limits. Powerful labor-based anti-Chinese associations such as the "Knights of St. Crispin" were formed which continued to exercise political influence well into the twentieth century. Unlike other migrant groups the Chinese imperial government was neither willing nor able to make diplomatic representations on behalf of its subjects, and the efforts to seek relief from discriminatory local and state legislation in the courts were rarely successful. Publicity over the involvement of Chinese as strike breakers in several prominent labor disputes in the East helped draw national attention to the issue, inducing the labor movement generally to adopt the anti-Chinese rhetoric of California.

Despite some opposition the Fourteenth Amendment, passed in 1870, which made "persons of African descent" eligible for naturalization, continued to exclude Chinese from citizenship, thereby providing a rationale for continued and worsening discrimination. By 1876 a joint Congressional committee was ready to recommend curbs on further Chinese immigration, but opposition from large employers delayed the inevitable for another few years. The law which was finally passed in 1882, the Chinese Exclusion Act, was the first restriction imposed on the free flow of immigration into the United States, preventing any new arrivals except merchants, teachers, students, and officials. By this time there were a little over 105,000 Chinese resident in America, virtually all in California and the other western states. (The figure of over 300,000 recorded arrivals included multiple voyages and many who had already returned home.) Anti-Chinese laws had become an easy vote winner for populist politicians who introduced a further series of discriminatory acts imposing ever tighter restrictions, with overwhelming public support throughout the West. The most serious of these was the 1888 Scott Act which denied reentry to over 20,000 Chinese who had left on temporary visits home,

Anti-Chinese feelings were running high c.1860. A Chinese cartoon figure is seen swallowing two men in three sketches.

THE GREAT FEAR OF THE PERIOD
THAT UNCLE SAM MAY BE SWALLOWED BY FOREIGNERS.

THE PROBLEM SOLVED.

1877 cartoon warning cigar makers not to use Chinese labor. Trade unions, fearful of competing against cheap Chinese labor, supported restrictions against Chinese immigration during the 1870s and 1880s.

a deliberate breach of written promises to permit reentry by the U.S. authorities. The exclusion acts were extended for a decade in 1892, then again in 1902, while the Deficiency Act of 1904 indefinitely barred additional Chinese immigration from all U.S. territories.

Despite this apparent victory for the nativist lobby violence against Chinese continued and even worsened. It was clear that for most leaders of anti-Chinese protest the goal was not merely to halt further immigration but to drive out those already there. In most towns and cities throughout California and states such as Idaho, Montana, Oregon, and Washington there were small Chinese enclaves, numbering a few hundred at most. Many of these fell victim to riots and attacks by lynch mobs intent on burning down the Chinese quarter and driving its residents out of town, often beating them up and killing one or two in the process. Although there were occasional arrests after such incidents very few convictions followed. In an incident which was exceptional only in its high death toll at least twenty-eight Chinese were killed and the whole community of some six hundred or so driven out of Rock Springs, Wyoming Territory, by an armed mob of white miners in late 1885. Individual attacks on Chinese men throughout the region claimed hundreds more lives—in his 1976 history of Idaho F. Ross Peterson estimated that in that state alone in the worst years of 1866–67 over a hundred died.

Chinese-American society in the exclusion years

The exclusion acts and the racist attitudes that prompted them had a far reaching impact on the shape of Chinese-American community over the decades that followed. The total number of Chinese in America peaked at only some 125,000 early in the 1880s (to put the nativist rhetoric about floods of Asians in perspective we should recall that by this time there were several million new European immigrants each year.) The existing extreme gender imbalance was frozen in place, creating a predominantly bachelor society (although a significant number had wives and children in China who were unable to join them.) Since this society was virtually starved of new migrants and unable to reproduce itself naturally the numbers then began a gradual decline, falling to around 60,000 by 1920, before rising again to 80,000 by 1940. Of

A meeting of the Workingmen's Party on the sandlot opposite San Francisco city hall. The party was formed during a recession and gave expression to the anger felt against Chinese immigrants on the west coast who were thought to be undercutting wages, 1879.

course the total population of California and the other western states increased exponentially over the same period, so that the proportion of Chinese in the population dwindled into virtual insignificance by 1940. The pattern of ethnic enclaves that normally characterized the early years of immigrant experience was artificially prolonged as external prejudice and the resulting lack of assimilation kept many Chinese in the comparative safety and familiar surroundings of urban "Chinatowns." Both the availability of economic opportunities and continuing hostility contributed to a gradual concentration of the Chinese community in larger cities, particularly San Francisco and Oakland, but also Los Angeles, New York, and in smaller numbers Seattle, Portland, Sacramento, Boston, and Chicago.

San Francisco had the largest Chinatown and was the center of community life for Chinese across America, serving also as headquarters for the distinctively Chinese forms of association based on locality and family that developed. Chain migrations between particular villages or wider regions in China and specific localities in the United States were common, with established migrants being joined by relatives from home, shopping with someone from the same locality, seeking out someone they knew when looking for work or hiring employees etc. Led by the wealthier merchants, many of whom had brought established capital from China, they formed associations called *huiguan*, which in America were known as "companies." The earliest American *huiguan* were founded in San Francisco at the start of the 1850s by the Sam Yap and Sze Yap communities. Often a *huiguan* would loan money to a potential migrant to finance his passage to America, later ensuring that any outstanding debt had been collected before he could return. Overlapping with these companies at a more local level were systems of clan associations grouping together those individuals notionally related on the basis of a shared surname. In smaller Chinatowns a single "family" clan often predominated, with new members attracted there by the potential and actual support and protection it offered. Where there were insufficient people to form a single clan association an adapted version of a traditional four-clan association was formed. Rivalries between these clans or four-clan associations were frequent and often bitter. Each clan acted as a social network and mutual benefit association, providing job opportunities for unemployed members whenever possible and relief when necessary. Disputes between clan members and with other clans were settled by meetings of senior members. Regular levies were made of working members to provide funds for such purposes as supporting the (few) widows and orphans, and buying tickets to allow the very old and indigent to return to China. One of their most important functions in the eyes of many Chinese was to provide assurance that the dead would be afforded a proper burial, that the necessary rites would be carried out at their grave, and the appropriate remains eventually returned to the ancestral burial site back in China. Often the clan association also provided the means by which letters and remittances could be transferred back to families in the home villages. At the apex of this network of clan and locality associations was the so-called Chinese Six Companies in San Francisco, who among other functions served as a court of appeal for inter clan disputes and acted as semi-official representatives of the Chinese community with the American authorities. Dominated by the wealthiest merchants, the Six Companies formed a single body, the Chinese Consolidated Benevolent Association (CCBA) in 1882 to spearhead their resistance to the anti-Chinese campaigns.

To hostile politicians and newspaper editors these institutions were a sinister "secret government" forever associated, however unjustly, with the darker side of Chinese-American organizational life, namely the secret societies that became known as tongs. Uniting men on the basis of a fraternal oath of allegiance that was supposed to cut across ties to clan and locality, these secret societies had played a significant political role in Chinese rebellions, and in America they did provide an alternative to the domination of the companies by wealthy merchants. However, whatever the exaggerations of anti-Chinese media it is also clear that the tongs did become heavily involved in the organization of gambling, opium trafficking and prostitution, all of which were a feature of the bachelor society of the major Chinatowns. Disputes between rival groups led to so-called "tong wars" in which numerous men fell victim to assassins known as hatchet men or highbinders. Lurid accounts of these events in the American press contributed to stigmatizing the largely law abiding Chinese community as a whole.

The exclusion acts did not entirely close off further Chinese immigration. Under the terms of the U.S.-China treaty merchants still had the right to bring in their wives and minor children, while American-born Chinese had rights of citizenship which could be extended to their minor children. Even these rights were frequently challenged by immigration officials and local legislatures and the role of the CCBA in sponsoring legal representation to defend them up to the Supreme Court was vital. In 1927 the Supreme Court extended the derivative rights of the offspring of American-born Chinese to include grandchildren. As those Chinese who were American citizens by birth reached adulthood and were able to return from visits to China with their children a system of "paper sons" developed to exploit this loophole, with the slots given to the children of ineligible clan members or sold to others. The destruction of immigration authority records in the fires that followed the San Francisco earthquake of 1906 greatly increased the opportunities for fraudulent entry of this type. The increasingly stringent immigration checks the U.S. authorities introduced in a usually vain attempt to detect these "paper sons" added to the bitterness of the Chinese community, although the days or even weeks of detention involved seldom attracted public comment. Between 1910 and 1940 Chinese immigrants were interrogated and detained at a processing center on Angel Island in San Francisco Bay, before that they had been held at a facility known as "The Shed" on the waterfront. Those who met the admission criteria, such as treaty merchants and students often had to produce two non-Chinese witnesses before they were granted admission. Even then Chinese-Americans were often vulnerable to being picked up in raids organized by immigration officials, held for weeks without bail, and in many cases deported. In total the U.S. authorities recorded nearly 95,000 Chinese "immigrants," an average of some 1,500 a year in the sixty years between the passage of the exclusion act in 1882 and the ending of exclusion in 1943, although many of these would have been accounted for by multiple journeys of merchants and returning former residents.

The late nineteenth- and early twentieth-century Chinese-Americans, even those who had attained citizenship by birth, were, with very few individual exceptions, living an almost wholly unassimilated life. To a large extent this was due to discrimination and the effects of the exclusion acts on family formation. The Chinese were segregated in schools and theaters,

A Chinese man hangs from a branch labeled "Freedon to All." Hanging to his pigtail are a tiger and an elephant bearing the words twenty years and ten years. The Tiger represents the Irish workers (Tammany Tigers) and the elephant the Republicans. In 1882 Congress passed the Chinese Exclusion Act, placing a ten-year moratorium on Chinese immigration, 1882.

Above: Chinese immigrants being taught English in Califronia, c.1885.

Opposite, Above: Cover of Harper's Weekly, *1887.*

Opposite, Below: A mob of white coal miners attacking Chinese immigrants who worked during a strike at the mines in Rock Springs, Wyoming, September 1885.

refused admission to most bars, hotels, and restaurants, prevented from owning land in many states, usually prohibited from marrying Caucasians, and effectively barred from many towns. Very few families formed as the gender ratio remained hugely imbalanced—in 1890 there were 26.8 males to every female and only three percent of the population was American born. Those few children born in America were mostly educated in Chinese at private schools or classes, or in the case of wealthy merchants sent back to China for education. As a consequence many aspects of the deeply conservative patriarchal society they had brought from China continued little changed, at least until they began to be transformed in China itself by the revolution of 1911. It was only then that the majority of Chinese-American men began to abandon their traditional dress, shaven head and queue, and women the bound feet, and the established social codes in favor of a slow adaptation towards American norms.

The economic life of Chinese-Americans was also affected by the racism of the labor movement and employers. Beginning in the 1870s it became increasingly difficult for Chinese to find employment in large factories or as organized contract laborers in industry or agriculture. Instead they had to seek whatever niches were available to them, predominantly in Chinese owned small businesses in service industries, giving rise to the familiar stereotype of the Chinese laundry man. Laundries required little complex expertise, they needed, at least until the development of dry cleaning, little in the way of expensive equipment, and they utilized long hours of low paid labor. Relatives and clan members could be relied on upon as they had few alternative sources of employment. Where necessary the business could be readily transferred if the owner decided to return to China. Small restaurants serving adapted dishes such as chop suey and chow mein at low prices to working men also became widespread. Other Chinese found a niche as shopkeepers in areas of the deep South and Southwest neglected by white retailers. Many of these businesses were founded with capital obtained by a rotating credit association, in which each member makes a weekly or monthly contribution which is drawn out by one member selected by lot or in turn. In California similar means, along with funds brought by wealthy merchants from China, supplied capital for a few medium and larger scale enterprises, including garment factories, canneries, and others. The Chinese owned Canton Bank lasted from 1907 to 1926, while a China Mail Steamship Company formed in 1915 survived only eight years. Despite their entrepreneurial heritage few Chinese at this period had the necessary capital and experience to create businesses in America that could break out of the barriers of prejudice that constrained the community as a whole, while the Chinese population itself was too small to support major businesses alone.

Adaptation: the second generation and after

Sufficient wives and "picture wives" had been admitted despite the exclusion acts for the percentage of the community born in America to rise gradually, finally reaching more than half by 1940. The new generation had to look beyond the existing social and organizational institutions that catered for the steadily aging bachelor society of the first generation, turning instead to public schools, Protestant churches, and Christian youth associations. Education in English became the norm and familiarity with the Chinese language slowly declined. The normal social past times of American youth of the day, such as sports and dancing became increasingly popular, although Chinese-American youth remained conservative. Family control over marriage choices was eased, as were clan loyalties. As in other immigrant communities the second generation became far more assimilated into American ways than their parents, stimulating considerable inter-generational conflict in the process. New second generation organizations were formed to combat continuing prejudice, among them the Native Sons of the Golden State, founded in 1895, and renamed the Chinese-American Citizen's Alliance in 1915. Short-lived Chinese language newspapers had been founded as early as the 1850s, but by the 1930s the small Chinese language press was supplemented by the first English language Chinese-American papers. More girls attended secondary schools and sought work outside the family home, while a few even made it to college. College attendance among Chinese American males increased although it remained low as a result of poverty and the limited employment opportunities. Attempts by banks and city authorities to work with or monitor the Chinese community provided careers for some, others provided professional services such as

Above: A market in San Francisco's Chinatown around 1900.

Opposite, Above: A banner on Grant Street, San Francisco, welcomes visitors to Chinatown, with its hundreds of Chinese shops, restaurants, and markets, c.1955.

Opposite, Below: A street in Chicago's Chinatown, September 1995.

doctoring, dentistry, and legal services to predominantly Chinese customers. A handful were able to transcend the barriers of prejudice and find work in the mainstream employment market. Two even found some success in Hollywood, the cinematographer James Wong Howe (1899–1976) and the actress Anna May Wong (1907–61.) Politically most Chinese-American organizations including the CCBA supported and contributed financially to the Kuomintang nationalist governing party in China.

Exclusion was finally abolished in 1943 in the hope of rallying Chinese sentiment in the course of the war against Japan. World War II itself saw some 8,000 Chinese-Americans serving in the U.S. armed forces, many of whom were able to benefit from the G.I. Bill in its aftermath. Moreover employment discrimination against minorities was considerably eased by manpower shortages, giving new and wider opportunities to many. Although China was given only a nominal annual immigrant quota of 105, a significant number of women were admitted in each of the postwar years as G.I. brides. Discriminatory state laws were gradually struck down by the Supreme Court, allowing the wealthier and more assimilated Chinese to move out from the urban enclaves. With a brief upset in 1957 when paranoia over Communist infiltration briefly revived the prospect of federal action against the Chinese community this advance continued over the remainder of the century. By 1970 twenty-six percent of Chinese men had four or more years of college, the highest proportion of any ethnic group. Chinese-American professionals flourished in science and technology, education and health. Outstanding achievements included the Nobel Prize for Physics won by C. N. Yang and T. D. Lee in 1957, and by S. Ting in 1976. I. M. Pei became an internationally recognized architect. Maxine Hong Kingston was among the first of a critically acclaimed body of Chinese-American women writers. However a high proportion of Chinese men remained in low paid service industries and Chinese women were disproportionately represented in low paid clerical and garment industry jobs.

New immigrants arrived in substantial numbers from Taiwan, Hong Kong, and the Chinese mainland after the immigration act of 1965 ended the quota system, with the Chinese-American population finally achieving gender balance by 1970. Chinatowns were

revived, serving as community amenities for the wider Chinese-American population as well as increasingly as tourist attractions for other Americans. The Chinese New Year became a major cultural and tourist festival in cities such as San Francisco and New York. Old prejudices have not totally disappeared but have certainly become far less overt and by the 1970s and 1980s Chinese-Americans had become generally accepted as one ethnic group among many rather than as a sinister exception singled out for special exclusion.

Japanese

The Japanese emigration to the Americas began rather late in the nineteenth century but eventually took on sufficient volume for Japanese-Americans to become the largest ethnic group of Asian origin in the U.S. by the 1970s. One of the unusual characteristics of Japanese immigration was the extremely uneven geographical distribution of settlers who mostly remained in the two states that saw the first arrivals—of the 600,000 or so Japanese-Americans in 1970 over a third still lived in Hawaii and another third in California. Until American ships lead by Commodore Perry reached Japan in 1853 the country had been in self-imposed isolation from overseas contacts for over two hundred years. The Emperor Meiji, restored in 1868, introduced a period of dramatic modernization and openness to western culture. Ordinary Japanese became free to travel abroad for the first time, and the hardships that accompanied the dislocation of traditional feudal society in the countryside encouraged growing numbers to seek better opportunities abroad. The generational aspects of Japanese society were echoed in the naming of migrant generations in America, the first being called *Issei*, the second *Nisei*.

Hawaii was both the earliest destination of pioneering Japanese migrants and later an important staging post on the way to America. Virtually from the start the Japanese government felt it necessary to exercise a degree of involvement in both the emigration process and the supervision of migrants abroad unlike that seen elsewhere. The first attempt to recruit con-

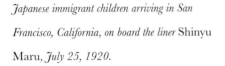

Japanese immigrant children arriving in San Francisco, California, on board the liner Shinyu Maru, *July 25, 1920.*

tract laborers in Japan to work on the sugar plantations of Hawaii, involving street vagrants unsuited to heavy agricultural labor, was a failure that drew the attention of Japanese officials. Arguably concerned far more with the image of Japan overseas than the personal welfare of emigrants, restrictions on the issuance of passports and visas only to individuals judged "suitable" was intended to stop Japan becoming an alternative to China as a demeaning source of cheap labor. Drawing mostly on the agricultural prefectures of Hiroshima, Yamaguchi, and Kumamoto thousands of laborers left for Hawaii, where by 1900 the 61,111 Japanese residents formed a staggering forty percent of the total population. Exclusively Japanese villages with schools, temples, and other institutions developed in the plantation districts. In the early decades of the twentieth century the conflict between preserving Japanese cultural values and assimilation was personified by the two best known community leaders to emerge in Hawaii, the radical nationalist Fred Makino (1877–1953) who edited the Japanese language paper *Hawaii Hochi* (founded 1912) , and the Christian pastor Reverend Taki Okemura (1865–1951) who advocated greater adaptation to American lifestyles. By the 1890s some Hawaiian Japanese began to seek alternatives to the harsh life of the sugar plantations by moving on to California but the number of Japanese residents in Hawaii itself continued to rise, reaching over 150,000 by 1940 and in excess of 200,000 by 1960. By the turn of the century however migrants were also moving in significant numbers directly to California, part of a larger exodus that also took Japanese to Peru, Bolivia, Brazil, and Canada.

By 1890 there were a little over 2,000 Japanese recorded in mainland United States, the majority probably merchants, students and diplomats. This figure had multiplied to over 24,000 a decade later, and in total the arrival of almost 300,000 Japanese immigrants was recorded before 1924. Taking into account returnees, deaths, and multiple entrants, the census bureau found only 111,010 Japanese residents in 1920, with a modest rise to 138,834 ten years later. Unlike in Hawaii Japanese never comprised even one percent of the population in California or any other state. As with the Chinese figures for annual immigration were tiny compared with arrivals from Ireland, Germany, Italy or many other European countries at the same period. The reaction of American nativists was to be similarly out of all proportion.

Important insights into the early Japanese presence on the West Coast have been uncovered in contemporary Japanese consular reports from San Francisco which relayed home the concerns of the small Japanese elite over what they perceived as the disreputable activities of most of the fellow countrymen and women. Anxious that Japan should not suffer the humiliation that had recently been visited upon China by the Exclusion Act of 1882, the reports perhaps over stressed the negative in their efforts to persuade the home government of the need to restrict or at least improve the "quality" of the migrants. As reported by Roger Daniels in his 1988 history of Asian immigration, the consul was particularly upset by what he regarded as the excessive number of Japanese gamblers, pimps and prostitutes. However his inquiries in the Pacific Northwest also revealed day laborers in lumber camps, saw mill operatives, and restaurateurs. Small restaurants serving cheap meals to working men became something of a specialty among this first group of Japanese immigrants—there were reported to be sixteen such establishments in Los Angeles in 1896, probably employing a majority of the city's 100 or so Japanese residents.

Despite the aspirations of the Japanese government it was as substitutes for Chinese contract labor that the first major influx of Japanese workers into California occurred in the 1890s. Many of these were agricultural workers from Hawaii whose contracts with the plantations had ended. Some of them had acquired sufficient English to be able to negotiate as labor contractors, recruiting work gangs of their fellow countrymen for seasonal jobs on California farms. The first groups were obliged to compete with the Chinese, often by undercutting their day or piece work rates, but by the end of the decade with many of the remaining Chinese having found urban employment they were able to push up their earnings, attracting inevitable complaints from the employers. According to one estimate by 1909 there were as many as 30,000 Japanese working in agriculture in California. The rapidly expanding economy of California at this period had an urgent need for cheap labor in a whole range of industries, allowing initially unskilled Japanese migrants to find employment in canneries, on the railroads, in meat packing, logging, salt-refining, mining and numerous other occupations. Japanese enclaves developed in many towns and cities, with the largest forming at the main

entry port of San Francisco. Within these was a network of small businesses supplying the needs of the community: rooming houses for new arrivals, laundries, small restaurants, shops selling imported produce, letter writers, money lenders, and inevitably brothels and gambling houses. Others ran businesses in the wider community, such as restaurants, groceries, and laundries. Many Japanese found work as domestic servants. However it was in agriculture that Japanese immigrants were most successful.

Japanese farm workers had spread out from California to the Pacific Northwest and to states such as Idaho, Colorado, and Utah. From casual laborers, a growing number had begun save sufficient from their earnings to lease land or purchase it outright, often with the assistance of funds obtained from rotating credit associations. Sugar beet was the most important crop developed by Japanese farmers in the Rocky Mountain area: Daniels reports that by 1913 a third of the beat crop in Idaho, almost 8,000 acres, was produced by Japanese farmers, who also had a further 10,000 acres devoted to other produce. In Colorado they farmed about 25,000 acres, half producing sugar beet. Most of this land was leased but the amount owned outright rose steadily. As there were insufficient Japanese laborers in this region other ethnic groups, particularly Mexicans, supplied part of the labor force for Japanese farms. In Washington aliens were prohibited from owning land, but Japanese farmers leased some 16,000 acres by 1914, most of it given over to berry and vegetable farming. Here the Japanese also controlled most of the retail distribution of their crops via market stalls, through wholesalers, retail market stalls especially in Seattle, and street peddlers. In California also Japanese farmers benefited from labor intensive high yielding techniques, with the quantity of land under their control rising exponentially from below 5,000 acres in 1900, to over 450,000 acres by 1919. In the same year it was calculated that their gross yield was over $67 million, amounting to about ten percent of the state's agricultural production. Most of this growing prosperity was accounted for by a substantial number of quite small farms but larger enterprises did develop. Notable among these was the business of George Shima, who achieved great wealth by cultivating potatoes on the previously virgin land of the San Joaquin delta. He was estimated to directly control almost 30,000 acres of land by 1913, as well as marketing produce for many other Japanese farmers. He employed a work force of up to 500 and by 1920 was said to control eighty-five percent of the Californian potato crop estimated to be worth more than $18 million. At his funeral in 1926 the mayor of San Francisco and the chancellor of Stanford University were among the pall bearers.

Anti-Japanese discrimination

Perhaps not surprisingly the increasingly conspicuous success of Japanese farmers was a factor in inflaming nativist and racist opposition to continuing Japanese immigration. The first significant anti-Japanese sentiment arose as early as 1891 when San Francisco newspapers began to mock and criticize the shabby state of the few hundred arrivals, with pro-labor journals such as the *Bulletin* and anti-Chinese politicians soon attempting to stir up nativist sentiment against the new "threat." In response the San Francisco school board passed a resolution in June 1893 requiring all Japanese pupils to attend the segregated Chinese school. Opposition to this arbitrary measure was led by the Japanese consul Sutemi Chinda, who noted that there were less than fifty Japanese in the school system, all of the well behaved young men. After appeals from white notables orchestrated by the consul the decision was reversed and anti-Japanese sentiment appeared to have subsided. This respite was however all too brief as criticism of the Japanese resumed at the turn of the century as a side effect of campaigns throughout the West for the renewal of the Chinese Exclusion Act. By the middle of the decade, despite the minuscule numbers of Japanese in America, press agitation for Japanese exclusion, lead by the San Francisco Chronicle, had reached a pitch that demanded action from state legislatures. Even more nakedly racist than the campaign against the Chinese (since the handful of Japanese at that time could pose no credible economic rivalry) labor unions spearheaded the anti-Japanese movement. At the same time the success of Japan in the Russo-Japanese War (1904–05) drew world attention to the country's claims of great power status. Although there is little evidence to suggest that President Roosevelt felt any more favorably disposed to the Japanese than other Americans of the day, he was aware of the Japanese government's sensitivity over the treatment of its citizens abroad. Prompted by concern over a renewed school segregation row in San

Opposite: A Congressional Committee looking over Japanese brides' passports at the Angel Island Immigration Station.

Opposite: Japanese immigrants arrive in San

Francisco on July 25, 1920, aboard the liner

Shinyu Maru.

Francisco, in a controversial and widely criticized speech of December 1906 he called on Congress to permit the naturalization of Japanese immigrants, noted the recent military achievements of Japan, and pointedly warned that "the mob of a single city [might] at any time perform acts of lawless violence which would plunge us into war." In fact no such naturalization proposal was ever presented to Congress (which would never have passed it anyway) and the President authorized immediate negotiations with the Japanese government on a "voluntary" restriction of immigration. Concerned above all to avoid the humiliation of another exclusion act the Japanese government readily agreed that it would cease issuing passports valid for continental United States to skilled or unskilled laborers. However those laborers who had already lived in America were permitted to return, and, crucially for the future of the Japanese-American community, new passports could still be issued to the parents, wives, and children of existing residents.

Rather than simply ending the flow of Japanese immigrants altogether as the nativist agitators had expected, the so-called "Gentlemen's Agreement" transformed it from an overwhelmingly male phenomenon to a predominantly female one. In the years before the agreement only a few of the more settled migrants had begun to form families, but in its aftermath many more followed suit. For some this involved bringing existing wives and children from Japan, while for many others proxy weddings arranged by their families brought so-called "picture brides" to America. Unlike the Chinese, who as we have seen were condemned to a shrinking bachelor society for many decades, this provision allowed the gender balance of the Japanese community to move from around ninety percent male at the time of the agreement to approximate parity by the late 1920s.

If the Gentlemen's Agreement had been intended by Roosevelt to defuse both domestic and international tension over Japanese immigration it cannot be regarded as a success. The continued, albeit numerically modest, inflow of Japanese, in combination with anxiety over the growing agricultural success of Japanese-Americans kept anti-Japanese sentiment in California inflamed, and the issue remained at the forefront of political invective throughout the western states. Such was the official concern about Japanese government reaction that President Woodrow Wilson called in the Japanese Ambassador to discuss events in California on only his second day in office in March 1913. The focus of agitation switched from exclusion to land ownership, with a series of anti-Japanese land bills in the Californian state legislature. As with much anti-Chinese discrimination, the basis of these measures was the racist provisions of the naturalization statue of 1870, which made only "white persons and persons of African descent" eligible for naturalization. In practice however, although a damaging institutional endorsement of populist racism, the 1913 Alien Land Act had little impact on Japanese-American agriculture. Although it prevented people who were ineligible for citizenship from owning agricultural land and limited them to leases which had a maximum duration of three years, the majority of land farmed by Japanese-Americans was already on shorter leases, and land which they owned was easily registered in the name of American born children, who were of course entitled to citizenship. The failure of the act to curb Japanese-American farming entrepreneurs encouraged anti-Japanese agitators in California to press for far harsher restrictions, which were imposed in 1920 after winning a three to one majority of popular votes throughout the state. Japanese nationals and corporations of which they owned a majority of stock, were then prohibited outright from further transfers of land, and from leasing land. Restrictions of the same type were imposed in Washington state in 1921. By this time however there were already sufficient native born Japanese who had American citizenship for the restrictions to be largely evaded and the number and acreage of land under Japanese-American control declined only slightly over the following decade. More importantly, the value and output of their farms multiplied over the same period.

Nativist hostility to all immigrants had received a significant boost via American participation in World War I, creating a backlash against "foreigners," which we have already seen had far reaching consequences in all immigrant communities. Momentum towards general restrictions on immigration was gathering pace. In 1917 an act was passed barring all Asian immigration except that of Filipinos (who were the American citizens) and the Japanese. Calls by western politicians for the Agreement to be rescinded gathered support nationally. However when the continued, albeit restricted, immigration that had been permitted under the

Angel Island immigration officials examine Japanese immigrants aboard the ship Shinyu Maru *before letting them disembark, 1931.*

Gentlemen's Agreement, was finally cut off in 1924 it was by the passage of the Immigration Act, which for the first time limited the influx of migrants to the United States through the imposition of a system of national quotas. Yet there was a final triumph for anti-Japanese hysteria when they were denied the minimum quota of a hundred persons a year to which the country should have been entitled by the addition of a clause, primarily targeted at Japanese, barring from entry all persons "ineligible for citizenship."

Japanese-American society

As we have seen, the Gentlemen's Agreement changed rather than halted the immigration of Japanese. From being primarily an inflow of single men seeking employment, it became a female immigration as the men already settled in America took advantage of the agreement's provision to either bring over their wife and small children, or, if they had not been married, to arrange a wedding with a so-called "picture bride." In contrast to the Chinese who were forced by the exclusion acts to remain a predominantly bachelor community, by the 1920s families had been formed and the second generation or Nisei Japanese-Americans were of growing importance. In total around 20,000 adult Japanese women entered America in the years between the agreement and the passage of the 1924 Immigration Act—a small number, but given the geographical concentration of Japanese settlement in the West, sufficient for viable family-based communities to be formed. While the number of Chinese in America had shrunk to little over 75,000 by 1940, at the same date there were some 125,000 Japanese-Americans, more than two-thirds of whom were citizens by birth. Despite the efforts of agitators, the ban on all Japanese immigration imposed in 1924 came too late to prevent this community taking shape.

The Japanese government's intense sensitivity to the implications for national status of the treatment accorded its citizens abroad, reflected in the Gentlemen's Agreement, also led it to sponsor the major cultural organizations of the first generation migrants. A network of regional and local associations was headed by the Japanese Association of America, based in San Francisco. Controlled by prominent Japanese-Americans approved by the Japanese Consul, these associations were delegated important official functions of the consulate. In particular they had the power to issue the documents necessary before a passport could be obtained allowing a wife to be brought to America. Buttressed by the influence these powers conferred, the associations saw their main role as encouraging the immigrants to assimilate, to adopt American modes of dress, to learn English, and to place their children within the American educational system. In this they seem to have reinforced tendencies towards rapid adaptation already widespread among Japanese-Americans, whose economic and educational attainments consistently outpaced the norm despite the discrimination they faced. This adaptability extended to religion. Although there were Japanese Buddhist temples, in general there was little serious effort made to establish Japanese derived religious traditions in America, and the majority of Nisei joined Christian Protestant denominations. Deprived of participation in mainstream American life for the Issei generation the Japanese associations provided the main forum through which men could compete and have their social achievements within the community recognized. Elections were often intensely competitive, and those who achieved leadership positions saw their role as exercising patriarchal supervision over the community. Funds were raised for charitable causes and for legal resistance to discrimination, as well as to provide social welfare functions. Other, less important social organizations were formed on the basis of areas of origin in Japan, while the first generation also supported women's societies, language schools, and numerous other associational activities.

As might be expected when there was a general pressure towards assimilation, language retention among the second generation was not high, and their social activities were adapted to their situation as American citizens widely seen as alien. Anti-Japanese sentiment throughout the West continued through the 1920s and 1930s, stimulated by elements of the press and by hostile labor organizations and civic groups. Brought up to be hard working and respectful, many Nisei were excellent students, with some achieving professional qualifications. Nevertheless, like their parents they were still held back by widespread discrimination in employment forcing the majority to seek work within the community in Japanese owned small businesses or agriculture. Others worked as lawyers, doctors, dentists, nurses, but rarely with clientele drawn from wider society. Separate organizations emerged to meet the needs of the second generation, with local associations defending Nisei interests grouped under the umbrella of the national Japanese-American Citizen's League founded in the 1920s. Generally excluded from regular socializing with other young people, Nisei developed a parallel network of activities such as athletics clubs, football, and baseball leagues, often with the assistance of institutions such as the Scouts, YMCA, and YWCA. Inevitably attitudes and behavior developed that were more in accordance with American norms than with the traditions of their parents, exacerbating intergenerational conflict. In part because of the fears aroused in the older generation by the Americanization of the youth, and also due to pessimism about prospects in America, it became common for Japanese-American families to send at least one son (or much more rarely daughter) to Japan where he could be raised by relatives and pass through the Japanese educational system. Known as *Kibei*, they were usually returned to the United States in their teens.

Japanese-Americans in World War II

Life in the small but relatively prosperous Japanese-American community throughout the west coast states was transformed by the events that followed the surprise Japanese attack on Pearl Harbor on December 7, 1941. More than 110,000 men, women, and children, some 70,000 of whom were American citizens, were forcibly incarcerated in detention camps without trial or due process, simply on the basis of their ethnic origin, in what has since become regarded as one of the biggest violations of constitutional rights in American history. Yet war against Japan need not have spelt disaster for the Japanese-Americans. After all no comparable measures were taken against the far larger number of German or Italian Americans, nor was their loyalty to the United States seriously questioned. The Japanese-Americans however were a small and vulnerable minority, already under regular pressure, as we have seen, from powerful interest groups and populist politicians. Too few to have any political weight and lacking influential support they provided an easy and popular target for public frustration and anger. Although government officials had no reason to doubt the allegiance of the Japanese-Americans and knew that there was no imminent prospect of a Japanese invasion of mainland America, they made no effort to defend or support them.

Apparently responding to fears of sabotage curfews and other restrictions were imposed on Japanese-American districts and some 2,000 Japanese included in a roundup of "enemy aliens" in the immediate aftermath of Pearl Harbor. These men, who were subsequently interned in camps in Montana, North Dakota, and elsewhere, constituted much of the leadership elite of Japanese-America, such as leading businessmen. officials of Japanese-American associations, language school teachers, even Buddhist priests. Their contacts with Japanese consular officials (made necessary by the Gentlemen's agreement and subsequent involvement of Japan in subsidizing Japanese-American cultural activity) was cited as evidence of subversive intent. Regular raids and searches of properties headed or occupied by "enemy aliens," in practice by any Japanese whether citizens or not, disrupted the leaderless community. Non citizens had their bank accounts frozen. Many of those who had succeeded in finding employment with white firms soon lost their jobs. Deprived of existing authority figures the second generation Japanese-American Citizen's League was soon at the forefront of efforts to assure America of their loyalty and patriotism, even at the expense of criticizing the older generation, and in some few cases informing the authorities of suspect individuals.

Although historians investigating military records have subsequently established that the armed force were quite relaxed about any potential threat from Japanese-Americans, political leaders cited wartime "military necessity" as justification for the mass detention that followed. Beginning on January 19, 1942, the U.S. Attorney General issued a series of orders which defined security areas along the Pacific Coast which had to be emptied of "enemy aliens." A month later the definition had been widened to "dangerous persons," implicitly including American citizens, and on February 19th, President Roosevelt signed an executive order ordering that they be removed and that relocation camps be built to house them. Over the following six months a total of over 110,000 Japanese-Americans, almost two thirds of them American citizens, were brought to temporary assembly centers then transferred to permanent camps. They were to be imprisoned for up to four years in these barbed wire ringed camps, built in desolate and inhospitable areas such as Tule Lake and Manzanar in California; Poston and Gila River in Arizona; Minidoka in Idaho; Heart Mountain in Wyoming; Granada in Canada; Topaz in Utah; and Rowher, and Jerome in Arkansas. The two smallest camps were Amache and Jerome, each of which held 7,500, while the largest Poston, held over 18,000. Each imposed identical and regimented conditions: communal barrack housing (albeit divided into family rooms), communal toilets and showers, mess hall food, uniforms. Inmates were paid $16 a month for manual labor, $19 for professional work. Boredom and the unfamiliar climate took their toll, with arguments, gambling, fights, and occasional strikes. An apparently confused elderly man who wandered out of the fences at Topaz was shot dead by a soldier when he ignored a call to halt.

Differences within the Japanese-American community were exacerbated by conditions in the camps. Generational conflicts, both within families and more widely were magnified by the circumstances. Rivalry for leadership between Issei and Nisei figures was overlaid by differing attitudes towards America and Japan. The cooperative, pro-American policy of the

JACL, maintained despite all provocation within the camps, was bitterly criticized, particularly by Kibei, many of whom had imbibed ideals of Japanese nationalism during their education at home. Violent attacks on "collaborators" became commonplace. One focus for these disagreements, as well as a major cause of uncertainty among ordinary inmates, was the procedures that permitted detainees to apply for leave clearance, and, if approved, to reestablish homes elsewhere (although not in the west coast states from which they had come.) The War Relocation Agency, which managed the camps, relied on questionnaires which required the signatory to renounce all allegiance to Japan and swear loyalty to the United States, conditions that divided the applicants, perhaps unsurprisingly after the treatment they had received. In all about a third were eventually permitted to leave, many of whom were able to find employment or enroll in college programs in the East or Midwest. Others left to join the army, especially after the draft was reinstated for Japanese-Americans at the start of 1944. In fact Japanese-Americans had a distinguished record of military service, with the 442nd Combat Team and the 100th Battalion, in which 33,000 Japanese-Americans from Hawaii (where there had been no mass detention) and the mainland, suffered 600 dead and over 9,000 casualties, becoming the most decorated units in American military history. Less well known than these feats in Europe, many Japanese-Americans also served, mostly as linguists, in the Pacific theater. The camps themselves were gradually wound up after the 1944 Supreme Court ruling in *Endo v. United States* that the detentions were unconstitutional. It was a sad reflection on their expectations of America that over 40,000 had to be virtually forced to leave the security of the camps in 1945

Japanese-Americans after the war

The war was of course a turning point in the lives of many Americans. This was true also for those Japanese-Americans whose experience of internment seemed to mark a radical break with life before and since. The agricultural land on which much prewar prosperity was based had largely gone with the expiry of leases, many had also lost homes and businesses. In total losses came to hundreds of millions of dollars. Nevertheless, despite apprehensiveness about public hostility, and resettlement elsewhere during the war, most Japanese-Americans returned to the Pacific coast, especially to California. By 1960 the state had around 157,000 Japanese-Americans. At first the old restrictions on employment opportunities were still in effect, but over the next few years a gradual easing of hostility became apparent. In part this may have been due to a shifting of racist agitation towards the far larger numbers of African-Americans and Mexicans who had been drawn west by labor shortages during the war. Many young Japanese-Americans were able to gain a college education, some financing it by work such as gardening, others through the G.I. Bill. There were major advances in 1952 as the State Supreme Court struck down the Alien Land Law and on a national level the new Immigration Act made all Asians eligible for naturalization. In turn this provision undercut much other state anti-Japanese and anti-Chinese legislation. Hawaii, where Japanese-Americans constituted thirty-seven percent of the population by 1950, provided the first forum for national political representation, with the election of Congressmen Matsunaga and Mink, and of Senator Daniel Inouye in 1962. Subsequently Japanese-Americans have been elected for mainland districts, the first being Congressman Mineta in 1972, and Senator Hayakawa in 1976. Japanese immigration resumed on a modest scale after the war, with a significant number of war brides during the occupation, and subsequently a few thousand immigrants annually. Since the 1980s increasing numbers of mostly shorter term migrants have followed the inflow of Japanese financial and industrial corporations into America. The success of the Japanese economy has also helped open up employment opportunities more widely as attitudes towards Japanese-Americans modified. Intermarriage with non Japanese increased markedly after the 1960s. In 1970 Japanese-Americans were the largest Asian population, with a total of nearly 600,000, while a decade later this had risen to a little over 700,000, but the total had been surpassed by the far more rapidly expanding Chinese-American and Filipino American communities.

CHAPTER 8 # Immigration after 1920

Opposite: Sheet music for an anti-immigrant Nativist song which proclaims "Citizen Know-Nothing" as "Uncle Sam's Youngest Son." Formerly called the American Party, the Know-Nothings received their name from their practice of secrecy, claiming to "know-nothing" when questioned about their politics. The party discriminated against immigrants and Roman Catholics in particular, and all foreign influence in general, 1854.

Massive immigration from Ireland, Germany, Scandinavia, Central Europe, and Italy transformed America in the nineteenth century, settling the new states of the west and populating the newly expanding industrial cities. Despite the huge contribution made by immigrants opposition to immigration was a persistent undercurrent in the political and popular discourse of the era. By the turn of the century earlier concerns about the impact of Catholics and Asians had broadened into widespread opposition to any further immigration. Nativists expressed a racially based hostility to the main immigrant supplying nations of the period as well alarm over the supposed economic impact of further arrivals. The early 1920s saw a series of federal legislative measures which for the first time imposed general numerical restrictions on immigration in the form of national quotas. At the peak of a mounting surge of nativist agitation, the quota system brought the century of immigration to a close. With minor adjustments it remained in force for over forty years, limiting but not ending mass immigration. After 1965 restrictions were modified and a marked overall increase in annual immigration figures occurred, which with a few fluctuations has continued to the present. The framers of the 1920s legislation were primarily concerned to cut off the inflow of non "Anglo-Saxon" peoples, as they saw it, by devising a quota system that favored earlier migrant nations such as the United Kingdom, Germany, and Scandinavia. Although the measures had the intended effect of limiting inflows from countries such as Italy and Poland, they were overtaken by events as the century progressed and the focus of migration shifted to new areas. Notable among these were western hemisphere sources including Central and South America, and the Caribbean, Asia, and the Soviet Union.

The quota system and its aftermath.

Although much of informed opinion throughout the nineteenth century recognized the vital contribution made by continuing immigration in opening up the new states to the west and in transforming the United States into a leading world power, anti-immigrant sentiment remained a continued undercurrent. In times of prosperity and national self confidence nativism had little general appeal. However when times were hard and sentiment uneasy the search for scapegoats and easy solutions to perceived problems made hostility to particular immigrant groups a convenient line. As they do in many parts of the world today populist politicians and the press repeatedly found that strident attacks on immigrants struck a chord which brought votes and sales. Historians have identified three phases of nativism in America. The first, dating from the late 1820s, was an upsurge of anti-Catholicism, as the massive influx of German and Irish (and subsequently Italian) Catholics was presented as a dangerous challenge to the Protestant heritage of the Founding Fathers. For several decades mob attacks on priests and churches became commonplace in eastern cities. The second phase, beginning in the 1870s, was directed against Asian immigrants, specifically the Chinese and later the Japanese. As we have seen there was little serious opposition to anti-Asian discrimination and the movement culminated in the bipartisan passage of the Chinese Exclusion Act of 1882 and the subsequent Gentlemen's Agreement with Japan. The third and most far reaching phase however was a more diffuse hostility to all immigrants whatever their religious or racial back-

A torchlight meeting of the Know-Nothings in New York City. 1854.

ground. It was this movement, prompted by the mass immigration of the 1880s and in particular the census of 1890, which was seen by contemporary observers as marking the end of the frontier era, that prompted a gradual increase in federal regulation of immigration, culminating in the quota measures of the 1920s. The apparent success of this third phase of nativism may be attributed to the nationalism that had inevitably accompanied United States participation in World War I, the pervasive unease about the pace of social change in postwar America, and the intellectual climate of the day that made racially restrictive immigration controls appear an acceptable solution.

At first Congress made no efforts to control, restrict, or regulate immigration into the United States. Attempts by several of the individual states to impose measures such as head taxes, made in response to anti-Catholic nativism were struck down by the Supreme Court in 1848, when it found that immigration came within the responsibilities limited to Congress to regulate commerce with other nations. Calls for Congress to exercise this responsibility by imposing restrictions were led in the pre Civil War decades by the American or Know Nothing party, whose primary aims were a limitation of the rights of aliens to hold political office and a proposed extension of the period of qualification for naturalization to up to twenty-one years. These policies failed to attract widespread support, and when in the aftermath of the Civil war Congress did consider naturalization, the Fourteenth Amendment, passed in 1868, imposed a uniform national citizenship open to all "persons born or naturalized in the United States." In 1870 the group eligible for naturalization was extended to include "persons of African descent" as well as "white Persons," a measure which by the standards of the day was intended to be liberal but was subsequently to provide the basis for far reaching legal discrimination against the Asian migrants it excluded from access to citizenship. For the first time there was a group of people in America, working to improve their life and that of their families, who were defined irrevocably as "aliens ineligible for citizenship."

As we saw in the previous chapter, the campaigns by Californian politicians, organized labor, and racist groups against Chinese and Japanese immigration enjoyed widespread national support. When Congress passed the first Chinese Exclusion Act in 1882 few voices were raised against it. The number of Chinese migrants, although significant in the then tiny labor force of California, were small relative to the huge inflows from Europe at the same period, and the exclusion act has sometimes been dismissed as a historical curiosity of minor significance. Yet, aside from its far reaching impact on the formation of a Chinese American community, it set a precedent for the exclusion from America for the first time ever of a group of people defined solely in terms of national origin. Subsequent Supreme Court rulings that this exclusion of a whole "class" of people was constitutional paved the way for further restrictions. Pressure for these also increased because the federal authorities felt constrained to take an ever increasing administrative role in processing the influx of migrants after a series of post-Civil War Supreme Court rulings struck down the rights of states in this area. Starting in 1882 a federal head tax of fifty cents was imposed (rising to $8 by 1917) in order to finance the processing on immigrants. In 1892 the New York city-run depot at Castle Gardens was replaced by the new federal facility on Ellis Island, which was to handle some twelve million immigrants over the following four decades. At the federal authorities assumed control over the reception of immigrants they acquired powers to exclude those deemed undesirable. The first of these were the prohibitions of contract laborers imposed by Congress in 1885 and 1887, although little serious effort was made to enforce this ban. More significant was the 1891 measure that excluded "all idiots, insane persons, paupers or persons likely to become a public charge, persons suffering from a loathsome or contagious disease, persons who have bee convicted of a felony or other infamous crime or misdemeanor involving moral turpitude." In a measure aimed at barring Mormons polygamists were also prohibited from entering the United States. Health checks at Ellis Island did lead to some sick migrants being returned, while the shipping com panies who had to bear the cost of deportation no doubt restricted numerous others from embarking at all. The "LPC" or "likely to become a public charge" clause certainly inconvenienced migrants but probably excluded relatively few. On average only around one percent of aspiring immigrants were refused entry or deported under these restrictions. In 1903 anarchists and others advocating violent means of achieving political change were added to the list of those excluded. Campaigners against immigration were anxious for more far reaching restrictions which would strike at the general bulk of immigrants rather than just the marginal limits set so far. Many saw the best way of achieving this as the introduction of a literacy test. This approach was in accordance with the racist nature of prevailing sentiment of the day which generally regarded the mostly southern and eastern European migrants of the late nineteenth and early twentieth century as intellectually and morally inferior to their northern European predecessors.

In the late nineteenth century, racism, which had of course earlier exercised an important impact on the slavery issue and the treatment of Native Americans, gained a new intellectual respectability. Darwin's insights into the competitive struggles of animal species in natural selection had been misapplied to so-called "races" in self-justificatory polemics which argued that the then prevalent dominance of white Anglo-Saxon Protestants was somehow the natural order of the world and reflected an innate superiority. "Races" could be ordered in a natural hierarchy which should not be challenged. Southern Europeans, Slavs, and Jews (not to mention Asians and Africans) were supposedly naturally inferior and excessive mixing with them might be expected to produce national disaster. From this perspective immigration was seen as posing a direct threat to the future of America. Typical of this school of intellectual racism was the Immigration Restriction League, founded by a group of Harvard graduates in 1894. The historian of immigration Roger Daniels notes that they were to become the most influential single group pressing for a restriction of immigration and cites one of their founders who in a statement typical of the movement asked whether America should be "peopled by British, German, or Scandinavian stock, historically free, energetic, and progressive, or by Slav, Latin, and Asiatic races, historically downtrodden, atavistic, and stagnant." Somewhat illogically literacy was seen as a key to "improving" the racial balance of the immigrant inflow, or failing that, to excluding the undesirable. Attempts to bring in such a test began during the deep economic depression of the 1890s, with the measure first passing the House in 1895. In

Uncle Sam putting the Quota Act in place. The act limited immigration to three percent of the number of foreign-born nationals in the census of 1910. This illustration from 1921.

1897, 1913, 1915, and 1917 it was also carried in the Senate but on each occasion fell to a presidential veto. In 1917 however the second veto exercised by President Woodrow Wilson was overridden by a substantial majority in both houses. By this time, although the direct effect of the war had been to dramatically reduce the annual numbers of immigrants, this was far outweighed by the nationalist anti-European backlash that accompanied it. As we have already seen in earlier chapters, a wave of anti-foreigner sentiment swept the country with the loyalty of even the longest established groups of "hyphenated Americans" being called into question. For the first time merely being an immigrant was sufficient for agitators to call into doubt one's commitment to America. Language tuition was abandoned in many immigrant groups, the foreign language press suffered a huge decline in titles and circulation, names were anglicized and attacks on foreigners frequent. In this climate there was little opposition to further controls on immigration despite the President's ethical objections. In fact however, like most previous measures, the literacy test had a quite limited impact on the number of immigrants. Literacy was to be assessed in any recognized language rather than just English (as some nativists had proposed), and by that time levels of education among people in Europe with sufficient funds to emigrate were generally high enough to qualify. Only a fraction of one percent of applicants ever failed the test.

Nevertheless the passage of the literacy test was symptomatic of the shifting climate of opinion in favor of those urging more far reaching restrictions. Also in 1917 a law was passed which closed of all further immigration by Asians other than Japanese and Filipinos. At the end of the war the obvious instability in Europe combined with a panicked reaction to the Bolshevik revolution in Russia left American opinion still wary of foreign involvement and paranoid about the potential dangers of foreign radicals within America. Alarmist reports suggested that millions of hungry refugees fleeing the desolation of postwar Europe were about to flood into America. In a response that can only be seen as panic the house passed a bill in December 1920 without holding hearings, which suspended all immigration for a year. The Senate responded by passing an "emergency" one year quota bill. Ignoring Western Hemisphere immigration, and the already restricted Asians, the bill limited the total inflow of Europeans to five percent annually of the total number of foreign born Europeans recorded by the 1910 census, with each country assigned a share in proportion to the number of their nationals recorded. There would therefore be a total quota of about six hundred thousand, most of which would be assigned to Britain, Ireland, Germany, and the Scandinavian countries. The House passed the bill with the percentage reduced to three percent, cutting the total number permitted to around 350,000. It was vetoed by President Wilson in his last days office but reintroduced two months later in a special session of Congress by the incoming President Warren G. Harding. In May 1922 the same quotas were extended for two more years. By 1924 these provided the baseline for debate by both sides, with opinion largely divided between those who wanted to maintain the existing quotas and the nativists, lead by House Immigration Committee chair Albert Johnson who favored far harsher controls. As intended the 1922 Act had cut immigration, with some 600,000 arrivals in each of the two years, around half of them from Europe. The nativists wanted to cut this back significantly and were open about their intention to restrict Italians and other "undesirable" groups still further. This was to be achieved by pushing back the baseline year from 1910 to 1890 (when of course the percentage of northern Europeans was far higher.) The 1924 Act as passed was a victory for the nativists. In the first phase of operation, which lasted until 1929 the baseline was to be 1890, and the total quota was reduced from three to two percent. As intended this cut the Italian quota from some 40,000 to only a few thousand, and the Polish quota similarly. The second phase furthered the racist agenda still more by proposing to base later quotas on a study of the racial origins of Americans going back to the eighteenth century, although the onset of the Great Depression thwarted its full implementation. At the same time the 1924 Act unilaterally rescinded the Gentlemen's Agreement with Japan and, in a deliberate snub, the Japanese were denied even the token quota of a few hundred to which they should have been entitled.

The effect of this legislation is entangled with other factors. Economic depression in the immediate postwar years and more seriously throughout the 1930s had a marked impact, not only reducing the numbers who wanted to came to America—which in the Great Depression of the 1930s hardly looked the land of opportunity—but also in inflating the numbers who returned to their countries of origin. World War II, beginning at the end of the 1930s, severely restricted transatlantic travel with obvious implications for immigration. Moreover the nativist drafters of the Immigration Act of 1924 had failed to recognize the significance of a gradual shift in the source of immigrants towards the Western Hemisphere, which remained unrestricted. Overall there was an annual average net immigration of nearly 440,000 each year from 1921 to 1924, which fell by almost exactly a half to around 220,000 per annum from 1925-30, primarily due to the impact of the quotas. After that numbers plummeted as the Great Depression was followed by war—there was even a net outflow each year from 1932 to 1935. In 1932 there were only 35,576 immigrants and 103,295 emigrants, giving a net figure of minus 67,719. Over the period from 1931 to 1945 the annual average net inflow was a mere 13,000 or so.

Before the Great Depression virtually ended immigration in the 1930s the quota act seemed to have worked much as its sponsors intended in cutting off the inflow of certain groups. Only around 15,000 Italians arrived per year, a drastic decline on previous numbers. Nations such as Germany favored by the quotas were able to send more than prewar levels, although others such as Britain never approached their annual quota. At the same time though the immigration from the Western Hemisphere, which had begun under the impact or wartime labor market shortages, began to take on a more lasting significance. Between 1925 and 1930 nearly half a million Canadians and over 250,000 Mexicans were recorded as entering the United States, almost certainly a figure distorted by repeat crossings but understating the true numbers passing over the long and then largely unguarded land borders. After 1930 the Depression both reduced the numbers able to afford the cost of emigration and more importantly made America seem a far less appealing destination. Additionally consulates were instructed to apply the LPC clause far more strictly cutting the number of potential entrants still further. These restrictions extended to refugees as well as normal migrants, making it difficult for German and Central European Jews facing persecution and genocide from the Nazis in the 1930s to obtain entry to the United States, although subsequently a number of those who did succeed in doing so were to make important contributions in the fields of both science and the arts.

Apart from the granting of a token quota to the Chinese in 1943 as a wartime ally, and similar gestures towards the Filipinos and Indians in 1946, the war years brought little change to immigration policy. In its aftermath however it was clearly necessary both to take some action to admit a limited number of refugees and other displaced persons and to modify some of the more blatantly racist exclusions of the quota system. The Displaced Persons Act of 1948 and a subsequent extension admitted some 415,000 persons over four years, many of them ethnic Germans and people from the Soviet occupied Baltic region. In 1952 the McCarran-Walter Act liberalized naturalization to include Asians and modified provisions for the reunification of families outside quota limits. However as President Truman noted in a critical veto message (which was overridden) it kept in place the deliberately discriminatory quotas. Both sides to these disputes over quotas largely failed to notice that events in the world had moved on and that the sources of immigrants were changing as a result. By the 1950s Europeans had fallen to little over half of total immigrants—legal migrants in the years from 1952 to 1965 totaled around 3.5 million, of which only about one third were covered by the quotas. Canadians were a still significant but declining source, but the real change was in the growing proportional and absolute numbers of Asians, Latin Americans, and later people of predominantly African ancestry from the islands of the Caribbean.

While the McCarran-Walter Act was still largely informed by the nativist prejudices of the 1920s, these sentiments were to become increasingly at odds with national opinion in the era of Civil Rights activism and social egalitarianism. By the early 1960s some kind of reform was clearly essential. John F. Kennedy sent Congress proposals that left the overall quota ceiling (then a modest 156,700) intact but proposed a number of other significant changes, including a five-year phase out of quotas, modification of remaining racially discriminatory measures including the allocation of all Asian applicants to their national quotas regardless of their previous domicile and the past exclusion of Jamaica and Trinidad and Tobago from the non-quota status accorded other Western Hemisphere nations. Although no action was taken during the Kennedy presidency a consensus for change of some form existed and immigration

Immigrants stand in line for one of many medical tests at the immigration processing complex of Ellis Island in New York Bay, August 1923.

reform became one of the first issues debated by Congress following the 1964 election. The measure finally passed, the Immigration Act of 1965, was signed by President Truman on Liberty Island in New York Harbor, a fitting setting for a measure which was to have an impact on immigration into the United States that went far beyond the apparently modest reforms intended by the drafters and backers of the act.

The act abolished the old system of national origins, replacing it with overall caps on numbers to be admitted from each hemisphere—170,000 per annum from the "Old World," 120,000 per annum from the "New World." No more than 20,000 would be allowed entry each year from any one Old World country. These limits were to remain in force until 1978 when the two quotas were merged and the 20,000 national cap extended to both hemispheres. The old LPC and ideological restrictions were kept in place, as was a modified but largely similar set of preference rules for the admission of non-quota immigrants such as spouses, children, and other close relatives of U.S. citizens and resident aliens, skilled workers, and refugees. Johnson and the acts proponents seem to have seen the measure as essentially a modest and overdue correction of the more discriminatory aspects of the old act, correcting its bias against southern and eastern European nations, while extending a measure of control to the Western Hemisphere. Probably as a result of a failure to correctly assess recent immigration trends its actual consequences were almost totally unanticipated. Certainly it seems unlikely that Congress would have passed the measure had it been aware of the marked increases in immigration from Latin America and Asia it would herald. Nevertheless what did occur was merely a continuation of developments that had been in place since the 1930s: immigration into the United States was once again on a marked upward trend, and migrants from the countries of Central and South America, and of Asia were playing an ever increasing part. From its trough in the Great Depression of the 1930s when only half a million people were admitted, the decade total doubled to a million in the 1940s, rose to 2.5 million during the 1950s, 3.3 million in the 1960s, 4.5 million in the 1970s, and 6 million in the 1980s. Contrary to expectations by the mid-1960s economic growth in Europe meant that there were relatively few migrants applying from the old donor nations, most of which never came close to filling their 20,000

annual cap. Instead the number of Chinese, Koreans, Asian Indians, and other Asians able to meet the LPC clause within the numerical ceiling or to qualify under one of the preference rules as a relative of a U.S. citizen increased markedly. Moreover with each person admitted as a resident alien a small cluster of relatives were entitled to preferential admission, with a further group eligible once the original migrant became a U.S. citizen, usually after five years. These people in turn conferred preference status on to others. The same process occurred in Latin America, with each individual admitted under the numerical ceilings opening up the prospect of a further number of relatives. In this way patterns of chain migration developed bringing in new migrants from Asia and Latin America in particular, and to a lesser extent people from the Caribbean. The official ceiling of 290,000 annual admissions was exceeded each year, often by over a hundred percent, as those eligible for admission under the preference rules exceeded those covered by the numerical limitation. A substantial additional number was admitted at various times as refugees, some an annual flow from long lasting trouble spots, others in large clusters in response to a particular emergency. Cubans, Vietnamese, Russian Jews, and Haitians were the largest numerical beneficiaries of admission under Presidential parole authority or the terms of the Refugee Act of 1980. In the first five years after the acts passage a total of over 450,000 refugees and asylum seekers were admitted. For the first time ever the United States officially recognized the right of asylum in accordance with its international obligations under the United Nations.

Perhaps as a consequence of the Mariel crisis of 1980, when over a few weeks some 125,000 Cubans were admitted in the full glare of media scrutiny, public debate about the extent and character of immigration resumed. In the closing years of the Carter administration economic weakness and the uncertain national mood were accompanied by a revival of nativistic concerns about the ability of the country to continue to absorb so many new immigrants. A bipartisan Congressional commission established in 1978 to review immigration policy was mainly concerned with reducing illegal entrants, calling in its 1981 report for a tightening of border controls, research into the possibility of introducing an identity card scheme, and an amnesty program to regularize the status of existing illegal immigrants. Although the

After a safe crossing, three immigrant women pose on the deck of a ship arriving in New York Bay, c.1920s.

overt racism that had characterized nativist discourse in the 1920s was now muted many of the old criticisms of migrants as unable to assimilate, as undermining the supposed cultural unity of the nation, as competing for jobs and driving down living standards were restated in the Congressional and media debates that followed. This time however there were at least some influential voices raised in support of continued large scale immigration, with many notable economists in particular pointing to the vital contribution made by immigrants to the continued economic growth of the nation. In the event it was five years before Congress succeeded in passing legislation, and the Immigration Reform Act of 1986 did not include proposed provisions to include relatives within the quotas and thus reduce overall numbers. Instead its impact was limited as its measures were directed primarily at unauthorized entrants. Under its terms employers were required to check the eligibility of all new employees to work in the United States, with sanctions including prison terms introduced for those who hired illegal aliens. An amnesty program for existing unauthorized immigrants was introduced, and provision made to allow crop growers easier terms for importing agricultural workers (by issuing green cards to up to a quarter of a million more temporary laborers. In a further sop to powerful southwestern agricultural interests the INS was explicitly forbidden from carrying out raids on workers in the fields, previously its most effective means of catching the illegal laborers all sides knew were essential to the regional economy. Although the amnesty program was take up by a total of 3.1 million aliens, the act as a whole did little to change the overall immigration picture. Further Immigration Acts were passed in 1990 and 1996, which once again modified a few details without substantially altering the nature or source of the inflow. Lottery programs were introduced which both regularized the status of a significant number of unauthorized immigrants from Ireland and opened up access in larger (but still relatively modest) numbers to Africans and other nationals who had lacked the relationships necessary to gain preferential admission through the general system.

Mexicans

In 1996 Mexicans were by far the largest group of immigrants legally admitted into the United States. The 163,572 Mexican immigrants in that year made up almost eighteen percent of all immigrants, some three times the proportion of the Philippines, the second largest source. They made up the largest component of a Hispanic population that was estimated at twenty-seven million by 1994, itself a dramatic twenty-eight percent increase from the 1990 figure. More recent statistics would show continued growth in the Mexican-American population at a similarly rapid rate. By 1990 Mexican-Americans also constituted substantially the largest foreign born group in the United States, with over one in five of all foreign born persons at that date being of Mexican ancestry.

The first significant Mexican-American population emerged in the mid-nineteenth century when, between 1845 and 1854 the United States annexed Texas, and northern Mexico, including what were to become the states of New Mexico and California. The few thousand Mexicans who opted to remain in the captured territory (and another small tranche bought in the Gadsden Purchase of 1854) were granted U.S. citizenship. Although divided by the Rio Grande along a substantial part of its 2,000-mile length, the border between the Unites States and Mexico that resulted from the nineteenth century changes remained largely open to those attracted north by the greater economic opportunities available in Texas and California. Several thousand Mexicans were drawn to California during the Gold Rush, while many more found agricultural employment in Texas before the turn of the century. Like the Chinese, Mexican miners in Gold Rush California were often the victims of racist attacks and a number perished in lynchings. Small but significant numbers of Mexicans continued to migrate over the border for shorter or longer periods over the remainder of the century. The long and open land border made any calculation of immigrant numbers problematic and census data often had definitional problems dealing with the gradations of different ethnic identities among long established communities along the border. Historians have regarded most of the early data as substantial underestimates and now put the Mexican-American population as high as 381,000 to 562,000 by 1900. To this day there are no accurate and agreed figures for the num-

Above: Two hundred new citizens pledge allegiance to the flag in Justice Burr's court. The new citizens were obliged to grasp the staff of the silkaline flag before receiving full citizenship papers, May 2, 1920.

Right: Mother and child being inspected by members of the Health Department. March 17, 1921.

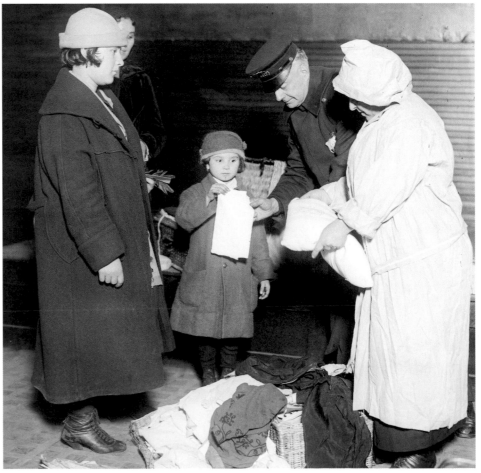

ber of Americans of Mexican ancestry as they remain subsumed by the census results in the larger category of Americans of Hispanic descent, a figure which includes Puerto Ricans, Cubans, and other Central and South Americans.

In the first three decades of the twentieth century Mexican immigration grew sharply as the turmoil created by economic change and political unrest in Mexico displaced large numbers of rural workers at the same time as higher wage levels and labor shortages in the expanding agricultural and industrial sectors of the Southwest drew laborers across the border. The worsening labor shortages during World War I widened the range of opportunities for Mexican workers further. This phase peaked in the 1920s when almost half a million Mexicans were granted permanent visas. At the same period, despite, or perhaps because of, a tightening of regulation at border posts, many thousands more entered the United States illegally. It was in the 1920s that professional gangs first developed to profit from smuggling Mexicans across the border in groups in order to supply contract labor to American farms and factories. As was to happen on several occasions throughout the twentieth century the Mexican workers that had been welcomed as cheap labor in factories and farms when work was plentiful found the situation very different when economic recessions made jobs scarce. After the start of the Great Depression there was growing hostility to Mexican immigrants throughout much of the Southwest as they were accused by labor organizations and the press of undercutting American workers and of being a drain on welfare resources. For the first time American consulates began to exclude large numbers of applicants using the literacy test, while news of the worsening situation to the north of course reduced the number of would-be migrants. In consequence the number of Mexicans in the United States actually declined by some half a million during the 1930s. Although a part of the repatriation was voluntary a substantial element was due to pressure and harassment by both federal and local officials, with many actual deportations.

The flow of migrants resumed again at the end of the 1930s with the start of World War II when the wartime demand for labor once again provided numerous opportunities. For the first time there was official recognition of the role played by Mexican workers in the Southwest when in 1942 an executive agreement between the two countries authorized the importation of short term contract laborers known as *braceros*. In the five years of the program there were around two hundred thousand *braceros*, most of them employed in agriculture or transportation. The need for their labor was exacerbated by the internment of Japanese Americans, who as we have seen played an important role in Californian agriculture. The scheme resumed in 1951 to meet new agricultural labor shortages that emerged during the Korean war, and was continued until 1964. In the peak year of 1959 almost 450,000 workers were admitted under the scheme. As before the majority were employed in California. Mexican labor became a vital input to agriculture across a large area of the southern United States, ensuring that large numbers of entry permits were granted even outside the *bracero* schemes.

Officially recognized immigration was only one element of the inflow from Mexico. From at least the 1930s there have also been large numbers of unregistered or illegal immigrants, pejoratively known as "wetbacks." Despite the fact that these undocumented migrants are equal essential to the standard of living of Anglo-Americans throughout the Southwest, providing cheap labor on farms, in factories, and increasingly since the 1950s, in domestic service, their presence has been at best tolerated by the authorities. Fear of deportation often prevented many of these workers from effectively protesting against exploitative employment conditions and poor wages. Sporadic federal efforts to round up and deport them led to harassment of legal and illegally resident Mexicans alike, creating a widespread distrust of officialdom. In the largest of these anti-illegals campaigns between 1950 and 1955 a total of 3.8 million people were expelled over the border, although as today many individuals were no doubt caught more than once. In 1986, for example, the Immigration and Naturalization Service claimed to have expelled 1.8 million Mexicans. Cynics have pointed out that high figures aid the INS in its annual budget applications and that for some of the many Mexican agricultural workers who are seasonal migrants deportation is a free and convenient way of traveling to the border on the way home!

Mexican immigration continued on a sharply rising trend over the remainder of the twentieth century, with Mexican-Americans the largest sector of a rapidly growing Hispanic

Immigrants at Commonwealth Pier show their despair as the bars to freedom drop and they are condemned to return to Europe and certain poverty, June 9, 1921.

American population. From the trough of the 1930s, the number of Mexican authorized arrivals rose to 60,000 in the 1940s, to 275,000 in the 1950s, over 440,000 in the 1960s, and two-thirds of a million in the 1970s. Many of those included in these figures would have been seasonal migrants counted many times, or workers who returned home after a number of years but the net effect has been a substantial and rapid increase in the Mexican-American resident population. Initially a predominantly male migration, although with a significant minority of young women who at first found employment in domestic service and other trades, by the 1970s as longer term residence in the United States became the norm increasing numbers of women and children began to join their men folk. This trend was reinforced by the changes in immigration legislation in favor of relatives. Although most Mexican immigrants were initially drawn to the agricultural sectors in California and Texas and to a lesser extent unskilled laboring positions in the booming new industries of the Southwest, over the years other employment opportunities elsewhere in the United States have broadened the pattern of settlement so that today there are measurable numbers of Americans of Mexican descent in virtually all states of the Union. As early as 1930 fifteen percent of Mexican-Americans lived outside the Southwest. Mexicans filled blue collar positions in food processing, construction, auto production, and the utilities, while women also worked in the textile and food packing industries in significant numbers. Mexican agricultural workers moved first to the Midwest, then spread to seek work in the Northeast and East coasts, while the railroads were early employers of Mexican workers in many parts of the nation. Over the first half of the twentieth century, Mexican-American neighborhoods grew up in many towns and cities, with the pattern of chain migration of relatives promoting rapid expansion. El Paso, San Antonio, and Los Angeles emerged as the largest of many Mexican-American urban communities. By 1970 eighty-five percent of Mexican-Americans lived in cities. For many these districts maintained a predominantly Mexican social environment facilitated by regular contacts with home and the frequent flows of migrants in both directions, limiting the extent of assimilation with Anglo American society. Despite the broadening of employment opportunities as the century progressed for most Mexican-Americans of both recent and long-standing American residence

occupational and social mobility was limited by relatively low levels of educational attainment and by persistent discrimination and until the 1960s segregation in schools and housing. A small middle class did develop but was largely restricted to serving the Mexican population. Flagrant racial bias was highlighted during World War II in the notorious Sleepy Lagoon case in which 17 Mexican-American youths in Los Angeles were wrongly convicted over the murder of another youth. Although the convictions were reversed on appeal in 1944 sensational media coverage of supposed youth gangs led to street harassment of young Mexican men by off duty servicemen culminating in the so-called "zoot suit" riots.

With the increasing numbers of Mexican-Americans in the second half of the twentieth century came a gradual decline in social exclusion and a corresponding improvement socioeconomic status. The percentage of men and women employed in agriculture and unskilled laboring positions declined steadily and the numbers finding openings higher status occupations from skilled and semiskilled industrial work to clerical, managerial, and professional careers rose sharply, particularly in the 1970s and after. Nevertheless both occupational surveys and income data show that Mexican-Americans are still disproportionately concentrated in lower status occupations and at lower income levels, so that progress towards full equality still has some way to go. Persistent inequality in educational provision, even after the official ending of segregation, has provided a major focus for the organizational efforts of the Mexican-American community. Mexican-Americans have also tended to be underrepresented politically with distrust of authority inculcated by years of bitter experience with the immigration service making many reluctant to become registered voters. In the 1960s and 1970s the Chicano movement emerged, stressing pride in Mexican identity and cultural heritage and seeking to promote greater solidarity and self awareness in the Mexican-American community with some success. The first significant political representation occurred also in the 1970s with the 1974 election to governorships of Jerry Apodaca in New Mexico and Raul Castro in Arizona. Since then Mexican-American voting has become more organized and has achieved considerable success at local and state levels, and is increasingly regarded as a major constituency in federal election campaigns. Also significant were the efforts of the United Farm

A group of children playing outside a tenement block in New York, c.1940.

Overcrowding in the hot summer of 1941. Here four children and their kitten are sleeping on a fire escape of their tenement building on Irving and Rivington Streets in the Lower East Side, May 23, 1941.

Workers led by César Chavez to organize agricultural workers in California to press for improved pay and working conditions.

Since the 1960s the numbers of Spanish language newspapers, radio and television stations serving the Mexican-American and other Hispanic communities have expanded rapidly. Although Mexican culture has made its largest impact on Anglo Americans through aspects such as cuisine and popular music, Mexican-American literature, film, and theater have also been critically acclaimed. The earlier reluctance of the American Catholic Church to cater for the interest of Mexican-Americans has been overwhelmed by the sheer numbers of new congregations at a time when religious attendance elsewhere has fallen sharply. Aspects of Mexican social life such as folk festivals, the importance of family ties, and of language maintenance have persisted despite on going assimilation due to the continual reinforcement provided by the steady flow of new migrants.

Puerto Ricans

By the end of the twentieth century there were around two million Americans of Puerto Rican ancestry, about a third of whom lived in New York, which by 1970 already had a Puerto Rican population that at over 800,000 was more than double that of the island's own capital San Juan. Aside from New York City the other two largest of the Puerto Rican communities found in many urban centers throughout the eastern and southeastern United States are Chicago, with around a hundred thousand, and Philadelphia, with more than 30,000 residents. As American citizens since 1917 Puerto Ricans have been free to travel to the United States mainland, but cultural differences and racial discrimination have still left them among the more deprived of immigrant communities.

Puerto Rico is a small Caribbean island some one thousand miles east of Florida which came into American possession in 1898 following the Spanish-American War. In 1917 the

Jones Act, passed in response to a growing movement for independence declared all Puerto Ricans to be U.S. citizens, although they have no vote in U.S. elections. Aside from a few political exiles opposed to Spanish rule there were very few Puerto Ricans in the United States before 1900. In the early decades of the twentieth century, improvements in health care and sanitation resulted in the island's population expanding rapidly, with the total doubling to over 2.2 million between 1910 and 1950. Not only was the small agricultural economy unable to provide work for the swelling numbers, but most work that was available was poorly rewarded and seasonal in nature. The situation was made worse by a number of devastating hurricanes and falling world prices for stable crops such as sugar, coffee, and tobacco. Although the depression in the 1930s limited the number who took the only easily available option of migration to the United States those who did arrive in the prewar years set the path for many more to follow, spreading news and remittances back home. From the start New York City was the focus of Puerto Rican immigration, with the number resident in the city reaching 61,000 by 1940. After the end of World War II cheap air flights provided the means for a rapid expansion of traffic in both directions, permitting the Puerto Rican community in America to grow dramatically. Easy transport links and unregulated passage also allowed the community to maintain regular ties with the homeland, with almost five million air passengers between the island and the mainland per year by 1973, by which time the resident population on the mainland was approaching 1.5 million. A pattern had developed of islanders spending one or more long periods employed or in schooling on the mainland but with a substantial minority ultimately settling back home.

In New York Puerto Ricans settled first around the Navy Yard in Brooklyn and in East Harlem, with later communities developing in the South Bronx, Manhattan's Lower East Side and Upper West Side, and Williamsburg in Brooklyn. Moving mostly into unskilled jobs vacated by earlier European migrants, the Puerto Rican community suffered heavily from the decline in such occupations in the 1970s which temporarily slowed the pace of arrivals. Language difficulties, poor health facilities, unemployment, inadequate housing, and the other problems that have confronted impoverished immigrant groups were exacerbated by racial

Many immigrants ended up in tenement blocks in New York; this photograph taken c.1920.

based tensions with both Euro and African-Americans. Although increasing numbers have found white collar employment in teaching, social work, and the professions they remain exceptions in a community that has yet to fully adjust to life in America. Community and social groups are active in helping this process, and in promoting Puerto Rican culture, although inevitably it is the island's musical heritage that has had the most widespread impact. Educational attainment levels, although rising, still lag well behind the national average, with the inevitable implications for continued poverty—in 1990 thirty-eight percent of families in New York lived in poverty, double the average for the city's population as a whole.

Filipinos

Small numbers of Filipinos have been coming to mainland United States since at least the start of the twentieth century but the vast majority have arrived since the national quota system was abandoned in the mid 1960s. Such has been the pace of immigration since then that The Philippines ranks second only to Mexico as a source of immigrants in the period after 1960. Over 1.3 million Filipinos were admitted to the United States between 1960 and 1995, and at 913,000 in 1990 they constituted the second largest foreign born group. Around a half (more by now but the statistics are not yet in) of all Filipino born immigrants arrived between 1983 and 1993.

The United States gained control over the Philippines after the Spanish-American War at the end of the nineteenth century. The archipelago had commonwealth status from 1935 until it was granted independence in 1946. Before 1924 a few hundred Filipinos were admitted to study at American schools with colonial government assistance, a number that expanded to around 14,000 self-financed students in the years before 1934. Most of these returned home to join a growing indigenous middle class. The other main group of Filipino migrants in the first half of the century was contract laborers recruited for the sugar plantations of Hawaii. Between 1909 and 1931 these totaled around 113,000, of whom almost half remained in Hawaii, some 39,000 returned home, and 18,600 moved on to settle on the West Coast of the U.S. mainland. Both those who came back to the Philippines with sufficient money to buy land in their home village and those who remained abroad but sent money and remittances had a widespread impact on those left behind. In 1910 the census bureau estimated that there were only around 400 Filipinos in mainland United States, but soon afterwards the restrictions imposed on Japanese immigration led to increased demand for Filipino agricultural workers. Most of the 50,000 or so that came in the following twenty years remained in Californian agriculture (with work in restaurants and domestic service in the off season) but a few settled in major cities such as Chicago, New York and Philadelphia. The Depression of the 1930s interrupted this flow and after 1934 Filipino immigration was restricted, with an annual quota set at only fifty. Although Filipinos supplemented Mexicans in Californian farm labor this insultingly low quota was half the previous low awarded any other nation. Significant numbers also worked in the merchant marine and in the lower ranks of the U.S. Navy. An overwhelmingly male population (the ratio of men to women was fourteen to one in California in 1930) that was largely transient in nature there was very little community formation in the prewar period. Filipinos suffered from the same anti-Asian racism and sporadic violence that had targeted the Chinese and Japanese, although while their country was an American colony they could not be similarly excluded, but they remained ineligible for full citizenship until 1946.

In the first decades after the war the quota was lifted to 100, allowing only a very modest inflow, mostly of wives, children, and unmarried women, which permitted the gradual formation of a small Filipino American community. This process was assisted by a substantial number of non quota immigrants, totaling over 32,000 in the thirteen years the act remained in force. However after the Immigration Act of 1965 the situation was transformed. With the abolition of the restrictive quota the way was open for many more people to emigrate to the United States. In place of the male blue collar workers who had previously been the leading part of Filipino migration, the gender balance became more even and a remarkably high proportion of around two-thirds were educated professional workers. Nurses and other medical professionals made up a large proportion of these, finding ready employment in the public hos-

Opposite, Above: A row of men sit under graffitti and an old poster on an ocher-colored plastered wall of a tenement building in a poor quarter of New York, c.1956.

Opposite, Below: Filipino women dancing in the annual New York Philippine Day Parade, June 1994.

After the outbreak of war in Europe, all immigrants to the U.S. were requested to fill in forms and have their fingerprints recorded in an effort to keep out fifth columnists. Here immigrants are crowding a Brooklyn post office at the start of the four-month registration period, August 9, 1940.

pital system. Other professionals tended to find that they had to work at levels below their qualifications, while large numbers of unqualified women found work in domestic service. Due to the high proportion of working women and professionals average family income among Filipino Americans is higher than most other recent immigrant groups and above the national average. Most recent migrants were already fluent in English and chose not to settle in distinctively Filipino ethnic enclaves. Consequently assimilation and intermarriage with non-Filipinos have been high. The chain migration of relatives permitted under the preference system of the post-1965 immigration law has tended to favor recent immigrant groups such as the Filipinos, permitting legal immigration on an extremely rapid scale, with the result that the Filipino American community has almost doubled in size each decade from 1960 to 1990 and continues to expand at a similar pace.

Koreans

The Korean-American community first came to public attention in tragic circumstances when Korean owned businesses were the primary target of looters during the Los Angeles riots of 1992. Although there were very few Koreans in America before 1960 they were another of the beneficiaries of the 1965 Immigration Act, after which numbers increased rapidly. By the census of 1990 there were almost 800,000 Koreans living in the United States.

The forerunners of the recent Korean emigration were a small number of students and other travelers who came to America in the nineteenth century. Among them were several key figures in the Korean independence movement, including Pak Yong-man (1881–1928), and Syngman Rhee who was the first Korean to earn a doctorate from an American university (Princeton, 1910) and later became the first president of the Republic of Korea in 1948. More significantly in terms of American immigration some 7,200 laborers were engaged as contract workers by the Hawaiian Sugar Planter's Association between 1903 and 1905. A few hundred of these later made their way to the mainland were they formed the nucleus of a tiny Korean-

American community. When Japan took over Korea in that year it forbade emigration, and later would-be migrants were excluded by U.S. laws prohibiting Asian immigration. This situation really only changed with the Korean war (1950–53) when large numbers of U.S. troops were permanently stationed in the country. In the immediate aftermath of the war, between 1952 and 1960 some 8,000 Korean refugees, orphans, and war brides were admitted, with a further 12,000 wives and children of U.S. servicemen following over the next five years. At the same time Korea was exposed to a massive dose of American culture, making the United States seem the natural destination for emigrants once changes in the law in 1965 made admission possible.

Following the passage of the 1965 Immigration Act at least 20,000 Koreans have entered the United States virtually every year, with non quota immigrants taking the total significantly higher. In contrast to the overwhelmingly female immigration of servicemen's families before the act, the newcomers were mostly drawn from the professional middle classes, including teachers, civil servants, lawyers, and doctors. At first many of them had been displaced from the north in the course of the Korean war and found it hard to adapt to the southerner dominated regime that followed. A high proportion had college degrees. Later, despite the rapid advances of the South Korean economy, greater contacts between the two countries and the Americanization of much of Korean educational and cultural life encouraged others to follow.

The majority of Korean immigrants settled in Los Angeles, but significant communities also developed in New York City and Chicago. Despite the concentration in the West, and in California in particular, around a fifth of all Korean-Americans live in the Northeast, the South, and the Midwest. Some of the wealthier and more successful professionals, such as doctors who could find work in the public hospital system, were able to quickly establish middle class lifestyles and buy homes in the suburbs. Many others settled in the thriving Koreatown district around Olympic Boulevard in Los Angeles and adapted to their new circumstances in America by following lower status occupations, particularly small businesses. Koreans became notably successful in running small grocery and other stores in declining neighborhoods of

A group of Armenian immigrants at Ellis Island; photo taken in the 1920s.

Opposite: Friends gather at the Cyclades Café, a Greek restaurant on the Lower East Side, New York City, to hear news from back home during World War II, July 1943.

cities across the nation—in El Paso for example there were reported to be more than thirty Korean owned stores by 1985. However tensions with African-American groups led to several well publicized disputes and store boycotts. As a result Korean businesses became a focus for mob attacks during the Los Angeles riots of 1992, in which over 2,300 shops were burned down causing losses totaling $350 million. Despite this setback Korean-Americans on the whole have been notably successful in adapting to American life. In the 1980s and 1990s the proportion in white collar employment in the group identified by the census as "managers, professionals, executives" has risen steadily, as has the percentage completing college education.

Korean Christian churches, most of them of Protestant denominations, have grown rapidly to cater for the religious needs of the Korean-American community, with church associations playing a recognized welfare role. One survey reported by Roger Daniels recorded 215 Korean churches in Southern California by 1979. Secular community associations have also attracted a large membership with each town or city where Koreans have settled having its own Korean Association sponsoring social functions and providing limited welfare services. The largest of these is the Korean Association of Southern California. A new type of association that has emerged among the post-1965 immigrants is the college or high school alumni group, called *tongch'ang'hoe* or *hakch'ang-hoe*. Members adopt a fictive kinship system, with earlier graduates exercising something of the authority assigned to older brothers and sisters in Korean culture. Korean sports associations and summer camps are also widespread, although language schools are declining in popularity. Korean language television, radio, and newspapers flourish, particularly in Los Angeles, although language retention among the growing second generation is not high. One paper, the *Shin-Han Minbo* (New Korea) has been published, albeit intermittently, since 1905. Korean restaurants are now a regular feature of major cities throughout America, although dietary patterns among Korean-Americans themselves have modified considerably. An important social event in many Korean families is the *chanch'i* party held to celebrate first and sixty-first birthdays. Classical musicians, of whom the violinist Kyung-Wha Chung is probably best known, have been prominent among the few Koreans to gain national and international renown.

The events of 1992 contributed to a downturn in Korean immigration in the early 1990s, although numbers picked up again later in the decade following the sharp downturn in the Korean economy in 1997.

Asian Indians

Like the other groups discussed in this chapter immigrants from the Indian subcontinent benefited significantly from the opening up of immigration rights that followed the passage of the 1965 Immigration Act. Only a few hundred Asian Indians, as they sometimes identify themselves in the United States, arrived as merchants or students before 1900. Around 7,000 predominantly Punjabi agricultural workers found employment on the West Coast between 1904 to 1923, where their presence provoked racist hostility and the rapid passage of executive and congressional exclusion measures that effectively halted almost all further immigration. Return migration to India was quite high and the population fell to less than 1,500 by 1946. After 1965 however growth in numbers was very rapid. Seventy-six thousand people of Indian descent were recorded in the census of 1970, a number that had risen to 200,000 by 1980, and over 800,000 by 1990.

The preference given to skilled workers and those with qualifications in short supply in the U.S. labor market favored India, where there was a large and well qualified English speaking middle class. Within the first decade of the acts passage almost 50,000 businessmen, and male engineers, scientists, doctors, dentists, and other professionals entered the United States, along with a similar number of wives and children, some of whom also had higher or professional qualifications. A number of Indians found teaching work in universities across America. In the 1980s and 90s many migrants were employed in the computer software and hardware industries. As a result of the relatively high levels of educational attainment Indians have the highest median and average incomes of any of the significant recent immigrant groups, although a trend towards less well qualified immigrants and a consequent increase in poverty

was apparent in the 1980s and 1990s. Adapting readily to life in America there was no need for the transitional ethnic enclaves that characterized early migrant experience for most other groups. Instead Indians have settled in a widely dispersed fashion across much of the United States although there are concentrations in New York City and neighboring towns, as well as in San Francisco and Los Angeles. Hindu temples have been established in New York and several other cities, as have religious facilities for Sikhs and Indian Muslims.

The first Asian Indian to sit in Congress was a remarkable if anomalous individual called Dalip Singh Saund who came to America from Amritsar in 1920. After earning three degrees including a Ph.D. in mathematics from Berkeley he turned to farming and ranching. Almost single handedly responsible for persuading Congress to lift the ban on Indians achieving citizenship in 1946 he was subsequently elected a judge and later a Congressman, serving until 1962.

Vietnamese and other Southeast Asians

In contrast to other Asian groups such as Filipinos and Asian Indians who qualified for admission to the United States due to preferences given to professionals and those with family links, the majority of Vietnamese arrived en masses in the period directly after the fall of Saigon in 1975. Most spoke little or no English, were totally unprepared for the transition to the United States, and consequently have found adaptation extremely difficult. A small minority was drawn from the more Europeanized elite of South Vietnam and arrived with sufficient resources or educational qualifications to become small business proprietors or even professionals. Districts known as "Little Saigon" emerged in major cities such as Chicago and the press reported a few academic success stories among the children of immigrant families. However most others had no knowledge of modern urban life and arrived with little or nothing, some of them after enduring long and hazardous sea voyages as "boat people." In total there were some 245,000 Vietnamese in America by the 1980 census, with further numbers of boat people and others admitted as a result of agreements with the Vietnamese government arriving subsequently. Other South East Asians also displaced by the war in Indochina included several hundred thousand Laotians and Cambodians and smaller numbers from ethnic groups such as the Hmong who had opposed communist rule. By the 1990s over a million Americans were of southeast Asian origin, most of them settled in California and other western states.

Cubans

Small numbers of Cubans lived in the United States throughout the nineteenth century and early twentieth century, including political exiles such as the independence leader José Marti (1853–95), and skilled cigar factory workers. Numbers increased towards the end of the 1950s to around 10–15,000 immigrants a year as the regime of the dictator Fulgencio Batista came close to collapse. After the overthrow of Batista by Fidel Castro's rebels in 1959 many who had benefited from his regime began to seek refuge in the United States. Despite the hostility between the two countries a direct air link continued until the Cuban Missile Crisis of 1962, allowing over 155,000 Cubans to claim admission as refugees. The influx slowed thereafter as refugees were confined to indirect means of travel and clandestine departures, but a further 30,000 were admitted in the three years to 1965. In 1965 an agreement was reached with Cuba under which those whose departure was approved could be airlifted to Miami, a procedure that brought a further 275,000 Cubans to America before the operation ended at the start of 1973. After that only a few migrants were able to escape in small boats or via third countries until the end of the decade when a further 125,000 arrived in a few weeks in the course of the chaotic "Mariel" crisis. After a dispute over the fate of several thousand Cubans who had claimed asylum in the Peruvian embassy in Havana Castro declared that all who wished to do so could leave for the United States. Cuban exiles in small boats carried out a dramatic televised "rescue" of friends, relatives, and numerous others, some of whom were at least encouraged to

A refugee makes boots at the Eversburg rehabilitation camp. A displaced person with a trade at his fingertips had more appeal to the immigration authorities than an unskilled worker, May 1950.

leave. This marked the last substantial influx of Cubans to date, although a number still gain entry each year either through officially approved departure or as refugees. Many of those allowed to leave have been of retirement age, contributing to the relatively elderly age profile of the Cuban-American community as a whole. By the end of the century there are at least a million Cuban-Americans, more than half of whom live in southern Florida. Cuban-Americans are almost totally urban dwellers, with other areas of high concentration including New York City, Newark, Jersey City, Los Angeles, and Chicago.

With the exception of those that arrived in America during the Mariel exodus, a high proportion of Cuban immigrants were drawn from the urban middle and upper classes who were the primary losers in the redistribution of resources that followed the communist revolution. Professionals, land owners, entrepreneurs, and government officials all chose to exile themselves in the early years of the revolution. Many of them had to start again at a lower level in the United States, although a minority brought their wealth with them. Press reports of dazzling success stories, such as that of Roberto Goizueta, who headed the Coca Cola Company until his death in 1997 have created the misleading impression that all Cuban-Americans are wealthy, when in fact many families still live on well below average incomes. As disenchantment with the Castro regime spread more widely they were joined by larger numbers of lower middle class and blue collar workers. Compared to the Cuban population as a whole the émigrés are disproportionately white, reflecting the racial basis of wealth distribution in pre-Revolutionary Cuba, and also to a degree a reluctance by blacks to emigrate because of their concern about race relations in America. Black Cuban-Americans have reported racial prejudice in Cuban areas of Miami and a majority choose to live elsewhere, particularly in the Northeast. There are also a small number of Cuban-Americans of Chinese descent.

Miami is the capital of Cuban-America, a city dominated and to a large extent created by the huge influx of Cubans since the 1960s. Many of the Cubans resettled elsewhere under U.S. government refugee programs subsequently returned to live there. Now a bilingual city with tens of thousands of Cuban owned businesses including banks, construction companies, and radio and television stations, the Cuban presence has made the city the gateway to

Latin America for U.S. businesses and a key bridge to the north for all aspects of economic activity, including illegitimate businesses, from South and Central America. Cuban music, night life, and restaurants have added to the tourist attractions of the city as well as serving the needs of the local community. For wealthy Cuban-Americans aspects of the aristocratic society life style displaced from Havana such as country clubs and social registers have been recreated in Miami.

The Catholic church in southern Florida has expanded dramatically over recent decades and now Spanish speaking services to Cuban parishes. Church associations are an important aspect of community life for many. Particularly since the Marial exodus there has also been a minority constituency for religious practices of Afro-Caribbean origin such as *Santeria*, the "way of the Saints." Cuban-Americans, like many other immigrant groups, have struggled to pass on to the second generation cultural values such as respect for family ties, strict supervision of unmarried women, and a high valuation of educational attainment with inevitably mixed success.

In the early years Cuban-American political interests were focused exclusively on influencing United States policy towards sustained opposition to the Castro regime. As more gained the vote their views exercised considerable influence over national policy towards their homeland, while smaller numbers played an active role in direct counterrevolutionary activity. In the 1980s Cuban involvement in electoral politics in Florida on behalf of both the Republican and Democratic parties increased. The first Cuban-American mayor of Miami, Raul Masvidal, was elected in 1985, with another man of Latino descent, Richard Martinez becoming Governor of Florida the following year. Ileana Ros-Lehten became the first Cuban-American woman to be elected to Congress in 1988. In the 1990s the lobby power of Cuban-American interests was powerful enough to tighten the economic embargo on Cuba still further through the Helms-Burton Act in the face of tentative moves in the opposite direction by the Clinton administration. Cuban-Americans moved to the center stage of national and international attention at the start of 2000 with the dispute between federal authorities and Miami Cubans over the Elian Gonzales asylum case.

A family of immigrants gaze at New York's skyline with mixed emotions. They are only three of the 30,000 people who were covered by blanket assurances of the CWS for eventual entry and citizenship, c.1950.

Above: A mass naturalization of minors in February 1954. There are seventeen nationalities represented in this group of fifty-one children seen saluting the flag in a courtroom in Brooklyn, New York.

Below right: A mural on the side of a building next to the One Stop Immigration business on Esperanza Street, Los Angeles, California, c.1994.

Opposite, Above: On October 3, 1979, Pope John Paul II stood in front of the Statue of Liberty and spoke in praise of immigrants as well as urging Americans to renew their birthright in freedom.

Opposite, Below: Mural next to the One Stop immigration business on Esperanza Street, Los Angeles, California, 1995.

Haitians

Haitians, like Cubans, have sought refuge in the United States from political oppression and endemic poverty in their homeland. Unlike Cubans however, their claims to refugee status have frequently been contested by the authorities and many clandestine migrants have been forcibly returned. After a history of sporadic and mostly small-scale emigration to the United States that dates back to as early as the sixteenth century a substantial increase in the immigration of Haitians has occurred since the 1960s leading to the formation of significant Haitian-American enclaves in several major cities. The Census Bureau recorded only 4,816 persons of Haitian birth in the United States in 1960s, 28,026 in 1970, rising sharply to 92,395 in 1980, before more than doubling again to 225,393 in 1990. Growth has continued since then, and it is worth noting that these figures are generally considered to be a substantial underestimate of the actual Haitian-American population. U.S. Marines occupied Haiti from 1915 to 1934, and a second invasion and brief occupation in 1994 was sparked as much by fears of a large exodus of refugees to the United States as political turmoil in the country itself.

The Haitian presence in America began in the sixteenth century when a number of French Haitian colonists and their slaves established rice plantations in South Carolina. Later it was a Haitian fur trader Jean Baptiste Point du Sable who founded the city of Chicago when he became the first permanent settler on the site in 1772. In the War of Independence a group of 800 Haitian "free men of color," as they were known, fought alongside Americans at the Battle of Savannah in 1779. During the Haitian revolution white planters and wealthy "mulattos" and their slaves, totaling some 50,000 people sought refuge in America, settling in Philadelphia, Boston, New York, Charleston, and New Orleans. Notable among them was the celebrated naturalist and illustrator John James Audubon (1785–1851). Subsequently James Savary, another émigré, who headed a battalion under General Andrew Jackson in 1814–15 became the first man of African descent to hold the rank of major in the U.S. Army. In the early twentieth century, particularly during the U.S. occupation, small numbers of mostly middle class Haitian émigrés settled in Harlem. A similar but larger scale exodus of predominantly well educated opposition supporters seeking refuge from the brutal regime of the dictator François "Papa Doc" Duvalier began after his election in 1957. Starting around 1970 as economic conditions in the already desperately poor island began to deteriorate further and political repression increased they were joined in America by increasing numbers of unskilled workers and rural poor. For many of these the only escape was by risking their lives in small

Some 10,000 immigrants take the American citizenship oath in a mass ceremony at Los Angeles Memorial Coliseum, California, June 22, 1981. The largest group of the seventy-three nations represented was from the Philippines— around 1,600.

boats headed for Florida, where those intercepted by U.S. coast guards were often interned for long periods and in many cases returned to their homeland.

With the arrival of poorly educated and impoverished rural migrants, many of whom were initially at least illegal immigrants, the Haitian community in the United States reproduced much of the social, racial, and economic divisions found in Haiti itself. The well educated, mostly light skinned, professional class tended to settle in one area, such as Queens in New York City, socialize together, adapt relatively easily to life in the United States, and achieve a degree of economic success and security. On the other hand districts of Brooklyn such as Crown Heights, Bedford Stuyvesant, and Brownsville became home to larger numbers of poor Creole-speaking Haitians who could obtain only low paid unskilled work, often found it hard to adapt to urban living, and consequently suffered all the associated ills of educational deprivation, poor quality housing, high crime rates and endemic drug abuse. For both groups family reunification has been a priority, with hard earned savings often put towards the costs of bringing additional family members to the United States. Federal concern over the extent of illegal Haitian immigration has been recurrent and prompted frequent clamp downs. Since the Reagan Administration it has been Coast guard policy to tow any intercepted boats back into Haitian waters. At the same time however recognition that for those already in the United States illegal immigrant status cut the poorest members of the community off from the welfare and other government assistance they urgently required has led to several amnesties that have regularized the position of many thousands of unauthorized entrants, most recently in 1998.

Other Caribbeans, Central and South Americans

Although there was no numerical restriction on immigration from the Western Hemisphere until the Immigration Act of 1965 (which imposed an annual quota of 120,000 persons), the numbers arriving in the United States from countries other than Mexico and Canada before that date were quite small. The 1940 census, for example, recorded only 7,000 Central Americans. Statistics on immigrants from Central and South America before the 1960s are poor as most surveys included them within a general Hispanic category. There was and remains considerable diversity both within and between countries in the continent and between the numerous islands of the Caribbean which would be reflected in any detailed study of immigrants from these sources but is beyond the scope of this volume. Here though we can

note that like the other peoples considered in this chapter, social and economic changes in their home countries since the mid-1960s immigration law reform have prompted a dramatic increase in numbers emigrating to the United States. Return emigration and regular two way movements have also been high in most cases but despite this there has been a dramatic increase in the numbers of Americans of Latin American or Caribbean ancestry. In total the foreign born population of Caribbean origin increased tenfold between 1960 and 1990, from 193,922 to 1,938,348. While Cubans (at 736,971 in 1990) and Haitians (1990 total 225,393) accounted for almost half this figure they were outnumbered by other Caribbean nations, of which the largest contributors were the Dominican Republic (347,858 in 1990), Jamaica (334,140 in 1990) and Trinidad and Tobago (115,710). The rate of increase in Central American immigration over the past forty years has been even more dramatic, as evidenced by the Census Bureau's "Other Central American" category, recording the numbers of foreign born other than Mexicans as having exploded from 48,949 in 1960 to 1,133,978 by 1990. El Salvador and Guatemala, two countries where large numbers of people have been displaced by civil war and internal repression, are the largest contributors to this growth, with totals of 465,433 and 225,739 respectively. Numbers from the more highly populated South American countries are slightly lower but still show a greater than tenfold rise, from 89,536 in 1960 to 1,037,497 in 1990, with Columbia (286,124), Peru (144,199), Ecuador (143,314), and Guyana (120,698) the largest sources. In many cases significant numbers of unauthorized migrants are not included in these figures.

Each of these countries has provided a smaller or larger community of immigrants in the United States that has developed its own distinctive settlement patterns and cultural life. By the late 1990s, for example, when the number of Dominicans living in the United States may have risen towards a million, they formed the largest foreign born group in New York City with a rapidly expanding enclave in the Upper West Side of Manhattan the second largest Dominican urban center in the world. Like the Italians or Irish immigrants over a century before a distinctive ethnic community has developed that, while marked by widespread poverty and deprivation, over time may be expected to ease the adaptation and assimilation of a new immigrant community into American life. In contrast most migrants from countries such as Argentina have been well educated professionals who have had neither the numbers nor the social necessity of forming urban enclaves but have adapted relatively easily to white collar positions dispersed across the country.

U.S. Border Patrol inspects a hole cut by illegal immigrants in the border fence between Mexico and the United States.

CONCLUSIONS: # Yearning to Breathe Free

At the start of the twenty-first century continued global imbalances in income and opportunity, often in combination with local wars and repression, still inspire many millions of people to seek better prospects for themselves and their families through migration. No one who travels in South and Central America, Eastern Europe, Asia, or Africa can be long unaware that for many people employment abroad seems to represent their best hope of progress. In consequence legal and illegal immigration into the United States continues at an extremely rapid pace. For those who have been able to reach America variations of the immigrant experience shared by earlier generations of migrants continue also. New ethnic enclaves form in the major cities, new languages are heard on the streets but the "melting pot" myth is now largely discredited. Instead each group evolves through an interaction with a changing American society that has both similarities and differences to the experiences of their predecessors, reflecting both their distinct cultures and the changing circumstances of the day. Inevitably some do so more rapidly and more "successfully" than others but all contribute both to the economic dynamism and to the cultural diversity of the country. As a result no survey of immigration into the United States can really be completed or concluded because it is an ongoing process. All we can do is remind ourselves of the story so far.

The Colonial era

Not unexpectedly the English were by far the largest group of immigrants in Colonial America, constituting about sixty percent of the population of European descent and somewhat less than half of the total population in 1790 (taking into account African-Americans but not the unknown number of Native Americans.) A minority, albeit an important one, of these English migrants were Puritans and Pilgrims emigrating in family groups in the seventeenth century. Most were yeomen, husbandmen and artisans impoverished by population increases, economic change or personal circumstances. Many were indentured servants, too poor to pay their own passage, who bound themselves and their families to labor contracts. Around 50,000 were convicts transported instead of imprisonment. The second largest group, comprising almost twenty percent of the total population in 1790, were the African American descendants of those who had survived the "Middle Passage," of whom around 690,000 were still enslaved, the remainders so-called "free persons of color." Other migrants from the British Isles, the Scots, "Scotch Irish," Irish, and a very few from Wales constituted the next largest constituent of the Colonial population, although their distinct and in some cases hostile traditions and histories make them far from a homogenous group. In the case of the Scots, for example, conflict with the English was the primary factor, with many people forcibly deported to the colonies in the aftermath of failed uprisings or for religious dissent. Others came "voluntarily" following changes such as the demilitarization of the Scots clans late in the eighteenth century when faced with the alternative of starvation at home.

German-speakers made up the second largest ethnic group of European descent enumerated in 1790, at 8.6 percent of the European population. German settlement in the Americas began in 1683 when a group of thirteen Quaker and Mennonite families settled in the newly established colony of Pennsylvania, to be followed during the Colonial era by other

President Harrison stands with Uncle Sam in front of a group of immigrants. Uncle Sam is drawing a line with his cane and saying "if we must draw the line, let us draw it at these immigrants." 1889.

groups of religious dissenters including Swiss Mennonites; Dunkards; Schwenkfelders; and Moravians. However the majority of German migrants at this period were members of the mainstream Lutheran or Reformed churches who began to arrive in large numbers until the years after 1710 when the so-called War of Spanish Succession between France and Britain led to French troops sacking Rhineland towns allied to the British. These Rhinelanders or Palatines (as they were called) were the forerunners of a growing flow of German-speaking immigrants, most of whom settled in the thriving colony of Pennsylvania after obtaining passage as indentured servants. The other nationalities who were represented by small but still numerically significant populations were the Dutch, French, Spanish, and Swedish, all of whom had themselves established colonies on the American mainland, albeit with varying degrees of success. While the Swedes were a tiny number from a brief and failed colony largely absorbed into the general population before the renewal of Swedish immigration in the nineteenth century, others such as the French Cajuns of Louisiana have preserved a distinct sense of ethnic identity to this day.

Into the century of immigration

The century after 1820 has been called the century of immigration. In a time of unprecedented population movements, both within countries and from one country to another, a massive migration of people from Europe to the United States transformed America beyond recognition. In total some 35,999,402 persons were recorded as entering the United States between 1820 and the passage of the National Origins Act in 1924. Almost eight million of them came in a single decade between 1901 and 1910. Emigration halfway across the world was not a decision to be taken lightly. It represented a choice and a risk, and studies suggest it was frequently the relatively more educated and enterprising members of a particular community, rather than the most impoverished and downtrodden who were willing and able to take that risk. Nevertheless poverty and lack of opportunities for advancement at home were primary motivating factors in an era during which the industrial revolution brought both rapid population growth and radical disruption of existing patterns of employment that ran ahead of the new demand for labor in factories. At the same time the geographical expansion of the

Many immigrants escaped extreme poverty in Europe only to find it again in America. These families in New York are living in slums, c.1890.

United States to the West, combined with the economic expansion of its own growing industrialization created a need for workers and farmers well beyond that which could be met by natural population growth. Linking the two were improvements in communications and transport. Efficient post and telegraph systems brought news of the prospects in America, exaggerated advertisements from export promoters, and letters home from those who had already left, to the remotest parts of Europe. The railways and canals made travelling to points of embarkation far easier, while the development of steam navigation and regular liner routes transformed the still difficult transatlantic passage. While most Americans in the nineteenth century recognized that continued immigration was essential to economic prosperity there were frequent outbreaks of hostility towards particular immigrant groups and concern about the supposed threats they posed to existing American ways. Anti-Catholic agitation in the mid-eighteenth century never succeeded in limiting the influx of Irish, German, or later Italian Catholics, but as we have seen opposition to the far smaller numbers of Chinese and Japanese immigrants in the West did lead to their exclusion.

In the period up to 1900 migrants from northeastern Europe made up the overwhelming majority of entrants, with a rapidly growing number of Italian shifting the balance towards southern Europe. In the final phase from 1900 to the 1920s immigration from north-eastern Europe fell while numbers from Italy and the countries of the crumbling Austro-Hungarian empire peaked, shifting the balance between the two areas close to equilibrium. At almost 6 million German-speakers constituted the largest single bloc of migrants during the century of immigration, followed by 4.75 million Italians, just under 4.6 million Irish, over 4.2 million from England, Scotland, and Wales, nearly 3.4 million from Russia and neighboring countries, 2.3 million from Scandinavia, and a total of 4.27 million from the various countries of the Austro-Hungarian empire.

The quota era

By the start of the 1920s hostility to any further immigration had spread from the regular nativist minority of organized labor and populist politicians to become almost a national consensus. World War I seemed to highlight the dangers of foreign involvement and had prompted a nationwide backlash against many aspects of immigrant language and culture. Racially based opposition to southern and eastern European immigrants was commonplace. The national mood was clearly set in favor of a strict limit on immigration and in response legislation was passed which for the first time imposed general numerical restrictions on immigration in the form of national quotas bringing the century of immigration to a close. However in retrospect it is clear that the quota period, which lasted from the early 1920s until 1965 marked only a relative pause in the history of immigration into the United States rather than the radical reversal of previous policy that its advocates had anticipated. The framers of the 1920s legislation were primarily concerned to cut off "undesirable" immigrants, by devising a quota system that favored earlier migrant nations such as the United Kingdom, Germany and Scandinavia. As intended the number permitted entry from countries such as Italy, Russia, and Poland fell sharply—only some 15,000 Italians were admitted per year between 1925 and 1930, compared with 222,000 in 1921. Yet the legislation failed to take into account changes in the pattern of immigration that were already becoming apparent, foremost among which was a shift towards Western Hemisphere sources. Between 1925 and 1930 nearly half a million Canadians and over 250,000 Mexicans were recorded as entering the United States.

Assessing the impact of the quotas is made problematic by the distorting impact of the Great Depression at the end of the 1920s and the war that followed. They did cut inflows by almost exactly a half to around 220,000 per annum from 1925-30 but after that in the early Depression era there was a net outflow each year from 1932 to 1935. Over the whole period from 1931 to 1945 the annual average net inflow was a mere 13,000 or so. After the war the Displaced Persons Act of 1948 and a subsequent extension admitted some 415,000 persons over four years, many of them ethnic Germans and people from the Soviet occupied Baltic region. In 1952 the McCarran-Walter Act liberalized naturalization to include Asians and modified provisions for the reunification of families outside quota limits but by the 1950s Europeans had fallen to little over half of total immigrants—legal migrants in the years from 1952 to 1965 totaled around 3.5 million, of which only about one-third were covered by the quotas.

New immigrants

The Immigration Act of 1965 abolished the old system of national origin quotas, replacing it with overall caps on numbers to be admitted from each hemisphere—170,000 per annum from the "Old World", and for the first time a limit of 120,000 per annum from the "New World" of the Western Hemisphere. Its passage set in place a continuation of developments that had been occurring since the trough of the 1930s: immigration into the United States was once again firmly on an upward trend, and entrants from the countries of Central and South America, and increasingly of Asia were playing an ever expanding part in the total. From its low point in the Great Depression of the 1930s when only half a million people were admitted, the decade total doubled to a million in the 1940s, rose to 2.5 million during the 1950s, 3.3 million in the 1960s, 4.5 million in the 1970s, and 6 million in the 1980s. However from around the mid-1960s economic growth in Europe meant that the old donor nations, mostly never came close to filling their 20,000 annual cap. Instead the expansion of educational facilities and economic growth in developing countries meant that the number of Mexicans, Chinese, Koreans, Asian Indians, and others able to meet the LPC clause within the numerical ceiling or to qualify under one of the preference rules as a relative of a U.S. citizen increased markedly. Subsequently each person admitted as a resident alien conferred entitled to preferential admission on a small cluster of relatives, with a further group eligible once the original migrant became a U.S. citizen, usually after five years. Patterns of chain migration developed bringing in more and more new migrants from Asia and Latin America in particular, and to a lesser extent people from the Caribbean. The official ceiling of 290,000 annual admissions was exceeded each year, often by over 100 percent, as those eligible for admission under the preference rules exceeded those covered by the numerical limitation. Others were admitted at various times as refugees, with Cubans, Vietnamese, Russian Jews, and Haitians the largest numerical beneficiaries of admission under Presidential parole authority or the terms of the Refugee Act of 1980. In the first five years after the acts passage a total of over 450,000 refugees and asylum seekers were admitted.

Immigration today

Despite some year on year fluctuations the number of immigrants officially admitted into the United States continues to increase and the trends in migrant sources noted since the 1960s are still apparent. A total of 915,000 legal immigrants were recorded in 1996, although the Immigration and Naturalization Service also estimates that around a further 200,000 people annually enter the country without proper authorization. Mexico, with 163,572 immigrants recorded, was by far the largest single country contributing to the total, followed by the Philippines at 55,876, India at 44,859, Vietnam at 42,067, China at 41,728, and the Dominican Republic at 39,604. European nations were the source of only sixteen percent of immigrants, largely accounted for by Ukraine (21,079), Russia (19,668), Poland (15,772), and the United Kingdom (13,624). Others such as Ireland, Germany, and Italy no longer feature among even the largest thirty sources. Africa, Central America (excluding Mexico), and South America now each contribute around five percent of annual immigrants, with number from Africa apparently on an upward trend.

As a consequence of the continued surge in immigration the number of foreign born persons in the United States is now at record levels. In 1990 there were 119.8 million foreign born individuals recorded, the highest total ever (although as a percentage of the total population the 7.9 percent figure was well down on the previous peak of around fifteen percent early in the century.) The switch from Europe to Asia and Latin America as immigrant sources is captured by figures recording that the proportion of foreign born persons from Europe fell from eighty-five percent in 1900 to only twenty-two percent in 190, while over the same period the proportion from Latin America rose from below 1.5 percent to forty-three percent and that from Asia also from below 1.5 percent to twenty-five percent. Moreover around one in four of all foreign-born persons in the United States in 1990 had arrived there only in the previous five years. Remarkably nearly half of all these foreign-born people live in either California or New York, while the population of Hialeah City, Florida is seventy percent foreign-born.

The ultimate irony. Fat, rich men stand at the dock to stop an immigrant from arriving. Shadows on the wall behind the men show their own immigrant fathers. Cartoon dated 1893.

J. Keppler

Index

ACKNOWLEDGMENTS

The publisher wishes to thank the following for supplying the photography for this book:

Front cover image and pages 10, 12 (top), 16 (both), 21 (both), 23 (top right), 24 (top), 25 (middle and bottom), 27 (both), 30 (top), 32 (all), 33 (top), 35 (both), 36 (bottom), 74, 75 (both), 78 (bottom), 79 (both), 102, 110, 118, 128, 129, 130, 153, 155, 156, 158 (bottom), 161, 162 (bottom), 163, 169, 181, 186, 189, 190, 198, 199, 201, 208, 210, 213, 225, 227 (both), 228 (both), 230, 237, 244 (top), 245 (top), 246, 249 and back cover image courtesy of © Bettmann/CORBIS;

Page 3 courtesy of © Roger Wood/CORBIS;

Pages 7 (both), 8 (both), 13 (bottom), 18, 22 (bottom), 23 (top left), 24 (bottom), 26 (bottom), 28, 29 (top and bottom), 31 (both), 33 (bottom), 34 (top and bottom), 36 (top), 39 (both), 40, 42, 43, 45, 46, 47, 51, 52, 57, 58, 61, 65, 66, 69, 71, 72 (both), 76, 77 (both), 78 (top), 81, 86, 91, 95, 96, 107, 131, 132, 133, 134, 135, 139, 157, 158 (top), 160 (bottom), 165, 166, 178, 202, 203, 204, 205 (both), 206, 207 (top), 219, 220, 222, 224, 233, 234 (top), 236, 240 (both), 243, 245 (bottom), 247 and 251 courtesy of Hulton Getty Picture Collection;

Pages 12 (bottom), 13 (top), 14, 15, 22 (top), 23 (bottom), 25 (top), 29 (middle), 30 (bottom), 37 (both), 98, 136, 144, 145 (top), 146, 162 (top), 200, 214, 250 and 253 courtesy of © CORBIS;

Page 19 (top) courtesy of Library of Congress, Prints & Photographs Division, Gottscho-Schleisner Collection;

Pages 19 (middle), 142, 143, 170, 173, 174 and 177 courtesy of Library of Congress, Prints & Photographs Division, Detroit Publishing Company Photograph Collection;

Page 19 (bottom) courtesy of © Joseph Sohm; ChromoSohm Inc./CORBIS;

Page 20 (top) courtesy of © Bob Krist/CORBIS;

Page 20 (bottom) courtesy of © Kevin Fleming/CORBIS;

Page 26 (top) courtesy of © Gail Mooney/CORBIS;

Page 85 courtesy of © Minnesota Historical Society/CORBIS;

Pages 115 and 147 and 152 courtesy of Library of Congress, Prints & Photographs Division, The Fred Hultstrand History in Pictures Collection, Institute for Regional Studies, NDSU, Fargo, N.D.;

Pages 121 and 185 courtesy of Library of Congress, Prints & Photographs Division;

Page 140 courtesy of Library of Congress, Prints & Photographs Division, Detroit Publishing Company Photographs Collection, Benjamin J Falk;

Page 141 courtesy of Library of Congress, Prints & Photographs Division, Theodor Horydczak;

Page 145 (bottom) courtesy of © Austrian Archives/CORBIS;

Page 148 courtesy of Library of Congress, Prints & Photographs Division, Farm Security Administration - Office of War Information Photograph Collection;

Pages 149 (all), 150 and 151 courtesy of Library of Congress, Prints & Photographs Division, Farm Security Administration - Office of War Information Photograph Collection, Dorothea Lange;

Page 160 (top) courtesy of © The Mariners' Museum/CORBIS;

Page 182 courtesy of Library of Congress, Prints & Photographs Division, Farm Security Administration - Office of War Information Photograph Collection, Fenno Jacobs;

Page 193 courtesy of Library of Congress, Prints & Photographs Division, Howard W Marshall;

Pages 196-197 courtesy of Library of Congress, Prints & Photographs Division, Panoramic Photographs Collection, © J D Givens;

Page 207 (bottom) courtesy of © Sandy Felsenthal/CORBIS;

Pages 231, 232 and 239 courtesy of © Weegee/International Center of Photography/Hulton Getty Picture Collection;

Page 234 (bottom) courtesy of © Michael S. Yamashita/CORBIS;

Page 242 courtesy of © Hulton-Deutsch Collection/CORBIS;

Page 244 (bottom) courtesy of © Steve Jay Crise/CORBIS.